A Reference Publication in Literature

Lawrence S. Thompson, *Editor*

CAROLINE DRAMA:
A Bibliographic History of Criticism

Rachel Fordyce

G. K. HALL & CO., 70 LINCOLN STREET, BOSTON, MASS.

Library of Congress Cataloging in Publication Data

Fordyce, Rachel.
   Caroline drama.

   (Reference publications in literature)
   Includes indexes.
   1. English drama--17th century--History and criticism
--Bibliography. I. Title. II. Series.
Z2014.D7F67   [PR671]   822'.5'09   77-20673
ISBN 0-8161-7952-2

PR
671
F67

This publication is printed on permanent/durable acid-free paper
MANUFACTURED IN THE UNITED STATES OF AMERICA

for
My Parents

Contents

	Entry	Page
INTRODUCTION		ix
ACKNOWLEDGMENTS		xv
LIST OF JOURNAL ABBREVIATIONS		xvii
GENERAL REFERENCE AND BIBLIOGRAPHIES	001-145	1
TEXTUAL CONSIDERATIONS	146-193	27
MAJOR CAROLINE DRAMATISTS	194-463	37
LESSER CAROLINE DRAMATISTS	464-593	93
INDIVIDUAL STUDIES AND COMPREHENSIVE WORKS .	594-773	119
STAGE HISTORY	774-829	157
INDEXES		
Subject Index		171
Persons, Plays and Places		183
Authors of Secondary Writings		195

Introduction

In 1936 Alfred Harbage, in his introduction to *Cavalier Drama*, stated that "Nearly all Cavalier plays are inferior in quality, and the historian's penalty for dealing with a body of literature which Time has justly submerged is self-evident. Cavalier plays are often so similar in theme that it is hard to describe them in such a way as to distinguish one from another, and their artistic weakness is so manifest that it is hard to concede the point with play after play without subjecting all to a monotonous drizzle of sarcasm."[1] Granted Harbage is addressing himself to court drama, a limited portion of Caroline Drama, in his pointedly critical judgment; nonetheless, his estimation of the Cavalier output has frequently become a catchall criticism for the entire body of late Renaissance dramatic material. That this is an unfortunate, perhaps hasty, and definitely a too general appraisal of the period is one of the reasons for the compilation of criticism that comprises this work.

Caroline Drama: A Bibliographic History of Criticism is designed to survey the major critical issues related to Caroline Drama as they have emerged over approximately the last 100 years, although there are necessary extensions into earlier criticism. The work implicitly, and explicitly when necessary, traces a critical issue, a type of criticism, or patterns of ideas from their inception to the present time. Every effort is made to cross-reference ideas, either in the entry itself, in the indexes, or both, without the vehicle of cross-indexing becoming burdensome. The intent of this bibliography is to show that although Caroline Drama has seen its "drizzle of sarcasm" it has also merited a sound and reasonably comprehensive body of thorough, methodical and enlightened criticism—the type of criticism that embodies standard literary analysis and evaluation, social history, stage history and methods of bibliographical enquiry.

The core of the bibliography is a conflation of works in English and foreign languages divided into six major sections: General Reference and Bibliographies, Textual Considerations, Major Caroline Dramatists, Lesser Caroline Dramatists, Individual Studies and Comprehensive Works, and Stage History. Quality, representativeness and lasting effectiveness were key factors in selecting the materials to be annotated. This does not mean to say that a work like Nason's

study of James Shirley,[2] because it has fallen into disrepute, will
not be included; it is included because of the substantial positive
and negative effect it has had on more contemporary critics of
Shirley. But generally speaking works are included because of their
continuing positive contribution to interpretation, analysis, criticism and the study of bibliographical techniques. Works included are
notes, articles, monographs, critical books, dissertations and editions of plays. In all cases the works were selected because of their
significance, effectiveness, or freshness of approach. Notes are included only when they further the body of knowledge related to Caroline Drama; queries are not included. Dissertations, especially those
that are editions of plays, are included only if they have a substantial amount of critical, biographical or bibliographical apparatus
attached to them. The same is true for standard editions of plays.
The content of these divisions is analyzed in the sections that
follow.

GENERAL REFERENCE AND BIBLIOGRAPHIES

Included in this section are standard bibliographies such as *PMLA*,
Abstracts of English Studies, *Annual Bibliography of English Language
and Literature*, Besterman's *A World Bibliography of Bibliographies*
and so forth. These are included to supplement the material of this
work and should be consulted by anyone interested in surveying all
tangential issues related to Caroline Drama. Also included in this
section are checklists, bibliographies of individual Caroline dramatists and of specific subjects such as costuming or ballads, as well
as encyclopedias and standard reference works for the period. A
typical entry reads:

029   CLARK, ALICE. *Working Life of Women in the Seventeenth
        Century*. London: Routledge, 1919. 335pp.
            Clark deals with the sociological and economic impact
        of women on trade, particularly in agriculture, textiles,
        crafts, and the professions. The study is derived from
        "women who move through [the period's] various scenes,
        either in the pages of the dramatists or as revealed by
        domestic papers or in . . . public records." Check the
        index and the abbreviated list of contents at the beginnings
        of chapters for sources.

The entry itself includes a number for indexing purposes, standard
bibliographical information, number of pages, and a statement on the
most salient issues of the book as well as its methodology. In this
section, I have not attempted to be critical of the material because
it is factual and intended to be used as a reference. To understand
how the sections relate to one another, one should read all entries
with an eye for key words, phrases, issues, topics, plays, persons
and so forth so that the entry can be used in conjunction with the
indexes at the end of the bibliography. With this in mind, one might
check the following nineteen terms in the index in association with

entry 029: agriculture; crafts; documents; economics; employment; history, political; history, social; householding; life, in cities; life, in the country; life, domestic; life, in London; professions; records, household; records, public; textiles; trade; women; and work.

TEXTUAL CONSIDERATIONS

Included in this section are works related to methods of studying bibliographical problems, textual studies, authorship, dating, printing, handwriting, sources, analogues, bibliographical style, copy-texts, form and conventions of text, types of editions, publication of research, authenticity, attribution, lost works, textual apparatus and general principles of bibliography. The purpose of this section is to coordinate in one place those works most specifically related to textual matters. It will be found, however, in the sections on Major and Lesser Caroline Dramatists, that many works included there touch on these subjects. Again, the indexes should be used liberally.

MAJOR CAROLINE DRAMATISTS

This section of the bibliography distinguishes Major Caroline Dramatists from Lesser Caroline Dramatists, for convenience and balance. The major dramatists in the Caroline period are Ben Jonson, John Ford, Philip Massinger, James Shirley, Richard Brome and Sir William Davenant. These men, generally speaking, are held in higher repute than lesser dramatists such as Thomas Rawlins, Lodowich Carlell, or Sir Aston Cockayne, and they are more actively and directly related to the period than authors such as William Cavendish, Duke of Newcastle, George Chapman or Thomas Killigrew. The annotation for the entries on Major Caroline Dramatists follows three patterns or a combination of the three. There are those entries which are annotated in a straight-forward, factual manner because of the nature of the material under discussion; occasionally misinformation in the work or related to the work is corrected. Frequently in this type of annotation there is cross-indexing to emphasize the fact that the work is one in a series directly related to a central critical or bibliographical issue. The second type of annotation is one in which the author of the work speaks for himself concerning his material, or the evaluation of another critic is included. The third type of annotation is a combination of factual information and my criticism. Concerning books, a conscious attempt has been made to note special features related to indexes, tables of contents, bibliographies or any other reference apparatus included in the book. Please *see* examples of the three types of annotations below.

436 STRUBLE, MILDRED CLARA. "The Indebtedness of Ford's *Perkin Warbeck* to Gainsford." *Anglia*, 49 (1926), 80-91.
     Struble takes J. LeGay Brereton's study of the origins of *Perkin Warbeck* in *Anglia*, 34 (1911), 194-234, and extends it. Brereton concluded that Ford's major source for *Perkin Warbeck* was Bacon's *History of King Henry the*

Seventh; to that Struble would add Gainsford's *True and
Wonderful History of Perkin Warbeck*, a little known work
appearing variously in the *Harleian Miscellany*. She feels
that "Ford would seem to have had before him as he wrote,
the histories of both Bacon and Gainsford, and to have
drawn therefrom about equally." The majority of the
article is concerned with the textual parallels, and with
"Ford's judicious selection from the accounts of several
historians, his skillful intermingling of varied source materials into a composite, harmonious adaptation, and, in
the last act, his vigorous rejection of the limitations of
the historian. . . ." *See also* John O'Connor's "William
Warner and Ford's *Perkin Warbeck*," *N & Q* (June 1955),
pp. 233-35; Michael Neill's "Ford and Gainsford: An Unnoticed Borrowing," *N & Q* (July 1968), pp. 253-55; and
Struble's introduction to *A Critical Edition of Ford's*
Perkin Warbeck, Seattle: University of Washington Press,
1924.

439   SWINBURNE, ALGERNON CHARLES. *Contemporaries of Shakespeare.*
      Ed. by Edmund Gosse and Thomas Wise. London: W. Henmann,
      1919. xii, 308pp.
         This work includes individual studies of the canon of
      Philip Massinger, John Day, Robert Davenport, Thomas Nabbes,
      Richard Brome, and James Shirley, as well as others. About
      Swinburne as critic, Gosse states, "No one who ever lived,
      not Charles Lamb himself, approached [Swinburne] in worship
      of the Elizabethans and Jacobeans or in textual familiarity
      with their writings. He had read and reread them all, even
      the obscurest; not one 'dim watchfire of some darkling hour'
      but he had measured what faint light and heat it had to
      give." What Gosse neglects to mention is the perceptive
      nature of Swinburne's criticism.

363   NASON, ARTHUR HUNTINGTON. *James Shirley, Dramatist: A
      Biographical and Critical Study*. NY: Arthur H. Nason,
      1915. xv, 471pp.
         One of the earliest studies of the life and works of
      James Shirley, Nason's suffers somewhat from an overlay of
      moralism that seems neither sympathetic, perceptive, nor
      critically valid in reference to the works themselves. The
      first part of the book covers the life of Shirley; the
      second covers the plays. He gives particular attention to
      *Love Tricks; The Wedding; The Witty Fair One; The Grateful
      Servant; The Traitor; The Humerous Courtier; Hyde Park;
      The Lady of Pleasure; The Ball; The Young Admiral; The Op-
      portunity; The Doubtful Heir;* and *The Cardinal.* He con-
      cludes that "In short, from Jonsonian and Fletcherian comedy
      of manners and humors, Shirley passed to Fletcherian and
      Shakespearean romantic comedy, dramatic romance, and roman-
      tic tragedy." An annotated bibliography of early works on

Shirley is included, as well as a lengthy alphabetical (by author) list of works containing references to Shirley. The book is thoroughly indexed.

LESSER CAROLINE DRAMATISTS

Considerable attention, particularly in recent years, has been given to the Lesser Caroline Dramatists. Frequently, however, the attention has been related more to matters of bibliographical interest than to literary criticism, although Henry Glapthorne, Sir Aston Cockayne, Thomas May, Abraham Cowley, Arthur Wilson, Sir William Berkeley, Thomas Killegrew, Thomas Randolph, Sir John Suckling, William Cartwright, Thomas Nabbes and Lodowich Carlell have all been given some critical attention. Now that there has been some agreement about matters of authorship and dating, these authors will probably receive more critical attention in the future. Thus far, there has been little attempt to analyze similar thematic and stylistic patterns among these authors. Authors such as Chapman and Heywood are included here not because they are lesser dramatists but because their careers are most naturally related to another literary period. One might also consider John Milton a lesser Caroline dramatist, and there are references to *Comus* as it relates to other masques in the period. But because of the contemporary tendency to treat Milton strictly as a Seventeenth Century or Restoration author, no attempt has been made to include an exhaustive list of references to *Comus*. For types of annotations, *see* the examples under Major Caroline Dramatists.

INDIVIDUAL STUDIES AND COMPREHENSIVE WORKS

Entries in this section are generally concerned with themes, genres, types of criticism, patterns of analysis and special topics. The works tend to encompass the entire period or a large portion of the period. Representative titles are Donald K. Anderson's "The Banquet of Love in English Drama (1595-1642)," Alfred Harbage's *Cavalier Drama: An Historical and Critical Supplement to the Study of the Elizabethan and Restoration Stage*, Theodore Miles' "Place-Realism in a Group of Caroline Plays," and John Streeter Manifold's *The Music in English Drama from Shakespeare to Purcell*. Also included here are comprehensive works specifically concerned with non-dramatic literature, or the literature of another place or time, but having a direct bearing on the study of Caroline Drama. Typical titles are Kathleen M. Lynch's *The Social Mode of Restoration Drama*, one-half of which is concerned with Caroline Drama, and T. E. Lawrence's *The French Stage in the XVIIth Century: A Study of the Advent of the Italian Order*. The latter is included for purposes of comparison and because of the latent *commedia* tendencies in Caroline comedy and tragi-comedy. Collections of essays are also included here.

STAGE HISTORY

The final section of this work is devoted to Stage History.
Matters related to theatres, construction of play houses, actors,
performances, audiences, scenery, acting companies, the profession of
the dramatist, pagentry, machinery, court, private and public performances and theatre history as literary evidence are included here.
Typical entries are E. K. Chambers' *The Elizabethan Stage*, Virginia
Gildersleeve's *Government Regulation of the Elizabethan Drama*, Leslie
Hotson's *The Commonwealth and Restoration Stage* and Allardyce Nicoll's
Stuart Masques and the Renaissance Stage, in which he gives attention
to eight Caroline masques. Also included are special interest topics
related to stage history such as John Freehafer's "Brome, Suckling
and Davenant's Theatre Project of 1639," and L. Stone's "Companies of
Players Entertained by the Earl of Cumberland and Lord Clifford,
1607-39." Because there is considerable overlap among topics related
to Stage History and those related to individual dramatists and thematic studies, the indexes should be consulted frequently.

INDEXES

There are three indexes appended to this work: the Subject Index, the Person, Plays and Places Index, and the Authors of Secondary
Writings Index. The combined entries of all three indexes include
over 10,000 entries plus cross-references. The Subject Index includes general topics; the Persons, Plays and Places Index includes
primary authors, characters, actors, acting companies and other persons related specifically to Caroline Drama, as well as place names
and short-title notations of plays. In the case of a person or play
that is frequently referred to by two or more titles, cross-indexing
is employed. The Authors of Secondary Writings Index includes a list
of all authors whose works are cited in this bibliography, whether or
not the work is included for annotation.

NOTES

1. *Cavalier Drama* (NY: MLA and London: Oxford University
Press, 1936), pp. vii-viii.

2. Arthur Huntington Nason, *James Shirley, Dramatist: A
Biographical and Critical Study* (NY: Arthur H. Nason, 1915).

Acknowledgments

At this point it is my distinct pleasure to acknowledge those persons and libraries in whose debt I am for both assistance and continuing encouragement. At the inception of this work I was indebted to John Velz, Catherine M. Shaw and James L. W. West III not only for their encouragement and perceptive criticism, but also for their aid in forming a methodology.

As the body of the work emerged, I was continually indebted to the dogged, patient and frequently inspired assistance of the staffs of the Folger Shakespeare Library, the Library of Congress, the Yale University Library, the Newman Library, and the libraries of the University of Pittsburgh, Carnegie-Mellon University and Duquesne University.

As the work finalized I had the remarkable good fortune to be assigned an assistant whose abilities as a conscientious proofreader and as a perceptive judge of content and style would be difficult to estimate. Suffice it to say, I am delighted to acknowledge the assistance of Rae Adams and to thank her and her husband, Dan, for their work on the typescript of this book.

During the course of this work, I received continual support, both financial and moral, from William C. Havard, Dean of the College of Arts and Sciences at Virginia Polytechnic Institute and State University, and from two department heads, Wilson C. Snipes and Hilbert H. Campbell. It is gratifying to work for and with these men.

And finally, to my son, Ehren, who has suffered patiently through the writing of a dissertation and two books in the course of his six short years, I can only say thank you.

List of Journal Abbreviations

BQR	Bodleian Quarterly Review
CBEL	Cambridge Bibliography of English Literature
CHEL	Cambridge History of the English Literature
CL	Comparative Literature
Coll Lang Assoc J	College Language Association Journal
Comp D	Comparative Drama
DAI	Dissertation Abstracts International
DNB	Dictionary of National Biography
EA	Études Anglaises
EIC	Essays in Criticism (Oxford)
ELH	Journal of English Literary History
ELN	English Language Notes (U. of Colo.)
ELR	English Literary Renaissance
Eng Miscellany	English Miscellany
Engl Inst Annual	English Institute Annual
ES	English Studies
E Studien	Englische Studien
Fortnightly Rev	Fortnightly Review
HLB	Harvard Library Bulletin
HLQ	Huntington Library Quarterly
JEGP	Journal of English and Germanic Philology
J of ELH	Journal of English Literary History
Lib Q	Library Quarterly
London Q	London Quarterly
M & L	Music and Letters (London)
MLA	Modern Language Association

MLN	Modern Language Notes
MLQ	Modern Language Quarterly
MLR	Modern Language Review
MP	Modern Philology
N & Q	Notes and Queries
Northwestern Missouri State Teachers Coll St	Northwestern Missouri State Teachers College Studies
Oxford Bibl Soc Proc & Papers	Proceedings and Papers of the Oxford Bibliographical Society
PBSA	Papers of the Bibliographical Society of America
PLL	Papers on Language and Literature
PMLA	Publications of the Modern Language Association of America
PQ	Philological Quarterly (Iowa City)
Proc Br Academy	Proceedings of the British Academy
Proc Oxford Bibl Soc	Proceedings of the Oxford Bibliographical Society
Ren D	Renaissance Drama (Northwestern U.)
Ren D, n. s.	Renaissance Drama, new series
Ren P	Renaissance Papers
RES	Review of English Studies
RES, n. s.	Review of English Studies, new series
RORD	Research Opportunites in Renaissance Drama
SB	Studies in Bibliography: Papers of the Bibliographical Society of the University of Virginia
SEL	Studies in English Literature, 1500-1900
Shak Sur	Shakespeare Survey
SHR	Southern Humanities Review
SN	Studia Neophilologica
SP	Studies in Philology
SQ	Shakespeare Quarterly
SRO	Shakespearean Research Opportunities
Texas St Lit & Lang	Texas Studies in Literature and Language

TLS	[London] Times Literary Supplement
TN	Theatre Notes
Univ of Colorado Stud, Ser in Lang & Lit	University of Colorado Studies, Series in Language and Literature

General Reference and Bibliographies

001   *Abstracts of English Studies.* Boulder, CO: National Council
      of Teachers of English, 1958- .
      Check the editorial note prefacing each number for a
      discussion of abstract policy, format, indexing, and the
      division of categories.

002   ADAMS, JOSEPH QUINCY, JR. *Bibliography, 1904-43.* Brattleboro,
      VT: E. L. Hildreth, 1943. 15pp.
      Adams lists 105 books, articles, long reviews, and ad-
      dresses for the thirty-nine-year period. Prefaced to the
      bibliography is a list of his editorial duties from 1916-
      1943.

003   _____, ed. *The Dramatic Records of Sir Henry Herbert, Master
      of the Revels 1623-73.* 1917; rept. NY: Benjamin Blom,
      1964. xi, 155pp.
      The first half of this book is a primary source of in-
      formation on censorship, licenses, and fees related to Eng-
      lish drama from 1622-42. Included are documents and facts
      concerning plays, presses, playhouses and their companies,
      musicians, and court drama. Information is drawn from Sir
      Henry Herbert's office-book and miscellaneous other docu-
      ments related to play production.

004   ALLEN, DON CAMERON. *The Star-Crossed Renaissance: The
      Quarrel about Astrology and Its Influence in England.*
      1941; rept. NY: Octagon Books, 1966. xi, 280pp.
      Allen's study is a history of the influence of astrology
      and related subjects on the literature, society, and insti-
      tutions of the English Renaissance.

005   ALLIBONE, SAMUEL AUSTIN. *A Critical Dictionary of English
      Literature, and British and American Authors.* Philadelphia:
      J. B. Lippincott, 1858-91. 2 vols.
      Allibone's dictionary contains over 37,000 articles on
      authors, and he enumerates over 93,000 titles. As a refer-
      ence work it is valuable because of its comprehensive na-
      ture - covering, as it does, pieces of biographical,

bibliographical, and critical information as were deemed of particular significance in the nineteenth century.

006　*Annual Bibliography of English Language and Literature.*
Cambridge:　Bowes and Bowes for the Modern Humanistic Research Association, 1920-　. Rept. vols. 1-33. NY:　AMS.
　　As well as listing articles, dissertations, and books, this annual bibliography covers significant reviews related to English language and literature.

007　APPERSON, GEORGE LATIMER.　*English Proverbs and Proverbial Phrases.　A Historical Dictionary.*　London and Toronto: J. M. Dent and Sons, 1929.　ix, 721pp.
　　Proverbs are alphabetically listed by key words or catch phrases, with at least one citation for where the proverb has appeared.　*See* the preface for a full statement on how proverbs are indexed.

008　ARBER, EDWARD, ed.　*A Transcription of the Registers of the Company of Stationers of London:　1554-1640.*　Privately printed, 1875-77.　5 vols.
　　Volume IV of this work contains the transcription for 1620-1640; Volume V is the index.

009　ARNOTT, JAMES F. and J. W. ROBINSON.　*English Theatrical Literature, 1559-1900: A Bibliography Incorporating Robert W. Lowe's* A Bibliographical Account of English Theatrical Literature [1888].　London:　The Society for Theatre Research, 1970.　xxii, 486pp.
　　Read the authors' preface for a concise statement about materials and methods for the bibliography.　The work has thorough cross-references; there are author, short-title, and place of publication indexes by Catherine D. Aird.

010　AUBREY, JOHN.　*Brief Lives.*　Ed. by Oliver Lawson Dick.
London:　Aecker and Warburg, 1949.　cxiv, 408pp.
　　Dick's lengthy introduction is a discussion of Aubrey's contribution to biography.　The editor discusses Aubrey's accuracies, inaccuracies, sources, and some related works. Each entry is prefaced by biographical material which Dick supplies.　There is a bibliography of other *Lives* and of articles related to Aubrey.　There is also a glossary of persons and a thorough index.

011　BAILEY, RICHARD WELD and DOLORES M. BURTON.　*English Stylistics: A Bibliography.*　Cambridge, MA:　MIT Press, 1968.　xxii, 198pp.

2

Berry, William Turner

One section of this book, "The Renaissance [to 1660]," includes references to major works, commentary, and general secondary sources related to Renaissance stylistics. This section should be read in conjunction with the one on "Cue Titles and Abbreviations." Many works are annotated, and the book is indexed by author.

012 BAKER, DAVID ERSKINE; ISAAC REED; STEPHEN JONES. *Biographia Dramatica*. London: Longman, Hurst, 1812. 3 vols: in 4 pts.
The work is an alphabetical listing, by author, including "historical and critical memoirs, and original anecdotes about authors and actors from early times to 1811." The Introduction to Volume I (pp. ix-lxxv) is a lengthy survey of late eighteenth century attitudes toward the history of the English stage.

013 BAKER, HERSHEL CLAY. *Hyder Edward Rollins: A Bibliography*. Cambridge, MA: Harvard University Press, 1960. 51pp.
After a brief biography of Rollins, Baker gives a chronological list of Rollins' works, as well as a list of dissertations written under him. The work is indexed topically.

014 THE BALLAD SOCIETY. *The Roxburghe Ballads*. Hertford: S. Austin and Sons, 1871-99. 8 vols. in 27 pts.
This collection is a comprehensive listing of early ballads. Parts 14, 15, 16, 17, and 20 are the Bagford Ballads; Volume VIII contains additional notes and ballads.

015 BERGERON, DAVID M. *Twentieth-Century Criticism of English Masques, Pageants, and Entertainments: 1558-1642*. London: Trinity University Press, 1972. 67pp.
Bergeron's bibliography contains 416 general and specific works on the English masque, pageant and entertainment. It is indexed by author and subject. There is also a brief supplement on the folk play and related forms with selected criticism by Harry R. Caldwell.

016 BERRY, WILLIAM TURNER and H. EDMUND POOLE. *Annals of Printing; A Chronological Encyclopedia from the Earliest Times to 1950*. London: Blanford Press, 1966. xix, 315pp.
Information is chronicled by date; citations are annotated and supplementary references are given. The work is liberally illustrated and indexed by author and work. A bibliography is included.

Besterman, Theodore

017 BESTERMAN, THEODORE. *A World Bibliography of Bibliographies.*
3rd rev. and enlg. ed. Geneva: Societas Bibliographica,
1955. 4 vols.
"The number of volumes recorded and separately collated
is . . . about 80,000, arranged under about 12,000 headings
and sub-headings."

018 BIGMORE, E. C. and C. W. H. BIGMORE. *A Bibliography of
Printing.* London: Bernard Quaritch, 1884. 2 vols.
Volume I is A-L inclusive; Volume II contains M-Z.
Entries are frequently annotated.

019 *Biographia Britannica, or, The Lives of the Most Eminent
Persons Who Have Flourished in Great Britain and Ireland,
from the Earliest Ages, down to the Present Times. . . .*
1747-66. Rept. Heldesheim: Georg Olms, 1973. 6 vols.
This work is an early reference dictionary to the
writers of England, Scotland and Ireland. It is more than
a mere compilation of records and information from Dempster,
Langbaine, Anthony à Wood, and others.

020 BISHOP, WILLIAM WARNER. *A Checklist of American Copies of
"Short-Title Catalogue" Books.* Ann Arbor: University of
Michigan Press, 1944. xvi, 250pp.
Bishop's work supplements Pollard and Redgrave, as does
David Ramage's *A Finding-List of English Books to 1640 in
Libraries in the British Isles* (1958).

021 BOHN, HENRY G., comp. *A Hand-Book of Proverbs.* London:
George Bell and Sons, 1879. xvi, 583pp.
Bohn's work is a compilation of earlier studies by Ray,
Fuller, Camden, Herbert, Trussler, and others. The table
of contents should be checked for categorical and geographical divisions of proverbs. Of most value is the
alphabetical listing of proverbs, pp. 281-583.

022 BRYDGES, SAMUEL EGERTON. *Censuria Literaria.* London:
Longman, Hurst, Rees, and Orme, 1805-09. 10 vols.
This work is sub-titled "Containing titles, abstracts,
and opinions of old English books, with original disquisi-
tions, articles of biography, and other antiquities."

023 BUCHAN, PETER. *Ancient Ballads and Songs of the North of
Scotland.* 1828; rept. Edinburgh: William Paterson, 1875.
2 vols.
Each ballad is accompanied by explanatory materials
housed in the "Notes" at the end of each volume. The table
of contents serves as an index to the ballads.

024   BUSH, DOUGLAS. *English Literature in the Earlier Seventeenth
      Century, 1600-1660.* 2nd ed. Oxford: Oxford University
      Press, 1962. 680pp.
      See particularly Chapter III, "The Successors of Spenser:
      Song-Books and Miscellanies," pp. 76-106.

025   *Calendar of State Papers, Domestic Series, of the Reign of
      Charles I.* Ed. by J. Bruce. London: Public Record
      Office, 1858-71. 22 vols.
      Each of the twenty-two volumes runs chronologically,
      with supplemental appendices by date and a full index.

026   *The New Catholic Encyclopaedia.* Ed. by staff of Catholic
      University. NY: McGraw-Hill, 1967. 15 vols.
      The index for this work is thoroughly comprehensive,
      and is found in Volume XV.

027   CHILD, FRANCIS JAMES, ed. *English and Scottish Ballads.*
      London: Sampson and Low, 1861. 8 vols.
      Book I contains ballads involving superstitions of
      various kinds: fairies, elves, water-sprites, enchantments,
      and ghostly apparitions; there are also some legends of
      popular heroes. Book II covers tragic love ballads; Book
      III, other tragic ballads; Book IV, love ballads not tragic;
      Book V, ballads of Robin Hood, his followers, and compeers;
      Book VI, ballads of other outlaws; Book VII, historical
      ballads; Book VIII, miscellaneous ballads, especially
      humorous ones. Book VIII also contains the index.

028   CHUBB, THOMAS. *The Printed Maps in the Atlas of Great
      Britain and Ireland, 1579-1870.* London: G. Philips,
      1927. xvii, 479pp.
      Chubb's book is a checklist of maps and cartographic
      materials; it is liberally illustrated.

029   CLARK, ALICE. *Working Life of Women in the Seventeenth
      Century.* London: Routledge, 1919. 335pp.
      Clark deals with the sociological and economic impact of
      women on trade, particularly in agriculture, textiles,
      crafts, and the professions. The study is derived from
      "women who move through [the period's] various scenes,
      either in the pages of the dramatists or as revealed by
      domestic papers or in . . . public records." Check the
      index and the abbreviated list of contents at the beginnings
      of chapters for sources.

030   CLARK, ARTHUR MELVILLE. "A Bibliography of Thomas Heywood's
      Works." *Proc Oxford Bibl Soc,* 1 (1925), 97-153.

Clark, E. C.

       Clark's study is a descriptive bibliography of Heywood's works from 1599-1675. The bibliography concludes with notations on Heywood's commendatory verses for published works, as well as a list of works edited by Heywood.

031   CLARK, E. C. "English Academical Costume." *The Archaeological Journal,* 50 (1893), 73-104; 137-149; 183-209.
       Clark gives a survey, primarily, of early academic costumes.

032   COURTNEY, W. L. "Oxford Plays down to the Restoration." *N & Q* (December 1886), p. 464.
       Courtney gives a list of university plays from 1547-1663, derived primarily from Halliwell's *List of Plays,* Wood's *Annals,* and Nichols' *Progresses of Queen Elizabeth and King James.* Ten plays are listed between 1626 and 1642.

033   CUNNINGHAM, C. WILLETT; PHILLIS CUNNINGHAM; CHARLES BEARD. *A Dictionary of English Costume.* London: Adam and Charles Black, 1960. 281pp.
       Part I is a dictionary of garments, dated in terms of their length of fashionableness; Part II "is a glossary of materials with the date they came into use." There is also a brief list of obsolete color names, prior to 1800. 303 line drawings are given to illustrate the text.

034   DARLINGTON, IDA and JAMES L. HOWGEGO. *Printed Maps of London* circa *1553-1850.* London: George Philip and Son, 1964. ix, 257pp.
       Included in this catalogue of printed maps are references to Ralph Agas' (?) *Civitas Londinum* and Cornelius Dankerts' . . . *London,* 1633, as well as his *The Cittie of London,* 2nd ed., *c.* 1645.

035   DAVIES, GODFREY. *The Early Stuarts, 1603-1660.* In *The Oxford History of England.* Vol. V, 2nd ed. Oxford: Clarendon Press, 1959. xxiii, 458pp.
       Davies approaches the Stuarts from a wide variety of topics, under the general categories of political and constitutional history, religious history, foreign relations, social and economic history, foreign trade and the colonies, education and science, the arts, and literature. In dramatic literature, he is particularly concerned with Jonson, decadence, Puritan assaults, dramatists' ridicule, and the closing of the theatres. There is a complete index.

036 DAWSON, G. E., ed. *Records, Plays and Players in Kent 1450-
1642.* In *Malone Society Collections.* Vol. VII. Oxford:
The University Press, 1965. xxxi, 211pp.
Dawson's introduction to his transcription is a discussion of the records themselves, the nature of the country
and the towns during this period, the kinds of entertainments that were about, the players in the towns, the problems of dating, the incompleteness of the records, and the
reconstruction of itineraries of acting companies.

037 DAY, CYRUS LAWRENCE and ELEANORE BOSWELL MURRIE. *English
Song-Books 1651-1702: A Bibliography.* London: The
Bibliographical Society, 1940. 439pp.
This work is an exhaustive bibliography of early English
song books. Of especial interest is the 4150-entry alphabetical list of incipits in the song books, particularly
useful for tracing musical settings for popular songs.
Check the introduction for a clarification on the organiza-
tion of the book. The work is indexed by composer, author,
singer, actor, tune, air, source, song book, printer, publisher, and bookseller.

038 DEWEY, NICHOLAS. "The Academic Drama of the Early Stuart
Period (1603-1642): A Checklist of Secondary Sources."
RORD, 12 (1969), 33-42.
Dewey's article supplements F. S. Boas' *University Drama
in the Tudor Drama* (1914). He cites 110 works, dividing
them in terms of "General Criticism and Scholarship" and
"Bibliography and Chronology."

039 DONOVAN, DENNIS. "Thomas Dekker: 1945-1965." In *Elizabethan
Bibliographies Supplements II.* London: Nether Press,
1967. Pp. 15-28.
Donovan supplies 168 citations.

040 _____. "Thomas Heywood: 1938-1965." In *Elizabethan
Bibliographies Supplements II.* London: Nether Press,
1967. Pp. 31-42.
There are seventy-three citations for the period.

041 DOWNES, JOHN. *Roscius Anglicanus.* Ed. by Montague Summers.
1929; rept. NY: Benjamin Blom, 1968. xiii, 286pp.
Downes' book is a contemporary source of information related to the performance and/or re-writing of Caroline plays
during the Restoration period. The main text should be read
in conjunction with the explanatory notes, which are the
majority of the work.

Fleay, Frederick Gard

042   FLEAY, FREDERICK GARD. *A Biographical Chronicle of the
        English Drama: 1559-1642.* London: Reeves and Turner,
        1891. 2 vols.
            Volume I contains, among other things, biographies of
        playwrights (Adamson-Jonson); Volume II contains biog-
        raphies (Jonson-Zouch), as well as descriptions of plays
        by anonymous Caroline playwrights.

043   _____. *A Chronicle History of the London Stage, 1559-1642.*
        London: Reeves and Turner, 1890. 424pp.
            Fleay's book is characterized by a substantial amount of
        factual material, much of which is verifiable. Chapters
        VI, VII, and VIII are most useful, the first two because
        they are concerned with Caroline theatres, acting companies,
        authors, and court performances, and the latter because it
        contains indexed lists to theatres, companies, actors,
        authors, university plays, pageants, and court plays.
        There is no cumulative index as such, but the majority of
        the book is an index.

044   FORD, WYN K. *Music in England before 1800: A Selected
        Bibliography.* London: The Library Association, 1967.
        128pp.
            Of particular note, in Part I, are sections on instru-
        ments and instrumental music, folk and church music, social
        conditions (as they affect Royal music), and seventeenth
        century music and drama. Part II is primarily an alpha-
        betized list of composers, musicians, and performers with
        accompanying lists of general and biographical entries.
        The book has an author index and concludes with a checklist
        of primary sources.

045   FULGHUM, WALTER B., JR. *A Dictionary of Biblical Allusions in
        English Literature.* NY: Holt, Rinehart and Winston, 1965.
        viii, 291pp.
            Fulgrum cites frequently alluded to words, phrases, and
        characters, and gives the origin of the Biblical term, a
        comment on what it means in context, and a citation for
        where it can be found.

046   FURNIVALL, FREDERICH JAMES. *Ballads from Manuscripts.*
        London: Taylor and Company, 1868-73. 2 vols.
            The full title of Furnivall's work reads like the table
        of contents; it is "Ballads from manuscripts. Ballads on
        the conditions of England in Henry VIII's and Edward VI's
        reigns (including the state of the clergy, monks and
        friars), on Wolsey, Anne Boleyn, Somerset, and Lady Jane
        Grey; with Wynkyn de Worde's *Treatise of a Galaunt* (AB.
        1520 A. D.)." The work is indexed.

Gomme, Alice Bertha

047   _____ and J. W. HALES, eds. *The Percy Folio*. London: De la
         More Press, 1905. 4 vols.
         The table of contents for each volume is its index to
         titles of ballads. Volume IV, pp. 335-39, contains a
         series of suggested readings and corrections of the first
         volumes.

048   GARDINER, SAMUEL R. *History of England from the Accession of
         James I to the Outbreak of the Civil War*. London:
         Longmans, Green and Company, 1883. 10 vols.
         Full tables of contents are given for each volume, and
         the work is indexed in Volume X. Dates are I: 1603-07;
         II: 1607-16; III: 1616-21; IV: 1621-23; V: 1623-25;
         VI: 1625-29; VII: 1629-35; VIII: 1635-39; IX: 1639-41;
         and X: 1641-42.

049   GASKELL, PHILIP. *A New Introduction to Bibliography*. Oxford:
         Oxford University Press, 1972. xii, 438pp.
         The work contains a good bibliography of relevant
         sources, pp. 392-413, and a thorough index. *See also*
         Ronald B. McKerrow's *Introduction to Bibliography for
         Literary Students* (1925), or the reprinted and corrected
         editions of 1927 and 1968; Fredson T. Bowers' *Principles
         of Bibliographical Description* (1949), and his *Textual and
         Literary Criticism* (1959); Vinton A. Dearing's *Methods of
         Textual Editing* (1962), in which he discusses the computer
         as an adjunct to the editing process; and William A.
         Jackson's *Bibliography and Literary Studies* (1962).

050   GODFREY, ELIZABETH. *Social Life under the Stuarts*. London:
         Grant Richards, 1904. 273pp.
         Godfrey's is a comprehensive survey of a wide variety of
         subjects related to the social order under the Stuarts. It
         is concerned with town and country life, dramatic, musical
         and artistic entertainments, science, medicine, supersti-
         tion, literary travel experiences, literary coteries, moral
         codes, and their effect on life. A precursor of Wright's
         Middle-Class Society, this volume is worth noting for its
         references to Caroline playwrights such as May, Suckling,
         and Davenant.

051   GOMME, ALICE BERTHA. *The Traditional Games of England,
         Scotland, and Ireland*. London: David Nutt, 1894-98.
         2 vols.
         The work is subtitled "With Tunes, Singing-Rhymes, and
         Methods of Playing According to the Variants Extant and
         Recorded in Different Parts of the Kingdom." A list of
         games covered is prefaced to the discussion of the games

Greg, W. W.

themselves. Games are listed alphabetically and cross-indexed by alternate titles.

052 GREG, W. W. *A Bibliography of the English Printed Drama to the Restoration.* London: Oxford University Press, 1939, 1951, 1957, 1959. 4 vols.
Volume I contains Stationers' Records Plays to 1616; Volume II contains plays 1617-1689, Latin Plays and Lost Plays; Volume III contains Collections, Reference Lists, and Appendices, including advertisements, prefatory materials, actor's lists, author lists, dedications, licenses, and so forth; Volume IV contains introductions, additions, corrections, and an index by title.

053 ____. *A Companion to Arber.* Oxford: Clarendon Press, 1967. vii, 451pp.
Greg subtitled his work "A Calendar of Documents in Edward Arber's Transcription of the Registers of the Company of Stationers of London 1554-1640, with Text and Calendar of Supplementary Documents." The subtitle summarizes the work's intent and content. Check the preface for Greg's rules for transcribing documents, and check the very thorough index for individual concerns.

054 ____. *A List of English Plays Written before 1643 and Printed before 1700.* 1900; rept. NY: Haskell House, 1969. xi, 158pp.
The descriptive list is arranged alphabetically by author. Greg includes "all the works of authors who are known to have written plays, whether extant or not, previous to [1642]." This is supplemented in Greg's *A List of Masques, Pageants, Etc. Supplementary to* A List of English Plays. London: Blades, East and Blades, 1902. xi, 35, cxxxi. This work concludes with a long essay intended as an introduction and appendix to *A List of English Plays.*

055 GRIERSON, HERBERT JOHN CLIFFORD. *First Half of the 17th Century.* Edinburgh and London: W. Blackison, 1906. xiv, 338pp.
Grierson surveys drama in Holland, England, France, Italy, and Germany during the first half of the seventeenth century. The work is indexed.

056 GROVE, GEORGE. *Dictionary of Music and Musicians.* Ed. by Eric Blom. 5th ed. NY: St. Martin's Press, 1954-1961. 10 vols.

Grove's *Dictionary* is the standard reference work for sources and information related to musicology, composers, compositions and terminology. The scope of all five editions has been "encyclopaedic and universal"; nonetheless, one might consult the third edition, in conjunction with the most recent edition, to ascertain eighteenth and nineteenth century attitudes toward music.

057   GUFFEY, GEORGE ROBERT, comp. "Ben Jonson, 1947-65." In *Elizabethan Bibliographies Supplements III*. London: Nether Press, 1968. Pp. 21-44.
Guffey's checklist is comprehensive for the eighteen-year span of the bibliography.

058   ____. "Thomas Randolph, 1949-65." In *Elizabethan Bibliographies Supplements III*. London: Nether Press, 1968. P. 47.
Guffey lists, over a sixteen-year period, the few works published on Randolph; these are primarily dissertations.

059   HALKETT, SAMUEL and JOHN LAING. *A Dictionary of Anonymous and Pseudonymous Literature of Great Britain*. Rev. by James Kennedy; W. A. Smith; A. F. Jonson. Edinburgh and London, 1926-34. 7 vols. Volume VIII (1900-50), and Volume IX (Additions to Vols. I-VIII), Ed. by Dennis E. Rhodes and Anna E. C. Simoni. Edinburgh: Oliver Boyd, 1956, 1962.
The entries are alphabetical, by short title; authors' names are included when known. General bibliographical details are included.

060   HALLIWELL, J. O. *A Dictionary of Old English Plays*. London: John Russell Smith, 1860. viii, 296pp.
Included are plays "existing either in print or in manuscript, from the earliest times to the close of the seventeenth century"; Latin plays written by English authors during the same period are also included. Works are listed alphabetically by title; each citation bears a note as to author, date, and so forth. The work concludes with a list of collections and an index to authors.

061   HARBAGE, ALFRED. *Annals of English Drama, 975-1700*. Philadelphia: University of Pennsylvania Press, 1940; rev. by Samuel Schoenbaum, 1964. First and second supplements to the revised editions, Evanston, IL: Northwestern University Press, 1966, 1970.
Harbage gives a chronological list of plays, by author, type, auspices, first and last edition, and two supplements

Harbage, Alfred

of extant and nonextant plays not included in the previous
list because of ambiguous dates. These are followed by individual indexes of English playwrights, English plays,
foreign playwrights, foreign plays, dramatic companies, and
a descriptive list of theatres. An appendix, "The Extant
Play Manuscripts, 975-1700: Their Location and Catalogue
Numbers," concludes the work.

062 _____. "Elizabethan and Seventeenth-Century Play Manuscripts."
PMLA, 50 (1935), 687-99.
Of particular interest is Harbage's alphabetical list of
manuscript plays from 1558-1700. He includes, when possible, the author, date, and location of the manuscript, as
well as whether or not it is an holograph or autograph--
when such information is available.

063 HARBEN, HENRY A. *A Dictionary of London*. London: Herbert
Jenkins, 1918. 641pp.
Harben's work is a topographical and historical dictionary of institution, building, street, and place names
with a geographical description of locations. In the case
of institutions, various locations are cited if the building location changes. The book includes citations for many
locations prior to the 1500's, but the majority of the work
is concerned with locations in the sixteenth through the
eighteenth centuries.

064 HARDISON, O. B. *The Enduring Monument: A Study of the Idea
of Praise in Renaissance Literary Theory and Practice*.
Chapel Hill: University of North Carolina Press, 1962.
Hardison's study is primarily related to classical
models of criticism, illustrated in Renaissance critical
works and poetry. However, as a reference work, it is important for the interpretation of the concept of praise and
the demonstration of the ways in which it is exhibited in
Renaissance literature.

065 HARVEY, PAUL, comp. *The Oxford Companion to English
Literature*. Rev. by Dorothy Eagle. Oxford: Clarendon
Press, 1967. x, 961pp.
This compendium is an alphabetical arrangement of
authors, their works and literary societies, as well as a
list of terms, concepts and allusions related to English
(and certain aspects of American) literature. The entries
are explanations as well as "sign posts" for further study.

066 HASTINGS, JAMES, ed. *Encyclopaedia of Religion and Ethics*.
NY: Charles Scribner's Sons, 1908-26. 13 vols.

Volume XIII contains the indexes: General Index, pp. 1-660; Index to Foreign Words, pp. 661-709; Index to Scripture Passages, pp. 710-11; and a list of authors of articles, pp. 712-57.

067 HAYDEN, HIRAM COLLINS. *Counter-Renaissance*. NY: Scribners, 1950. xvii, 705pp.
Ostensibly, Hayden's work ends with death of Bacon in 1626 (the outside limit he puts on the English Renaissance); nonetheless, because it is a study of the idea of counter-Renaissance, and based on the literature of the time, it serves as an excellent background for the study of the history of ideas during the reign of Charles I.

068 HAZLITT, W. CAREW. *Hand-Book to the Popular, Poetical, and Dramatic Literature of Great Britain, from the Invention of Printing to the Restoration*. London: John Russell Smith, 1867. xii, 701pp.
Works are catalogued by author; the hand-book concludes with a list of additions, mostly dramatic in nature.

069 _____. *A Manual for the Collector and Amateur of Old English Plays*. London: Pickering and Chatto, 1892. viii, 284pp.
The subtitle of this work is "Edited from the material formed by Kirkman, Langbaine, Downes, Oldys, and Halliwell-Phillipps, with extensive additions and corrections." The plays are listed alphabetically by title; each citation includes a brief statement about the play.

070 HILER, HILAIRE and MEYER HILER, comps. *Bibliography of Costume*. 1939; rept. NY: Benjamin Blom, 1967. 911pp.
This work is an exhaustive compilation of bibliographical information by author, type, country, concept, and term, in an alphabetical listing. Consult the introduction for aid in interpreting and finding information.

071 HOENIGER, F. DAVID and JUDITH F. M. HOENIGER. *The Development of Natural History in Stuart England: From Gerard to the Royal Society*. Charlottesville: University Press of Virginia for the Folger Shakespeare Library, 1969. 54pp.
This monograph is divided into sections on background, on Sir Thomas Browne, and on the founding of the Royal Society, and it concludes with a list of suggested readings and a series of nineteen plates.

072 HOLE, CHRISTINA. *English Home-Life, 1500-1800*. London: Batesford, 1947. vii, 184pp.

Holzknecht, Karl J.

       This work can be used in conjunction with *The English Housewife in the Seventeenth Century* (1953) by the same author. Both are thorough surveys of domestic attitudes and practices during their respective time frames; both are liberally illustrated and indexed.

073   HOLZKNECHT, KARL J. *Outlines of Tudor and Stuart Plays, 1497-1642.* London: Methuen, 1963. viii, 442pp.
       For each author treated, Holzknecht includes a brief biography, a critical comment, and a bibliography related to the plays by that author which he summarizes. In the latter part of the work, he summarizes the following plays that are relevant to this study: *'Tis Pity; The Broken Heart; Perkin Warbeck; The Lady of Pleasure; The Cardinal; Love and Honor; The Jovial Crew; The Maid of Honor;* and *The Fair Maid of the West, Part II.* Also included is a tabulated quick reference to the standard anthologies in which the plays appear. The book has a character index and an index of plays and playwrights.

074   HOWARD-HILL, TREVOR H. *Bibliography of British Literary Bibliographies.* Oxford: Oxford University Press, 1969-
       Check the table of contents for the breakdown of categories. The volumes are copiously indexed.

075   HOWELL, WILLIAM SAMUEL. *Logic and Rhetoric in England, 1500-1700.* Princeton: Princeton University Press, 1956. vii, 411pp.
       After an introduction, Howell devotes his study to the background of scholastic logic, the three patterns of traditional logic, the English Ramists' dialect and rhetoric, the counter-reform, and the new systems of logic following Bacon, Hobbes, Lamy, Glanville, and Descartes.

076   INSTITUT PÉDAGOGIQUE NATIONAL. *La Vie théatrale au temps de la Renaissance.* Paris: Institute Pédagogique National, 1963. xviii, 234pp.
       This bibliography contains 460 annotated sources, plus others related to the Continental Renaissance. The table of contents is following p. 234.

077   JACOB, GILES. *The Poetical Register: or, The Lives and Characters of the English Dramatic Poets.* 1719; rept. NY: Garland Publishing Company, 1970. xxviii, 452pp.
       Giles acknowledges his indebtedness to Langbaine while trying to correct the latter's faults and "prejudices." The work contains an alphabetic register of the dramatists, a brief section on "Modern Dramatick Poets" (*c.* 1717); and

Langbaine, Gerald

Jacob gives a list of plays by anonymous authors, and an index of the plays.

078 JORDAN, W. K. *The Charities of London, 1480-1660: The Aspiration and the Achievements of the Urban Society.* London: George Allen and Unwin, 1960. 463pp.
This work is a good reference book which can be used in conjunction with *Philanthropy in England, 1480-1660,* and *The Charities of Rural England, 1480-1660,* both by the same author. The books are thoroughly indexed and documented.

079 KINLOCH, GEORGE RITCHIE. *Ancient Scottish Ballads.* London: Longman, Rees, Orme, Brown and Green, 1827. xiv, 270pp.
Kinloch's volume contains historical and explanatory notes for all ballads and the appendix contains the airs for many of them.

080 LABARRE, E. J. *A Dictionary of Paper and Paper-Making Terms.* Amsterdam: N. V. Swets and Zeitlinger, 1937. 313pp. plus specimens of paper.
Chapter III, Part I of Labarre's dictionary is concerned with the history and process of papermaking in Europe. Part II is a discussion of the manufacturing of a great variety of types of paper; the dictionary (pp. 95-260), follows. Included are indexes to French, German, Dutch, and Italian terms, as well as forty-five samples of paper.

081 LANGBAINE, GERALD. *An Account of the English Dramatick Poets.* 1691; rept. NY: Garland Publishing Company, 1973. 589pp.
This work is a reprint of the complete edition of 1691, rather than the 1699 edition which was abridged by Charles Gilden. As Arthur Freeman points out in his brief preface to this edition, "this book was indispensable to any scholar of the earlier English drama, and it remains . . . a source for otherwise lost traditional information, and as a classic of seventeenth-century literary criticism." Langbaine attempts in his "Accounts" to correct and update Winstanley. An index to the plays and a brief appendix that "compleat[s] the Account of all Plays that have been printed as far as this present Time" follows.

082 _____. *Momus Triumphans; or, The Plagiaries of the English Stage; and The Lives and Characters of the English Dramatick Poets.* 1688 or 1689; rept. NY: Garland Publishing Company, 1972. 7, 32, 182pp.
These works should be read in conjunction with 081.

15

Literature of the Renaissance:

083   *Literature of the Renaissance: A Bibliography and Index.*
       [Title varies]. Chapel Hill: University of North Carolina
       Press, 1922- .
          This bibliography is reprinted from *Studies in Philology.*

084   *The London Stage, 1660-1800: A Calendar of Plays, Entertain-
       ments and Afterpieces, Together with Casts, Receipts, and
       Contemporary Comment Compiled from the Playbills, News-
       papers, and Theatrical Diaries of the Period.* Comp. by
       William Van Lennep; Emmet L. Avery; Arthur H. Scouten;
       George W. Stone; Charles B. Hogan. Carbondale: Southern
       Illinois University Press, 1965-68. 11 vols. in 5 pts.
       Introductions only, Carbondale: Southern Illinois
       University Press, 1968. 5 vols.
          See the table of contents for each of the five parts for
       the contents of the introductions and to check the extent
       of the theatrical seasons covered in that particular volume.
       Each part is thoroughly indexed.

085   McKERROW, RONALD B. *A Dictionary of Printers' and Publishers'
       Devices in England and Scotland 1485-1640.* London:
       Cheswick Press, 1913. liv, 216pp.
          Within the introduction to McKerrow's book is an explana-
       tory note on the arrangement of the work; the book proper
       contains a list of 428 printer's devices, an appendix of
       untraced devices, notes on the transfer of devices, and
       facsimiles. There are five indexes to various subjects.

086   McNAMEE, LAWRENCE FRANCIS. *Dissertations in English and
       American Literature; Theses Accepted by American, British,
       and German Universities, 1864-1964.* NY: Bowker, 1968.
       xi, 1124pp. Supplement I (1964-68). NY: Bowker, 1969.
       x, 450pp.
          McNamee's works are standard references for subjects
       covered in American, British, and German dissertations.

087   MADAN, FALCONER. *A Chart of Oxford Printing, 1468-1900.*
       Oxford: Oxford University Press, 1904. 51pp.
          Madan briefly covers the annals of Oxford printing to
       1900, lists Oxford printers and publishers, mentions many
       incidents and curiosities of the press itself, gives sta-
       tistics on the output of the press, gives the first occur-
       rence of unusual type, and concludes with a chart exhibiting
       the number of books printed or published at Oxford until
       1900. The chart is also broken down by theological and
       classical publications.

Nares, Robert

088 _____. *Oxford Books: A Bibliography of Printed Works
Relating to the University and City of Oxford or Printed
or Published There, I.* Oxford: Clarendon Press, 1895.
365pp.
Approach the bibliography *via* the index at the conclusion of the work.

089 MARSHBURN, JOSEPH H. *Murder and Witchcraft in England,
1500-1640, as Recounted in Pamphlets, Ballads, Broadsides,,
and Plays.* Norman: University of Oklahoma Press, 1971.
xxiii, 287pp.
Marshburn's work is a series of forty-seven case histories of murder and witchcraft in England from 1550 to
1635, five of which are related to the Caroline period.
The work is a thorough history and analysis of contemporary
materials related to the subject, and as such it is valuable
for the background materials it includes, as well as the
insights that are given into the social, religious and
economic aspects of the English Renaissance. Twenty-five
illustrations are included, and a lengthy list of auxiliary
entries of incidents, by date.

090 MONRO, ISABEL and DOROTHY E. COOK. *Costume Index.* NY: H. W.
Wilson, 1937. 338pp.
This work is a tightly-compacted, useful, but confusing
index to costume terms. The key must be consulted before
the main entries can be interpreted. *See* 091.

091 _____ and KATE M. MONRO. *Costume Index Supplement.* NY: H. W.
Wilson, 1957. 210pp.
Like the work above, this book is a subject index to
plates and to illustrated texts related to costume. It has
the same weaknesses, but almost doubles the amount of useful materials.

092 MORPURGO, J. E., comp. *Life under the Stuarts.* London:
Falcon Educational Books, 1950. 189pp.
This volume contains essays, by various hands, on constitutional history and political ideas, on religion,
London life, country life, economics, education, science,
poetry, the theatre, prose, literature, art, architecture,
music, sport, and dress. It is liberally illustrated.

093 NARES, ROBERT. *A Glossary of Words, Phrases, Names and
Allusions in the Works of English Authors, Particularly of
Shakespeare and His Contemporaries.* 1905; rept. Detroit:
Gale Research Company, 1966. ix, 982pp.

[Nichols, John Gough]

The glossary, in alphabetical order by significant word, includes a definition for each term or phrase and a literary reference.

094 [NICHOLS, JOHN GOUGH]. "A Bibliographical List of Lord Mayors' Pageants." In *London Pageants*. London: J. B. Nichols and Sons, 1837. Pp. 93-122.
Note the years 1626-1639 and the introductory, narrative description of Lord Mayors' pageants as they were affected by Heywood, Taylor, Tatham, and Jordan.

095 NUNGEZER, EDWIN. *A Dictionary of Actors and of Other Persons Associated with the Public Representation of Plays in England before 1642.* 1929; rept. NY: Greenwood Press, 1968. 437pp.
The author's purpose for his dictionary is "to assemble all the available information regarding actors, theatrical productions, stage attendants and other persons known to have been associated with the representation of plays in England before 1642." A typical entry includes historical data, the company and/or plays the person was associated with, and quotations related to the person.

096 PARKES, JOAN. *Travel in England in the Seventeenth Century.* Oxford: Oxford University Press, 1923. xvi, 354pp.
Parkes' book is a thorough analysis of travel and its conventions in the seventeenth century. She discusses the general geography, population and the state of the country, roads, bridges, the watch, postage by land and water, inns, alehouses, general lodgings, highwaymen and other trials and tribulations.

097 PARTRIDGE, A. C. *The Accidence of Jonson's Plays, Masques and Entertainments.* Cambridge: Bowes and Bowes, 1953. xiv, 333pp.
The book includes a "Chronological List of Plays, Masques and Entertainments," and is a thorough morphological study of Jonson's dramatic work. The book also contains an appendix of comparable uses in Shakespeare.

098 PATTISON, BRUCE. *Music and Poetry of the English Renaissance.* London: Methuen, 1948. x, 220pp.
Pattison's purpose is "to demonstrate that the relationship between [poetry and music] was not only intimate but such as could have existed at no other time; that environment and tradition kept poets and composers in close touch; that literary points of view helped to shape literary forms, and that the structure and content of lyric poetry owed

much to music." Check the index for frequent references to
Caroline dramatists.

099 PENNEL, CHARLES A. and WILLIAM P. WILLIAMS. *Elizabethan
Bibliographies Supplements VIII*. London: Nether Press,
1968. 52pp.
 The bibliographies are "Massinger, 1937-65," pp. 15-37;
"Ford, 1940-65," pp. 37-43; and "Shirley, 1945-65," pp. 43-
47.

100 PLANCHÉ, JAMES ROBINSON. *A Cyclopaedia of Costume or
Dictionary of Dress*. London: Chatto and Windus, 1876-79.
2 vols.
 Volume I, "Dictionary," is an alphabetical listing of
terms and concepts related to costume from earliest record-
ings through the eighteenth century. The volume is copiously illustrated with prints and plates. Volume II, "A
General History of Costume," is a chronological exploration
of costume from B.C. 53 through the eighteenth century.
Chapter X, "Theatrical, Allegorical, and Fanciful Costumes,"
is extensive and of value here. Consult the table of contents as well as the index for source materials.

101 *PMLA*. NY: Modern Language Association of America, 1884-
Rept. "Bibliography," 1921-66. NY: AMS.
 The titles of these annual bibliographies vary.

102 POLLARD, ALFRED WILLIAM and GILBERT R. REDGRAVE. *A Short-
Title Catalogue of Books Printed in England, Scotland and
Ireland, and of English Books Printed Abroad, 1475-1640*.
London: B. Quaritch, 1926. xvi, 609pp.; rept. 1946, 1950,
1963, and is presently being revised.
 See Paul G. Morrison's *Index of Printers, Publishers and
Booksellers in . . . STC, 1475-1640* (1950).

103 POLLOCK, FREDERICH and FREDERIC WILLIAM MAITLAND. *The History
of English Law*. 2nd ed. Cambridge: The University Press,
1923. 2 vols.
 Volume I is an analysis of early English legal history
from Roman law to the Middle Ages. Volume II discusses
the doctrines of English law through the Middle Ages, the
condition of man, and jurisdictions and communities.

104 RAMAGE, DAVID. *A Finding-List of English Books to 1640 in
Libraries in the British Isles, Excluding the National
Libraries and the Libraries of Oxford and Cambridge*.
Durham: G. Bailes and Sons, 1958. xiv, 101pp.

Rollins, Hyder Edward

>The preface to Ramage's compilation must be read before
>the list is approached, and one should note that books are
>listed by the *STC* numbers for the 1926 edition. The work
>is supplemented by a list of books not found in the *STC*.

105 ROLLINS, HYDER EDWARD. *An Analytical Index to the Ballad-
Entries (1557-1709) in the Registers of the Company of
Stationers of London.* 1924; rept. with foreword by Leslie
Shepard. Hatboro, PA: Tradition Press, 1967. xv, 324pp.
In his index, Rollins includes 3081 ballads by title,
as well as licensing and publication information. Ballads
are indexed by incipits when these are known. There is
also an index of names and subject.

106 _____, ed. *Cavalier and Puritan: Ballads and Broadsides
Illustrating the Period of the Great Rebellion, 1640-1660.*
NY: New York University Press, 1923. xv, 532pp.
A lengthy introduction and full texts of the ballads are
given. There is an index of titles, first lines, refrains
and tunes, and a glossorial index. Numerous illustrations
from the original broadsides are given.

107 _____, ed. *Old English Ballads, 1553-1625. Chiefly from
Manuscripts.* Cambridge: The University Press, 1920.
xxxi, 423pp.
Full texts of the ballads are included, plus bibliographical information. The work is indexed by first lines, by
titles, and by tunes (when known). A glossary is included.

108 _____, ed. *The Pepys Ballads.* Cambridge, MA: Harvard
University Press, 1929-32. 8 vols.
Rollins states that "the ninety ballads reprinted in the
two initial volumes of my edition of Samuel Pepys' collection were chosen upon an arbitrary but logical basis: they
include only printed ballads, earlier in dates than 1640,
which do not appear in the Ballad Society's *Roxburghe Ballads* and *Bagford Ballads,* or in my *Pepysian Garland.*"
There is no index, but each ballad is prefaced with a
statement to its origin.

109 ROUTH, CHARLES RICHARD NAIRNE, ed. *They Saw It Happen: An
Anthology of Eye-Witnesses' Accounts of Events in British
History 1485-1688.* Oxford: Blackwell, 1956. xv, 220pp.
Approximately one-third of the book is devoted to docu-
ments accounting events during the reign of Charles I.
Each account is prefaced with a transition statement about
the document, and a statement on its source.

110   SAINTSBURY, GEORGE E. B. *History of English Prosody.*
       1906-10; rept. NY: Russell and Russell, 1961. 3 vols.
       See particularly Volume II, Books V-VI, and chapters on
       "The Battle of the Couplets," "The Decay of Dramatic Blank
       Verse," and passing references to Caroline lyricists.

111   SHARP, HAROLD S. and MARJORIE Z. SHARP. *Index to Characters
       in the Performing Arts.* NY: Scarecrow Press, 1966.
       2 vols. in 5 pts.
         The purposes of this work are "to identify a given play
       character with the play in which he or she appears; to tell
       something about the character; to indicate the author or
       authors of the play, and to show as accurately as possible,
       the year in which the play was written, produced, copy-
       righted or published. Approximately 30,000 characters are
       listed from about 3600 plays with 1400 authors." The
       listings are from the fifth century B.C. through 1965.

112   SHUTTLEWORTH, BERTRAM. "W. J. Lawrence: A Handlist." *TN,* 8,
       9, 10 (1953-56), p. 52 ff.
         The eight-segment checklist continues, variously,
       through the three volumes.

113   SIBLEY, GERTRUDE MARIAN. *The Lost Plays and Masques: 1500-
       1642.* Ithaca, NY: Cornell University Press, 1933. 205pp.
         Sibley's checklist is alphabetically arranged by the
       title of the play, and includes as much source and critical
       material on the play as is available to the author: a com-
       prehensive book indexed to names, pseudonyms, and initials
       of authors mentioned.

114   SKEAT, WALTER W. *A Glossary of Tudor and Stuart Words,
       Especially from the Dramatists.* Ed. with addns. by A. L.
       Mayhew, 1914; rept. NY: Burt Franklin, 1968. xviii,
       461pp.
         For each alphabetically listed term a definition is
       given, as well as a variety of literary allusions.

115   SMITH, WILLIAM GEORGE, comp. *The Oxford Dictionary of
       English Proverbs.* Introduction by Janet E. Heseltine.
       2nd rev. Ed. by Paul Harvey. Oxford: Clarendon Press,
       1948. xxxii, 740pp.
         The proverbs are listed alphabetically, with variants
       and a citation as to where they appear.

116   SPARKES, JOHN C. L. and REV. ALFRED J. CARVER. *Catalogue of
       the Cartwright Collection . . . at Dulwich College.*
       London: Spottiswoode, 1884. 55pp.

Steensma, Robert C.

> This work is of particular note because of a reference
> (p. 3) to a catalogue of the collection of William Cart-
> wright's work with "quaint descriptions" that are "highly
> interesting."

117 STEENSMA, ROBERT C. "Jonson: A Checklist of Editions,
   Bibliography and Criticism 1947-64." *RORD*, 9 (1966), 29-46.
   Steensma lists 288 entries and gives a thorough index
   for his work.

118 STEPHEN, LESLIE and SIDNEY LEE. *The Dictionary of National
   Biography*. London: Smith, Elder and Company, 1885-1901.
   69 vols. 1908-09. 22 vols.
   This work is supplemented periodically. The 1951-60
   supplement contains an index covering the years 1901-60.
   The work is the most complete source of British, Irish, and
   Colonial biography to date. *See* corrections and additions,
   cumulative, in *The Bulletin of the Institute of Historical
   Research*.

119 STONEHILL, CHARLES A.; H. WINTHROP STONEHILL; ANDREW BLOCK.
   Anonyma and Pseudonyma. 2nd ed. London: C. A. Stonehill,
   1927. 4 vols.
   Although most references are to anonymous authors of the
   eighteenth and nineteenth centuries, there is still a size-
   able number of seventeenth century references.

120 STRATMAN, CARL J. *Bibliography of English Printed Tragedy,
   1556-1900*. Carbondale: Southern Illinois University Press,
   1966. xx, 843pp.
   To a certain extent Stratman's work overlaps Greg,
   Harbage, Bentley, and Nicoll, but "they do not confine any
   phase of their investigations to tragedy, nor do they attempt to list all editions of a particular tragedy when the
   play falls within the province of their study." Stratman
   does these things and he also mentions 175 tragedies not
   listed in any earlier bibliography.

121 *Studies in Philology*. Chapel Hill: University of North
   Carolina Press, 1917- .
   See "Recent Literature of the English Renaissance" in
   volumes from 1916-1970.

122 TANNENBAUM, SAMUEL A. *Beaumont and Fletcher: A Concise
   Bibliography*. NY: Tannenbaum, 1938. 94pp.
   Of the 1628 entries, several apply to Fletcher's two
   collaborations performed in the Caroline period. The work
   is extensively indexed.

Tillyard, E. M. W.

123   _____. *John Ford: A Concise Bibliography*. NY: Tannenbaum,
1941. 26pp.
This bibliography contains 385 works related directly
and indirectly to the dramatic works of John Ford. Tannenbaum ranks Ford's plays in terms of popularity, based on
frequency of publication. From first through sixth are
*The Broken Heart; Perkin Warbeck; 'Tis Pity; The Lover's
Melancholy; The Witch of Edmonton;* and *Love's Sacrifice.*

124   _____. *Philip Massinger: A Concise Bibliography*. NY:
Tannenbaum, 1938. 39pp.
This is a 676-entry bibliography of materials current to
about 1935; there is an excellent index to names and subjects. Entry 506 is missing.

125   _____. *Thomas Heywood: A Concise Bibliography*. NY:
Tannenbaum, 1939. 43pp.
This is an indexed, 715-entry bibliography; except for
the enumeration of Heywood's works, very few entries relate
to the author's Caroline plays, pageants or dialogues.

126   TANNENBAUM, SAMUEL A. and DOROTHY R. TANNENBAUM. *James
Shirley: A Concise Bibliography*. NY: Tannenbaum, 1946.
42pp.
This is a well-indexed bibliography of 591 entries, with
many references to criticism before 1900. Also included is
a list of thirty-four poems in praise of Shirley.

127   _____. *Thomas Randolph: A Concise Bibliography*. NY:
Tannenbaum, 1946.
The work contains 347 entries, most of which are related to Randolph's plays. There is also a list of twenty-
six poems in praise of Randolph.

128   TAYLOR, ARCHER. *Renaissance Reference Books: A Checklist of
Some Bibliographies Printed before 1700.* Berkeley and
Los Angeles: University of California Press, 1941. 24pp.
This checklist of approximately 400 entries is based on
the work of Besterman and Spargo.

129   TILLYARD, E. M. W. *The Elizabethan World Picture.* NY:
Vintage Books, 1950. 116pp.
Tillyard's work is an outline and an overview for the
study of order, sin, the great chain of being, and a system
of correspondences. It should be read in conjunction with
Arthur O. Lovejoy's *The Great Chain of Being: A Study of
the History of Ideas* (1953).

Trevelyan, George Macaulay

130 TREVELYAN, GEORGE MACAULAY. *England under the Stuarts.*
London: Methuen, 1910. xiii, 466pp.
This work is a standard reference to the social, political and economical history of England from 1603-1715. Of
general concern are Chapters I-III, V-VII because of the
information related to upper and middle class culture and
social functions, industry and commerce, humanitarianism
and "the personal government of Charles I, 1629-40."

131 USTICK, W. LEE. "Changing Ideals of Aristocratic Character
and Conduct in Seventeenth-Century England." *MP*, 30 (1932),
147-66.
Although Ustick's article is not concerned with drama
as such, his catalogue and analysis of books of manners and
attitudes toward aristocrats is of value because of the
parallels with seventeenth century dramatic themes.

132 VENN, JOHN and J. A. VENN. *Alumni Cantabrigienses.* Part I.
Cambridge: Cambridge University Press, 1922. 4 vols.
Part I is a "biographical list of all known students,
graduates, and holders of office at the University of
Cambridge, from earliest times" until 1751.

133 WATSON, GEORGE, ed. *The New Cambridge Bibliography of English
Literature.* Vol. I. Cambridge: Cambridge University
Press, 1974. xxix, 2491pp.
The new *CBEL* is the standard reference bibliography for
sources related to English literature. The index is still
in preparation.

134 WELSFORD, ENID. *The Fool: His Social and Literary History.*
1935; rept. Gloucester, MA: Peter Smith, 1966. xv,
381pp.
The latter chapters of Welsford's study, on the stage-
clown and the harlequin tradition, are significant here
although the entire work is a thorough history and background of the fool in literature. There is a bibliography
and a complete index.

135 WILLEFORD, WILLIAM. *The Fool and His Scepter: A Study in
Clowns and Jesters and Their Audience.* Evanston:
Northwestern University Press, 1969. xxii, 266pp.
Willeford addresses himself and his book to the questions "Why is the fool . . . such an often recurring figure
in the world and in our imaginative representations of it?
Why do fools from widely diverse times and places reveal
such striking similarities? Why are we, like people in
many other times and places, fascinated by fools?"

136   WILLEY, BASIL. *The Seventeenth Century Background: Studies in the Thought of the Age in Relation to Poetry and Religion.* London: Chatto and Windus, 1949. viii, 315pp.
        Willey's book gives a thorough background for the study of religious and quasi-religious philosophies of the seventeenth century in terms of its literature. Of particular note is Chapter VIII, "Rational Theology--The Cambridge Platonists."

137   WILLIAMS, FRANKLIN B., JR. *Index of Dedications and Commendatory Verses in English Books before 1641.* London: The Bibliographical Society, 1962. 256pp.
        Williams includes dedications as well as "other material found in preliminary leaves, such as epistles by editor, printer, or bookseller. The volume should be of use to students of patronage, publishing conditions, bibliography, and literary, social, and political history." The work is indexed by dedicatory author's names, by institutional and geographical citations, and by anonymous, bibliographical, and variant dedications. Check the general introduction and prefatory material before each section for additional information on organization.

138   WING, DONALD. *A Gallery of Ghosts: Books Published between 1641-1700 not Found in the* Short-Title Catalogue. NY: MLA of America, 1967. vi, 225pp.
        Check the foreword and list of sources to determine the extent of Wing's identification of "ghosts."

139   _____. *Short-Title Catalogue of Books in England, Scotland, Ireland, Wales, and British America and of Books Printed in Other Countries 1641-1700.* NY: Index Committee of the MLA of America, 1972. Only Volume I has been printed to date.
        Until this edition is completed, refer to *STC*. NY: Columbia University Press, 1945-51. 3 vols. in 6 pts. *See also* Paul G. Morrison's *Index to Printers, Publishers, and Booksellers in . . . STC* (1955).

140   WINSTANLEY, WILLIAM. *The Lives of the Most Famous English Poets.* Intro. by William Riley Parker. Gainesville: Scholars' Facsimiles and Reprints, 1963. viii, 221pp.
        As Parker points out in his introduction, "The work has obvious faults and limitations, which probably account for its never having been reprinted since its appearance in 1687. Almost forty per cent of it is largely or entirely derivative. . . . Nonetheless the book builds on the information" which it borrows.

Wood, Anthony A̋.

141   WOOD, ANTHONY A̋. *Athenae Oxonienses*. Ed. by Philip Bliss.
London: Printed privately, 1813; rept. Hildeshein: Georg
Olms, 1969. 4 vols.
    The work is "An exact history of all the writers and
bishops who have had their education in the University of
Oxford. To which are added the *fasti,* or annals of the
said university" from 1500 to approximately 1810. This
work should be read in conjunction with Joseph Foster's
Alumni Oxonienses. 4 vols. covering the years from 1500-
1714.

142   WOODFILL, WALTER L. *Musicians in English Society from
Elizabeth to Charles I.* Princeton: Princeton University
Press, 1953. xv, 372pp.
    Woodfill's is a thorough history and evaluation of musi-
cians and musicianship and their relationship with other
arts, as well as to institutions and society in general.
See also the appendices on the appointment of London waits,
on entries related to music from household records and mu-
nicipal records, and selected references to the kings'
employment of musicians.

143   WOODWARD, GERTRUDE LOOP and JAMES G. McMANAWAY. *A Check-List
of English Plays 1641-1700*. Chicago: Newberry Library,
1945; supplemented by Fredson T. Bowers, Charlottesville:
University Press of Virginia, 1949. 155pp.
    "Plays are listed alphabetically under the names of
their authors, anonymous plays under their titles, with a
minimum of cross references to translators and adaptors."
Short titles are used, "and the place of publication is
noted only if it is not London."

144   WRIGHT, THOMAS. *Dictionary of Obsolete and Provincial
English*. 1857; rept. Detroit: Gale Research Company,
1967. 2 vols.
    Wright's dictionary is a quasi-etymological study of
obsolete words and phrases from 1300 to 1900. At least
one literary citation is given for each entry.

145   YOUNG, STEVEN C. "A Check List of Tudor and Stuart Induction
Plays." *PQ,* 48 (1969), 131-34.
    Young gives a list of about sixty-five entries for in-
duction plays between 1497-1642, of which fifteen are between 1625/26 and 1642. He also, briefly, analyzes the
various functions of the induction in plays stating that
"the induction has been the most neglected of the numerous
introductory dramatic devices . . . and [it] presents the
most challenging problems of uniting introductory material
and a play."

Textual Considerations

146 BEARLINE, LESTER A., ed. *A Mirror for Modern Scholars:*
     Essays in Methods of Research in Literature. NY: Odyssey
     Press, 1966. xiv, 395pp.
         This work contains twenty-five essays on bibliographical
     problems, textual studies, authorship and dating, biography,
     sources and analogues, style, historical periods, history
     of ideas, historical interpretation, form and convention,
     and the publication of research. A bibliography of addi-
     tional sources related to these topics is included.

147 BENTLEY, GERALD EADES. "Authenticity and Attribution in
     Jacobean and Caroline Drama." *Eng Inst Annual* (1942),
     pp. 101-118.
         Bentley suggests criteria and principles for determining
     authenticity of attributed authorships for the more than
     200, lost or found, anonymous plays before 1642.

148 BLANEY, PETER W. M. "The Prevalence of Shared Printing in
     the Early Seventeenth Century." *PBSA*, 67 (1973), 437-42.
         Blaney discusses the practice of "simultaneous shared
     setting" and running-titles related to the publication of
     plays from 1600-1650.

149 BOWERS, FREDSON T. "Marriot's Two Editions of Randolph's
     Aristippus." *Library*, 4th ser, 20 (1940), 163-66.
         From internal evidence, Bowers determines that Thomas
     Harper in fact published two separate editions of Randolph's
     Aristippus in 1630. The second is a "line for line and
     page for page reprint of the other" with no corrections
     and new errors.

150 _____. "Multiple Authority: New Problems and Concepts of
     Copy-Text." *Library*, 5th ser, 27 (1972), 81-115.
         Bowers, updating earlier work by Greg, Dearing, McKerrow
     and others, considers numerous issues related to the selec-
     tion of a copy text and its ancillary issues.

Bowers, Fredson T.

151 _____. "A Possible Thomas Randolph Holograph." *Library,*
4th ser, 20 (1940), 159-62.
Bowers comments on Trinity College, Cambridge MS.3.12
(James 592), which contains a poem by Randolph, signed
"Tho: Randolph" and which he believes is a holograph.

152 _____. *Principles of Bibliographical Description.* Princeton:
Princeton University Press, 1949. xvii, 505pp.
While this book is thoroughly indexed, the most efficient
description of materials covered is located in the table of
contents. Bowers' purpose is to "survey the principles of
descriptive bibliography with relatively full detail, to
discuss difficulties, and especially to coordinate what has
been written about the problems with the solutions which
have been evolved in practice."

153 _____. "Problems in Thomas Randolph's *Drinking Academy* and
Its Manuscript." *HLQ,* 1 (1938), 189-98.
Bowers gives a thorough survey of the criticism regarding *The Drinking Academy,* then shows the association of it
with *The Fairy Knight.* He concludes with a note on dating.

154 _____. "Thomas Randolph's 'Salting.'" *MP,* 39 (1942), 275-80.
Bowers sets the date of Thomas Randolph's early dramatic
monologue late in September or early in October 1627. The
major issue of the article, however, is whether or not the
existing manuscript is a holograph.

155 BROWN, JOHN RUSSELL. "The Rationale of Old-Spelling Editions
of the Plays of Shakespeare and His Contemporaries." *SB,*
13 (1960), 49-67.
Brown re-states and re-analyzes the rationale for old-
spelling texts. He also discusses the methodology and
applicability of the facsimile reprint, the old-spelling
critical edition, the photographic and modernized edition.
He is in sympathy with the latter. This article should be
read in conjunction with Arthur Brown's "The Rationale of
Old-Spelling Editions of the Plays of Shakespeare and His
Contemporaries: A Rejoinder," *SB,* 13 (1960), 69-76.

156 DAWSON, GILES E. and LETITIA KENNEDY-SKIPTON. *Elizabethan
Handwriting 1500-1650.* NY: W. W. Norton, 1966. ix,
130pp.
The work is concerned preeminently with the seventeenth
century secretarial hand. The introduction is a discussion
of the survival of manuscripts, the mechanics of writing,
editorial principles, and methods of study. The text is
accompanied by plates, with transcription and brief

annotations for each of the fifty plates. A list of books
for further reading and reference is included.

157 DEARING, VINTON A. "Concepts of Copy-Text Old and New."
Library, 5th ser, 28 (1973), 281-93.
Dearing analyzes the selection of the copy text and
elaborates on the idea of W. W. Greg in his "The Rationale
of Copy-Texts," *SB*, 3 (1950-51), 21f.

158 EVANS, GWYNNE B. *"Comedies, Tragi-Comedies, with other Poems
by William Cartwright:* A Bibliographical Study." *Library*,
4th ser, 23 (1943), 12-22.
Evans surveys the history of Humphrey Moseley's edition
of Cartwright's works (1651); she then analyzes the order
of printing of the text. Particular attention is given to
The Ordinary and *The Siege*.

159 FEHRENBACH, ROBERT J. "The Printing of James Shirley's *The
Polititian* (1655)." *SB*, 24 (1971), 149-52.
Fehrenbach discusses Moseley's 1655 edition of Shirley's
play by comparing it with the 1655 edition of *The Gentleman
of Venice*. He concludes that it was printed in both octavo
and quarto issues, probably as soon as *The Gentleman of
Venice*, which was also printed in simultaneous issues,
cleared the press. "As the octavo sheets of the latter
probably were printed before the quarto sheets, there is
no reason to believe that the process would have been
changed for *The Polititian*."

160 FOXON, D. F. "The Varieties of Early Proof: Cartwright's
Royal Slave, 1639, 1640." *Library*, 5th ser, 25 (1970),
151-54.
Foxon supports and emends, with examples from Cartwright's play, the work of D. F. McKenzie in "Printers of
the Mind. . . ." *SB*, 22 (1969), 1-75, and Charlton Hinman's *The Printing and Proof-Reading of the First Folio of
Shakespeare* (1963).

161 GREG, W. W. *English Literary Autographs, 1550-1650*. London:
Oxford University Press, 1932. 3 vols.
Among the numerous plates with transcriptions in the
volume are autographs of Philip Massinger, Benjamin Jonson,
Thomas Killigrew, Sir William Davenant, and those of the
master of the revels.

162 _____. "More Massinger Corrections." *Library*, 4th ser, 5
(1924), 59-91.

Greg, W. W.

Greg updates the work of Cruikshank in *Philip Massinger* (1920), and discusses the autograph corrections of a collection of Massinger plays from 1623-32. He analyzes the manner in which the corrections are made, giving particular attention to *The Bondman; The Renegado; The Emperor of the East; The Roman Actor;* and *The Picture*. Finally, he discusses subsequent editions of Massinger's works and their corrections. For a continuation of this discussion, *see* A. H. Cruikshank's "Massinger Corrections," *Library,* 4th ser, 5 (1924), 175-79.

163   ____. "The Printing of Mayne's Plays." *Oxford Bibl Soc Proc & Papers,* 1 (1927), 255-62.
Discussing *The City Match* and *The Amorous War,* Greg notes that their bibliographical interest is greater than their literary one because of their press practices.

164   ____. *Some Aspects and Problems of London Publishing between 1550 and 1650.* Oxford: Clarendon Press, 1956. v, 131pp.
Greg discusses ordinances affecting the book trade, the stationers' records, licensing for the presses, entrances, and copyrights. In his chapter "Imprints and Patents," he discusses the interpretations of imprints, privileges and patents; and in the chapter "Two Minor Problems," he discusses the hand of the master of the revels and blocked entries. The work is thoroughly indexed.

165   ____. *"The Triumph of Peace:* A Bibliographer's Nightmare." *Library,* 5th ser, 1 (1946), 113-26.
Greg, in his discussion of bibliographical problems in Shirley's Inns of Court Masque, distinguishes between the evidence he obtained by studying the British Museum copies of *The Triumph* and the evidence obtained by Emma Unger and William A. Jackson as noted in the Pforzheimer Catalogue, 1940.

166   HARBAGE, ALFRED H. "Elizabethan-Restoration Palimpsest." *MLR,* 35 (1940), 287-319.
Harbage's thesis is that "Certain playwrights after 1660 secured in manuscript unprinted plays written before 1642, modernized them, and had them produced and published as their own; hence a number of Restoration plays hitherto considered original are actually adaptations of 'lost' Elizabethan plays." He then proceeds to track down some of the culprits. In the process Harbage offers some interesting speculations; for instance, "Brome is less a Jonson in buckram than a Ford in motley."

167 HARGREAVES, GEOFFREY D. "'Correcting in the Slip': The
     Development of Galley Proofs." *Library,* 5th ser, 26
     (1971), 295-311.
          Although Hargreaves is principly concerned with proofing
     and correction practices in the eighteenth and nineteenth
     centuries, he discusses the seventeenth century origins of
     galley proofs and analyzes compositors' practice.

168 HECTOR, LEONARD CHARLES. *The Handwriting of English
     Documents.* London: E. Arnold, 1958.
          Of particular value are Chapter I, "The Equipment of the
     Writers" on writing surfaces, paper, formats, pens, and
     inks, and Chapter VI, "English Handwriting since 1500," on
     secretary hands, humanistic hands, the emergence of the
     round hand, and the distinctive departmental hands. In-
     cluded are plates of various hands, with transcriptions,
     a bibliography, and an index.

169 HENSMAN, BERTHA. *The Shares of Fletcher, Field and Massinger
     in Twelve Plays of the Beaumont and Fletcher Canon.*
     Salzburg: Institut für Englische Sprache und Literatur,
     1974. 2 vols.
          An extremely well-documented study in identification of
     sources--it is not, however, indexed.

170 HILL, T. H. "Spelling and the Bibliographer." *Library,* 5th
     ser, 18 (1963), 1-28.
          Hill gives numerous principles for analyzing Elizabethan
     and seventeenth century texts in terms of spelling. He
     works principally with the evidence from compositors to
     determine the orthographic differences and similarities
     between "spelling-habit" and "spelling-pattern."

171 McILWRAITH, A. K. "Did Philip Massinger Revise *The Emperor
     of the East?"* *RES,* 5 (1929), 36-42.
          McIlwraith concludes that the one appearance of the
     character "Favorinus" instead of Paulinus (III.4.41) "was
     an oversight soon set right at the press." He then dis-
     cusses sources for the Massinger play. *See also* J. E.
     Gray's "The Source of *The Emperor of the East,"* *RES, n.s.,*
     1 (1950), 126-35.

172 _____. "The Manuscript Corrections of Massinger's Plays."
     Library, 5th ser, 6 (1951), 213-16.
          This is the fifth and the last in a series of discussions
     related to Massinger autograph corrections in some of his
     plays published between 1623 and 1632. For previous dis-
     cussions *see* J. E. Gray's "Still More Massinger Corrections,"
     Library, 5th ser, 5 (1950), 132-39, and back.

McIlwraith, A. K.

173 _____. "Pen-and-Ink Corrections in Books of the Seventeenth
       Century." *RES*, 7 (1931), 204-07.
           McIlwraith notes corrections in Massinger's *The City
       Madam*, and suggests that the anonymous printer of that play
       may have been Jane Bell.

174 _____. "The Printer's Copy for *The City Madam*." *MLN*, 50
       (1933), 173-74.
           McIlwraith supports his earlier assertion, in *RES*, 7
       (1932), 206, that "the quarto of *The City-Madam* was printed
       from a manuscript . . . which was most likely in Massinger's
       autograph."

175 _____. "Some Bibliographical Notes on Massinger." *Library*,
       4th ser, 11 (1930), 78-92.
           Of particular interest is McIlwraith's bibliographical
       examination of *The Picture* and *The Maid of Honor*, and their
       variations among states.

176 McKENZIE, D. F. "Printers of the Mind: Some Notes on
       Bibliographical Theories and Printing-House Practice."
       SB, 22 (1969), 1-75.
           McKenzie thoroughly questions and analyzes previous as-
       sumptions and hypothesis concerning seventeenth- and
       eighteenth-century printing houses and printing practices.

177 McMANAWAY, JAMES G. "Latin Title-Page Mottoes as a Clue to
       Dramatic Authorship." *Library*, 4th ser, 26 (1945), 28-36.
           McManaway is concerned with the dating of *Dick of Devon-
       shire* (not earlier than 18 July 1626), and other biblio-
       graphical information related to the play. He questions
       the ascription of authorship of the play to Heywood, and
       suggests on the strength of internal evidence, that the
       author may have been Robert Davenport. He is confident,
       however, that *Dick of Devonshire* and *The Bloody Banquet* are
       by the same hand.

178 MIDDLETON, BERNARD C. *A History of English Craft Bookbinding
       Technique*. NY: Hafner Publishing Company, 1963. 307pp.
           The intent of this work is to move the history of book-
       binding "from the backwaters of art history into the main-
       streams of bibliographical research," and for that reason
       the information related to all aspects of bookbinding is of
       particular interest to the literary and bibliographical re-
       searcher. Middleton is concerned primarily with bookbinding
       in the sixteenth, seventeenth, and eighteenth centuries,
       and the work is indexed.

179   ORAS, ANTS. *Pause Patterns in Elizabethan and Jacobean Drama:
An Experiment in Prosody*. Gainesville: University of
Florida Presses, 1960. 90pp.
In his discussion of Renaissance prosody, Oras analyzes
patterns in Jonson, Dekker, Ford, Brome, Shirley, Davenant
and others. The tables and graphs (pp. 33-88) should be
consulted. A final note on sources is included.

180   POVEY, KENNETH. "Working to Rule, 1660-1800: A Study of
Pressmen's Practice." *Library*, 5th ser, 20 (1965), 13-54.
Of particular interest is data given to support Povey's
thesis "that in English practice the inner forme was usually
printed first." Numerous related articles on the same subject are cited in the footnotes.

181   SAYCE, R. A. "Compositorial Practice and the Localization of
Printed Books, 1530-1800." *Library*, 5th ser, 21 (1966),
1-45.
The stated purpose of Sayce's article is "to suggest
methods of placing and dating printed books which do not
depend on a specialized knowledge of the history of printing." The product of his methods is "the detection of
pirated editions, the determination of the order of editions, the study of clandestine publications, of the work
of heterodox authors, and of the movement of ideas all depend on knowing when and where books were printed. . . ."

182   SCHOENBAUM, SAMUEL. *Internal Evidence and Elizabethan
Dramatic Authorship: An Essay in Literary History and
Method*. Evanston: Northwestern University Press, 1966.
xx, 281pp.
Pp. 231-56 are an extensive list of "monographs, articles, editions, *etc.*, concerned directly or indirectly
with questions of authorship attribution in Elizabethan
drama." Schoenbaum's work is an intensive study of scholarship related to authorship and collaboration. He argues
persuasively for "historical perspective and impartial
methodology."

183   SIMPSON, PERCY. *Proof-Reading in the 16th, 17th and 18th
Centuries*. London: Oxford University Press, 1935. xii,
251pp.
Simpson discusses authors' proof-reading, early proofs
and copy, correctors of the press, and the Oxford Press and
its correctors. The work is thoroughly documented.

184   SISSON, C. J. "Bibliographical Aspects of Some Stuart
Dramatic Manuscripts." *RES*, 1 (1925), 421-30.

Stevenson, Allan H.

Sisson states that *Believe as You List* "furnishes pre-
cise examples of the type of error made by an author in
original composition, by an author copying his own draft,
and by a scribe copying an author's original text." *See
also* W. W. Greg's *Dramatic Documents from the Elizabethan
Playhouses*. Vol. I (1935). Pp. 233-35.

185   STEVENSON, ALLAN H.   "New Uses of Watermarks as Bibliographical
       Evidence." *SB,* 1 (1948), 149-82.
           Stevenson makes a case for a more elaborate and subtle
       use of watermarks as bibliographical evidence and calls
       attention to "the significance of variant or dissimilar
       watermarks for bibliographical study."

186   _____.   "Paper as Bibliographical Evidence." *Library,* 5th
       ser, 17 (1962), 197-212.
           Stevenson justifies the use of watermarks and paper as
       dependable bibliographical evidence. The major portion of
       his discussion is devoted to analyzing the methodology of
       studying paper and the application of the methodology.

187   _____.   "Shirley's Publishers: The Partnership of Crooke and
       Cooke." *Library,* 4th ser, 25 (1945), 140-61.
           Stevenson examines the remarkable publication of thirteen
       first quartos of Shirley's plays between 1636 and 1640 -
       the time during which Shirley was residing in Ireland.
       Primary to his examination is an analysis of the methods
       of William Cooke and Andrew Crooke.

188   SYKES, H. DUGDALE.   "Elizabethan and Jacobean Plays:
       Suggested Textual Emendations." *N & Q* (October 1917),
       pp. 441-42.
           Two suggested emendations that Sykes gives are concerned
       with Massinger's *The Roman Actor* (II.2.38) and Glapthorne's
       Argalus and Parthenia (IV.1). He also shows how Glapthorne
       repeats lines from *Argalus* in *The Lady Mother*.

189   TANNENBAUM, SAMUEL A.   "Corrections to the Text of *Believe as
       You List*." *PMLA,* 42 (1927), 777-81.
           Tannenbaum compiles a fairly substantial list of correc-
       tions to *errata* in Arthur Symons' text of Massinger's
       Believe as You List.

190   TANSELL, G. THOMAS.   "Editorial Apparatus for Radiating Texts."
       Library, 5th ser, 29 (1974), 330-37.
           Tansell questions Greg's and Bowers' rationale concerning
       some of their editorial apparati, and offers his own sug-
       gestions and solutions.

191   THOMPSON, ELBERT N. S. "Elizabethan Dramatic Collaboration."
      E Studien, 40 (1909), 30-46.
         Thompson suggests reasons for the popularity of col-
      laborations, and then reviews the major collaborations
      through Massinger.

192   TURNER, ROBERT K. "Act-End Notations in Some Elizabethan
      Plays." *MP,* 72 (1975), 238-47.
         The author makes statistical reference to *The Soddered
      Citizen; Believe as You List; The Lady Mother; The Benefice;
      The Court Secret; The Queen of Corsica;* and others.

193   VAN DAM, BASTIAAN A. P. *Chapters on English Printed Prosody,
      and Pronunciation.* Heidelberg: Carl Winter, 1902. 206pp.
         Of particular note is Chapter I, "High-Handed Ways of
      Elizabethan and Jacobean Printers," and Van Dam's syntacti-
      cal analysis of printing practice. Although the work does
      not exceed 1622, it is of value as a post-Fleay study in
      methodology.

Major Caroline Dramatists

194   ADDIS, JOHN. "Massinger and Molière." *N & Q* (28 October 1865), p. 348.

Addis notes a striking similarity between a passage in Massinger's *Emperor of the East* (IV.4) and Molière's *Malade Imaginaire* (III.14).

195   ALI, FLORENCE. *Opposing Absolutes: Conviction and Convention in John Ford's Plays*. Salzburg: Institut für Englische Sprache und Literatur, 1974. iii, 109pp.

After an introduction which surveys Ford scholarship to date, Ali gives individual attention to *The Lover's Melancholy*; *The Queen*; *'Tis Pity She's a Whore*; *Love's Sacrifice*; *The Broken Heart*; *Perkin Warbeck*; *The Fancies, Chaste and Noble*; and *The Lady's Trial*. She concludes that "the moral issues in Ford's plays do not present themselves as abstract philosophical questions which, in the realm of ethics, attempt to discover what is essentially and eternally true. . . . The conflicts are realized externally in the clash between people of opposing view points on specific issues in apparently particular places and times."

196   ANDERSON, DONALD K., JR. "The Date and Handwriting of a Manuscript Copy of Ford's *Perkin Warbeck*." *N & Q* (September 1963), pp. 340-41.

Anderson discusses the imagery, primarily in the climactic fifth act of *'Tis Pity She's a Whore* (as it relates to the banquet), and heart imagery (related to spiritual and physical definition) in Acts II, III and IV of *The Broken Heart*. He concludes that these plays exhibit "a masterful handling of imagery." It is "sustained, contributing to the unity and reinforcing the theme of each play; it is dynamic, progressing from the figurative to the literal; and it is often ironic." There is a continuation and amplification of these points in a similar work by Robin Davril, *Le Drame de John Ford* (1954), pp. 444-52.

197   _____. "Kingship in Ford's *Perkin Warbeck*." *ELH*, 27 (1960), 177-93.

37

Anderson, Donald K., Jr.

> Anderson's thesis is that by "Illustrating the pragmatic
> viewpoint of such theorists as Machiavelli and Bacon, Ford
> portrays his ideal king in the person of the wise and
> eminently practical Henry VII, and so considerable is the
> playwright's attention to competent and incompetent govern-
> ing that *Perkin Warbeck* might well be called a lesson in
> kingship." Anderson feels that kingship is one of the
> major, if not the major, concerns in *Perkin Warbeck,* and
> "this is revealed both by the structure of the play and by
> his deviations from original sources."

198   ____. "*Richard II* and *Perkin Warbeck*." *SQ,* 13 (1962),
       260-63.
> Anderson notes a resemblance between two scenes in
> *Richard II* and *Perkin Warbeck*: "the final scene of Ford's
> fourth act and the second scene of Shakespeare's third
> act." He shows the similarity of language as well as plot,
> concluding that "Ford may have had *Richard II* in mind when
> he wrote *Perkin Warbeck* [because] the latter is an extension
> of Shakespeare's chronicle plays, with which Ford must have
> been familiar. . . ." Anderson states finally that "the
> possibility of a more specific influence is indicated by
> the similarities in situation, characterization, and
> language. . . ."

199   ANDREWS, CLARENCE EDWARD. *Richard Brome: A Study of His Life
       and Work.* NY: Henry Holt, 1913. viii, 134pp.
> The work contains a chronology of Brome's plays, a par-
> tially descriptive list of Brome's works, a discussion of
> Brome as dramatist, as well as the sources and influences
> for his works. Special attention is given to the influence
> of Shakespeare, Jonson, and Dekker on Brome. Two appendices
> are concerned with the sources for the satire in *The Anti-
> podes.* Andrews' "The Authorship of *The Late Lancashire
> Witches,*" in *MLN,* 28 (1913), is reprinted here.

200   ANKLESARIA, SHIRIN SAROSH. "Ben Jonson: The Biographical
       Tradition and Its Relation to Critical Appraisal." *DAI,*
       35:5386A (Cornell University), 1974. 250pp.
> The author's purpose is to discover "the relation between
> the biographical tradition of Ben Jonson and critical com-
> ment on his works up to 1900." He covers commentary by
> Aubrey, Gilchrist, Gifford, Hazlitt, Schlegel, Taine,
> Symonds, and Swinburne, among others.

201   ARNOLD, JUDD. *A Grace Peculiar: Ben Jonson's Cavalier
       Heroes.* University Park: Penn State University Press,
       1972. 86pp.

Barber, Laird Howard, Jr.

Arnold methodically discusses Jonson's plays from *Every Man in His Humor* through *The Magnetic Lady* to discover the direct and indirect spokesmen for Cavalier ideas. He is more concerned with the Ben Jonson who belonged "to the witty fellowship of the Mermaid in Bread Street" than the "choleric, self-consciously learned neoclassicist, the creator of . . . savagely indignant moralists."

202   BABB, LAWRENCE. "Abnormal Psychology in John Ford's *Perkin Warbeck*." *MLN*, 51 (1936), 234-37.
Babb surveys the pervasive tendency of Perkin Warbeck toward extreme melancholia and notes Urswick's discussion of Warbeck's conduct and state of mind. In particular, Babb notes that Urswick likens Warbeck to "witches,/Possess'd even [to] their deaths deluded. . . ." (V.ii)

203   BACON, WALLACE A. "The Literary Reputation of John Ford." *HLQ*, 11 (1948), 181-99.
Bacon briefly discusses Ford's reputation from 1661 to the present and finds it "reasonably safe to begin with the assumption that three plays for which Ford is most widely known are *The Broken Heart; Love's Sacrifice;* and *'Tis Pity She's a Whore*." The majority of the article is devoted to standard details of criticism related to these three plays. He also notes the role of Platonic love in Ford's work.

204   _____. "The Magnetic Field: The Structure of Jonson's Comedies." *HLQ*, 19 (1956), 121-53.
Bacon concurs with T. S. Eliot's sentiments on Jonson's reputation in *The Sacred Wood: Essays on Poetry and Criticism* (1932). He then reviews scholarship related to Jonson's comedies, giving some attention to *The Staple of News; The New Inn;* and *The Magnetic Lady*. The thrust of his own criticism is what he calls a "magnetic field" - that dynamic quality of lead characters in the comedies who attract the action and other characters, as well as the reader.

205   BARBER, LAIRD HOWARD, JR. "An Edition of *The Late Lancashire Witches* by Thomas Heywood and Richard Brome." *DAI*, 23:1695A (University of Michigan), 360pp.
Barber collates the 1634 editions, Halliwell's edition (1853), and Pearson's reprint (1874) to the copy text, which is a "Xerox" copy of the Huntington Library quarto of the first edition. There is a brief introduction and an appendix of contemporary materials.

Barish, Jonas A.

206   BARISH, JONAS A., ed. *Ben Jonson: A Collection of Critical
       Essays*. Englewood Cliffs, NJ: Prentice-Hall, 1963. 180pp.
          This work contains thirteen essays by various authors,
       a chronology and selected bibliography. Of particular note
       here are L. C. Knight's "Tradition and Ben Jonson," pp. 24-
       39; Harry Levin's "An Introduction to Ben Jonson," pp. 40-
       59; Edmund Wilson's "Morose Ben Jonson," pp. 60-74; Ray L.
       Heffner's "Unifying Symbols in the Comedy of Ben Jonson,"
       pp. 133-46; and Dolora Cunningham's "The Jonsonian Masque
       as a Literary Form," pp. 160-74.

207   _____. *Ben Jonson and the Language of Prose Comedy*.
          Cambridge, MA: Harvard University Press, 1960. viii, 355pp.
          Barish thoroughly analyzes the vitriolic, venomous, lyri-
       cal and docile speech of the characters in Jonson's plays.
       Check the index for individual references to late plays.

208   _____. "Feasting and Judging in Jonsonian Comedy." *Ren D,
       n.s.*, 5 (1972), 3-35.
          The majority of Barish's article is concerned with Jon-
       son's early work, but he concludes it with discussions of
       The Staple of News which he sees as a "restatement of the
       old comic moral where the knavish lawyer is circumvented by
       having his own tactics turned against him," and *The New Inn*
       which "forges once more the link between comedy and feast-
       ing, this time with considerable intricacy [because] it
       consists of a feast within a feast within a feast. . . ."

209   _____. "*Perkin Warbeck* as Anti-History." *EIC*, 20 (1970),
       151-71.
          Barish, re-affirming T. S. Eliot's estimation of Perkin
       Warbeck's personality, notes that most critics "have as-
       sumed that Ford too was presenting the story from the point
       of view of the Tudor-Stuart establishment as a tale of an
       impostor rebelling against a legitimate monarch. They have
       refused to suspend disbelief long enough to take Perkin's
       claims seriously because they have assumed that Ford could
       not have taken them seriously." He rejects all conventional
       interpretations of Warbeck's characterization.

210   BAS, GEORGES. "James Shirley, pasteur dans le Hertfordshire."
       EA, 15 (1962), 266-68.
          Bas gives numerous new pieces of information related to
       Shirley's taking orders and to his position in Hertford-
       shire. He continues the study of A. C. Baugh in "Some New
       Facts about James Shirley," *RES*, 7 (1931), 62-66.

Baum, Helena Watts

211 _____. "Shirley et 'Th' untun'd kennel': une petite guerre
des théâtres vers 1630." *EA*, 16 (1963), 11-22.
Bas' article is a continuation of Michael Grevelet's
"Th' untun'd kennell: note sur Thomas Heywood et le
théâtre sous Charles Ier," *EA*, 7 (1954), 101-06.

212 BASKERVILL, CHARLES READ. "Bandello and *The Broken Heart*."
MLN, 28 (1913), 51-52.
Baskervill is the first to note similarities between
John Ford's *The Broken Heart* and Bandello's story of Livio
and Camilla. *See also* Arpad Steiner's "Massinger's *The Pic-
ture*, Bandello and Hungary," *MLN*, 46 (1931), 401-03.

213 _____. "The Source of the Main Plot of Shirley's *Love Tricks*."
MLN, 24 (1909), 100-01.
Unlike Emil Koeppel (*Ben Jonson's Werkung.* . . .) who
sees Jonson's *Silent Woman* as the source for Shirley's *Love
Tricks*, Baskervill notes the structural and topical simi-
larities between Shirley's play and Riche's *Farwell to
Militarie Profession*, of which the eighth history is the
story "Of Phylotus and Emilia."

214 _____. "The Sources of Jonson's *Masque of Christmas* and
Love's Welcome at Welbeck." *MP*, 6 (1908), 257-69.
Baskervill notes the *Masque of Christmas*' indebtedness
to *The Knight of the Burning Pestle*, sword-dance traditions,
and others; he also points out similarities between *Love's
Welcome* and *The Masque of Christmas*.

215 BAUGH, ALBERT C. "Further Facts about Shirley." *RES*, 1
(1931), 62-66.
Baugh gives additional information about Shirley's wife
(Elizabeth), his daughter (Mary), and the family into which
he married. He also covers Shirley's study for the MA
degree, and the fact that Shirley was at one time in orders.
See 216.

216 _____. "Some New Facts about Shirley." *MLR*, 17 (1922),
228-35.
Baugh updates biographical information given in Nason's
*James Shirley, Dramatist: A Biographical and Critical
Study* (1915). In some cases he emends Nason's assumptions;
he also adds to and fortifies others. He confirms the fact
that Shirley took a BA from Cambridge in 1617.

217 BAUM, HELENA WATTS. *The Satiric and the Didactic in Ben
Jonson's Comedy*. Chapel Hill: University of North
Carolina Press, 1947. vi, 192pp.

Bawcutt, N. W.

> Having discussed the Renaissance theories of the func-
> tion of poetry, Baum treats Jonson's theory of comic poetry
> from the point of view of moral and aesthetic values. She
> lists as the objectives of his satire: avarice, lust,
> drunkenness, witchcraft and Puritans. The work concludes
> with a chapter on Jonson's achievement of a dramatic tech-
> nique. The work is well-indexed.

218   BAWCUTT, N. W. "Seneca and Ford's *'Tis Pity She's a Whore*."
      N & Q (June 1967), p. 215.
      Bawcutt shows similarities between the pseudo-Senecan
      play *Octavia* and *'Tis Pity She's a Whore*.

219   BENNETT, A. L. "The Early Editions of Massinger's Plays."
      PLL, 1 (1965), 177-81.
      In the hope that someone will undertake to re-edit
      Massinger, Bennett lists the editions and locations (some
      not given in the STC) of Massinger's seventeen plays.

220   BENTLEY, GERALD EADES. *Shakespeare and Jonson: Their
      Reputations in the Seventeenth Century Compared*. Chicago:
      University of Chicago Press, 1945. 2 vols.
      This work, in three parts, shows new allusions to
      Shakespeare, new Jonson allusions, and relevant allusions
      to other Jacobean and Caroline dramatists. The work is
      well-indexed by author, title, and subject. There are fre-
      quent references to Brome, Shirley, Randolph, Nabbes,
      Massinger, May, Mayne, and others.

221   BLACK, FORREST EDWARD, JR. "The Nature of Evil in the
      Tragedies of James Shirley." *DAI*, 36:2212-13A (Bowling
      Green State University), 1975. 198pp.
      Treating Shirley's five tragedies--*The Maid's Revenge;
      Love's Cruelty; The Traitor; The Politician;* and *The Car-
      dinal*--Black concludes that the plays display "an over-
      riding concern with causes and effects of worldly evil."

222   BLAND, D. S. "A Word in Shirley's *The Cardinal*." *RES, n.s.*,
      4 (1953), 358-59.
      Bland is concerned with interpreting the Duchess' re-
      joinder to the Cardinal in which she says his "praise has
      too much *landscape* [my italics]."

223   BLANEY, GLENN H. "Conventions, Plot, and Structure in *The
      Broken Heart*." *MP*, 56 (1958), 1-9.
      Blaney elucidates "the means by which Ford stresses his
      stand on the matter of love and marriage." He describes
      The Broken Heart as "a problem play, centrally depending

for its structure and for its statement of the theme of
romantic love upon the motives of betrothal and of marital
enforcement in violation of a pre-contract of betrothal."
He concludes that *The Broken Heart* was written "in protest
against the practice of enforced marriage in seventeenth-
century society. *See also* his "The Enforcement of Marriage
in English Drama 1600-1650," *PQ*, 38 (1959), 459-72.

224 _____. "Massinger's Reference to the Calverley Story." *N & Q*
(January 1954), pp. 17-18.
      Blaney is concerned with Massinger's reference, in *The
Guardian*, to the crime committed by Walter Calverley in
Yorkshire (1605) related to fraud and brutality in wardship.

225 BLEVINS, JAMES RICHARD. "Moral and Ethical Ambiguity in the
Plays of John Ford." *DAI*, 31:2867A (George Peabody College
for Teachers), 1970. 191pp.
      Blevins is especially concerned with a discussion of
Ford's *The Queen*; *'Tis Pity She's a Whore*; *Love's Sacrifice*;
Perkin Warbeck; and *The Broken Heart*. The work suggests
"some possible reasons for Ford's failure to achieve moral
and ethical coherence in his works."

226 BLISSETT, WILLIAM; JULIAN PATRICK; R. W. VON FOSSEN, eds.
A Celebration of Ben Jonson. Toronto: University of
Toronto Press, 1973. xiii, 194pp.
      Of particular interest are contributions by Clifford
Leech: "The Incredibility of Jonsonian Comedy"; Jonas
Barish: "Jonson and the Loathèd Stage"; George Hibbard:
"Ben Jonson and Human Nature"; and D. F. McKenzie: "*The
Staple of News* and the Late Plays."

227 BOUGHNER, DANIEL C. *The Devil's Disciple: Ben Jonson's Debt
to Machiavelli*. NY: Philosophical Library, 1968. 264pp.
      Boughner's first four chapters discuss Machiavelli's
theory of comedy and the structure, plot, and characterization in his works. The author then applies his early study
to the plays of Jonson. Of particular note is the final
chapter "Back to Satan: *The Devil Is an Ass*," in which he
feels Jonson turned back to his earlier theories of comedy
and his influence by Machiavelli.

228 BRADFORD, GAMALIEL. "The Women of Philip Massinger and John
Ford." In *Elizabethan Women*. Ed. by Harold Ogden White.
NY: Houghton Mifflin, 1936. vii, 242pp.
      Bradford's study is the most relevant one in this work,
however there are also articles related to the general education, home and social life of Renaissance women. Check

Bradley, Jesse Franklin

the author index for references to Shirley, Davenant, and other Caroline dramatists.

229   BRADLEY, JESSE FRANKLIN and JOSEPH QUINCY ADAMS, eds. *The Jonson Allusion Book, 1597-1700*. New Haven: Yale University Press, 1922. vi, 466pp.

Bradley and Adams trace "the materials . . . related to Jonson's career as a man of letters, and [disclose] the estimates of his genius as expressed by his contemporaries and immediate successors." The allusions are listed chronologically. The work also serves as an allusion book to many Caroline dramatists. It is indexed by author and work.

230   BRERETON, J. LE GAY. "The Sources of Ford's *Perkin Warbeck*." *Anglia*, 34 (1911), 194-234.

Brereton contends that Ford used more sources than were originally thought for *Perkin Warbeck*. To the previously noted source of Bacon's *History of King Henry the Seventh*, Brereton adds Hall's *Chronicle* and Holinshed's *Chronicles*. For an extension of this discussion *see* Mildred C. Struble's "The Indebtedness of Ford's *Perkin Warbeck* to Gainsford," *Anglia*, 49 (1926), 80-91.

231   BRIGGS, WILLIAM DINSMORE. "Ben Jonson: Notes on *Underwoods XXX* and on *The New Inn*. *MP*, 10 (1913), 573-85.

Briggs shows that "Lovell's discourse on 'true valour' in *The New Inn* is directly connected with *Underwoods XXX* through the fact that certain important lines in it are almost identical with lines in the epistle 'to Sachville, Earl of Dorset.'"

232   _____. "The Influence of Jonson's Tragedy in the Seventeenth Century." *Anglia*, 35 (1912), 277-337.

Briggs draws parallels between Jonson's tragedies and Massinger's *The Fatal Dowry*; *The Roman Actor*; *The Bondman*; *The Renegado* and others, Nathaniel Richards' *Messallina*, Ford's *Perkin Warbeck*, Denham's *The Sophy*, May's *Cleopatra*, *Julia Agrippina*, *Julius Caesar*, and *Antigone*, as well as a variety of other Caroline plays. He concludes that "many of the authors of these plays borrowed hints and suggestions, sometimes passages, from Jonson's dialogue, and it becomes evident that we have to do here with a definite Jonsonian influence more extensive" than was thought previously. *See also* Emil Koeppel's *Quellen-Studien zu den Dramen Ben Jonson's, John Marston's und Beaumont's und Fletcher's* (1895).

233   BRISSENDEN, ALAN. "Impediments to Love: A Theme in John Ford." *Ren D*, 7 (1964), 95-102.

Burelbach, Frederick M., Jr.

Brissenden is concerned with the analysis of sexual themes in Ford and "contemporary attitudes toward such a highly complex moral issue as sex." He shows how a future study should touch on these issues in *The Broken Heart*; *The Lover's Melancholy*; *The Queen*; *The Lady's Trial*; *The Fancies, Chaste and Noble*; *Love's Sacrifice*; *'Tis Pity She's a Whore*; *The Unnatural Combatant*; *The Revenger's Tragedy*; and others.

234   BROME, RICHARD. *The Antipodes.* Ed. by Ann Haaker. Lincoln: University of Nebraska Press, 1966. xxi, 138pp.
Haaker's preface to the edition is a thorough survey and critical evaluation of the play. The introduction includes a discussion of the date and sources for *The Antipodes*, an analysis of the play, and a word on the text. The text is followed by a chronology.

235   _____. *A Jovial Crew.* Ed. by Ann Haaker. Lincoln: University of Nebraska Press, 1968. xxi, 144pp.
As in the edition above, Haaker follows the general Regents format for the introduction and edition of *The Jovial Crew*. She specifically discusses the performance of the play, and the fact that it occurred as the theatres were closing.

236   BURBRIDGE, ROGER T. "The Moral Vision of *The Broken Heart.*" *SEL*, 10 (1970), 397-407.
Burbridge concludes that "Evil remains . . . the force inimical to human identity. In *The Broken Heart* it becomes something inactive yet terribly destructive, a narrowing of vision on the part of people who refuse to mix joy with suffering, who are unable to adjust to a world without black-and-white values. Their inability to compromise renders them incapable of accepting the reality of human weakness, and finally incapable of being human."

237   BURELBACH, FREDERICK M., JR. "'The Truth' in John Ford's *The Broken Heart* Revisited." *N & Q* (June 1967), pp. 211-12.
Burelbach reviews some critical materials and sources related to Ford's lines "What may be here thought Fiction, when time's youth/ Wanted some riper years, was known a Truth. . . ." He also suggests that Penthea's story has its origins in Castiglione's *The Courtier*. *See also* R. Jordan's "Calantha's Dance in *The Broken Heart*," *N & Q* (August 1969), pp. 294-95, and Michael Neill's "New Light on 'The Truth' in *The Broken Heart*," *N & Q* (June 1975), pp. 249-50.

Carsaniga, G. M.

238   CARSANIGA, G. M. "'The Truth' in John Ford's *The Broken
         Heart*." *CL*, 10 (1958), 344-48.
              Carsaniga suggests that there are at least two acceptable
         sources for *The Broken Heart*: Sidney's *Astrophel and Stella*
         and "the extraordinary artifice contrived for murder by a
         Lucchese merchant" noted in Girolamo Cardano's *De Rerum
         Varietate* and elsewhere. *See* 237.

239   CARVER, ANN AUGUSTA CATHEY. "The Plays of John Ford: A
         Critical Analysis." *DAI*, 29:3127-28A (Emory University),
         1968. 336pp.
              Carver is concerned only with those plays that Ford
         wrote independent of his contemporaries. She is particu-
         larly concerned with *The Lover's Melancholy*; *The Broken
         Heart*; *Love's Sacrifice*; *Perkin Warbeck*; *The Fancies,
         Chaste and Noble*; and *The Lady's Trial*.

240   CHALFONT, FRAN CERNOCKY. "Ben Jonson's London: The Plays,
         the Masques, and the Poems." *DAI*, 32:6922A (University of
         North Carolina at Chapel Hill), 1971. 313pp.
              Chalfont's dissertation is essentially a concordance or
         "topographical dictionary" which was "achieved by collect-
         ing and commenting upon all of the London place-names
         mentioned in his plays, masques, and poems."

241   CHAMPION, LARRY STEPHEN. "The Comic Intent of Ben Jonson's
         Late Plays." *DAI*, 22:2784A (University of North Carolina
         at Chapel Hill), 1961. 252pp.
              The purpose of Champion's dissertation is "to defend
         the comic intent" of the late works "as consistent with
         [Jonson's] earlier and more popular productions." He is
         concerned specifically with the satire and parody in *The
         New Inn*, *The Staple of News*, and *The Magnetic Lady*.

242   _____. *Jonson's Dotages: A Reconsideration of the Late
         Plays*. Lexington: University of Kentucky Press, 1967.
         156pp.
              Champion's first two introductory chapters set the stage
         for an extended discussion of *The Devil Is an Ass*; *The
         Staple of News*; *The New Inn*; and *The Magnetic Lady*. He
         concludes the work with a chapter entitled "Popular Taste
         and the Late Comedies: A Refusal to Compromise." "The
         primary purpose of [this work] is to demonstrate that Jon-
         son's comic intent, his theory of art, and his manipulation
         of material both for instruction and entertainment, is pre-
         cisely that of his acknowledged masterpieces, and that the
         plays can hardly be branded 'dotages' of a 'washed-out
         brain.'" *See* 241.

Collins, Howard S.

243 _____. *"The Magnetic Lady*: The Close of Jonson's Circle."
SHR, 2 (1968), 104-21.
Champion notes that Jonson's last play "reads like the
final exertion of a dramatist who has stubbornly devoted
himself to the higher aims of satiric comedy and who has
seen his public at best only partially receptive." He
views it as an effective "dramatic portrayal of his *ars
poetica* [and] in its sweep of dramatic devices it illus-
trates a remarkable summation of Jonson's comic technique."

244 CHAPMAN, EDGAR LEON. "The Comic Art of James Shirley: A
Modern Evaluation of His Comedies." *DAI*, 26:351-52A
(Brown University), 1964. 221pp.
Chapman states that his "study makes a comprehensive examination of Shirley's comedies and offers a revaluation
based on modern theories of comedy. The study begins with
a sampling and critique of earlier criticism, and proceeds
to a new analysis of Shirley's debt to the comic tradition
of Fletcher. For convenience, Shirley's comedies are then
divided into three major categories - apprentice work, romantic comedies, and London comedies." These analyses show
"that Shirley, within his limits, was a much more original
craftsman than is generally believed."

245 CLARK, WILLIAM S. "The Relation of Shirley's Prologue to
Orrey's *The General*." *RES*, 6 (1930), 191-93.
Clark is concerned with a prologue entitled "To a Play
Here Called *The General*" published in a collection of Shirley's poems in 1646. He disputes J. O. Halliwell-Phillips'
contention that Shirley was the author of *The General* and
attributes the play to Roger Boyle, Earl of Orrey. He also
contends that the play was written in Dublin in 1661 and
acted in 1662. *See also* his articles in *RES*, 2 (1926), 206,
and *MLN*, 42 (1927), 381-82, as well as Allardyce Nicoll's
History of Restoration Drama (1929), p. 379.

246 COLLINS, HOWARD S. *The Comedy of Sir William Davenant*. The
Hague and Paris: Mouton, 1967. 179pp.
After a short biography of Davenant, Collins analyzes
the plays as (1) comedy of humors; (2) comedy of intrigue;
(3) comedy of manners. Collins sees Davenant as "a man of
flexible and unprejudiced intellect" capable of encompassing
"the varieties of taste in comedy that was characteristic
of seventeenth-century audiences. . . ." Having defined
comedy in the seventeenth-century, he explores it in *The
Wits* and *News from Plymouth*, and traces comic elements in
eight Caroline tragedies and tragi-comedies. The remainder
of the book is devoted to Davenant's early Restoration

Cousins, Kathryn McCambridge

plays. *See also* Collins' dissertation, "The Comedy of Sir
William Davenant," *DAI*, 23:3369A (Brown University), 1960.
206pp.

247   COUSINS, KATHRYN McCAMBRIDGE. "The Role of the Narrative in
James Shirley's Tragicomedies." *DAI*, 30:5404A (Fordham
University), 1970. 183pp.
Cousins appraises the role of narrative action in *The
Wedding; The Young Admiral; The Duke's Mistress; The Royal
Master; The Gentleman of Venice; The Doubtful Heir; The
Imposture;* and *The Court Secret.*

248   CRABTREE, JOHN HENRY, JR. "Philip Massinger's Comedies."
DAI, 20:3725A (University of North Carolina at Chapel Hill),
1959. 315pp.
Crabtree is concerned primarily with the didactic and
moralistic elements in Massinger's *A New Way to Pay Old
Debts; The City Madam; The Great Duke of Florence;* and *The
Guardian.* He concludes that they are "exemplary" dramas
"designed primarily to teach by dramatizing moral lessons."

249   CRINÒ, ANNA MARIA. *James Shirley, drammatougo di corte.*
Verona: no publisher, 1968. 171pp.
The five chapters of this work are concerned with (1)
biography; (2) comedies; (3) tragicomedies; (4) tragedies;
(5) masques, and what Dr. Crinò terms "morali." She makes
frequent references to Shirley's contemporaries and predecessors. *See also* R. S. Forsythe's *The Relations of Shirley's Plays to Elizabethan Drama* (1914); W. W. Greg's *Two
Studies in James Shirley;* and J. P. Feil's "Shirley's Years
of Service," *RES,* 8 (1957).

250   CROWTHER, J. W. "The Literary History of *A Jovial Crew.*" In
Studies in English Renaissance Literature. Ed. by W. F.
McNeir. Baton Rouge: Louisiana State University Press,
1962. Pp. 132-48.
Crowther feels that *A Jovial Crew* "In its general good
humor, delight in carefree life close to nature, and sympathy for the poor and oppressed, as well as its lyric
quality and its moral and philosophical undertones, is a
romantic comedy with something of the spirit of the period
of about 1600, as represented, for example, in *As You Like
It.*" He also analyzes aspects of *The Court Begger; The
Damoiselle; The Northern Lasse; The Sparagus Garden; The
English Moor; Covent Garden Weeded;* and *The Antipodes. See*
R. J. Kaufmann's *Richard Brome: Caroline Dramatist* (1961),
for a divergent interpretation of *A Jovial Crew.*

251   CRUIKSHANK, A. H.   "Massinger Corrections." *Library*, 4th ser,
       5 (1924), 175-79.
           Cruikshank further supports the authenticity of a Mas-
       singer autograph collection. For earlier discussion of
       this subject *see* 252 and W. W. Greg's "More Massinger Cor-
       rections," *Library*, 4th ser, 5 (1924), 59-91.

252   ____. *Philip Massinger*. Oxford: Blackwell, 1920. vii,
       228pp.
           Cruikshank gives considerable attention to *The Bondman*,
       The City Madam, *Emperor of the East*, *The Fatal Dowry*, *The
       Roman Actor*, and *The Renegado*, and frequently cites other
       Caroline dramatists. Included are twenty appendices re-
       lated to the minor actors in Massinger's plays, the in-
       fluence of Shakespeare on Massinger, *Believe as You List*,
       the authorship of *The Fatal Dowry* and *The Virgin Martyr*,
       and alliteration in Massinger's works and those of others.
       The work also includes an index and a facsimile of the
       British Museum MS of *Believe as You List* (V. 2), pp. 85-116.

253   CRUM, MARGARET. "A Manuscript of Ford's *Perkin Warbeck*: An
       Additional Note." *N & Q* (March 1965), pp. 104-105.
           Crum's note gives evidence to support Donald K. Ander-
       son's contention that Bodleian MS Rawl. poet. 122 was pro-
       duced in 1745. *See N & Q* (September 1963), pp. 340-41.

254   DAVENANT, SIR WILLIAM. Love and Honour *and* The Siege of
       Rhodes. Ed. James W. Tupper. Boston: D. C. Heath, 1909.
       362pp.
           Prior to the two edited plays, Tupper gives a brief
       biography of Davenant, and an extended analysis of the
       dramatic canon of Sir William Davenant, pp. xi-xlvii. The
       work concludes with a brief bibliography and a glossary.

255   ____. *The Shorter Poems, and Songs from the Plays and
       Masques*. Ed. by A. M. Gibbs. Oxford: Clarendon Press,
       1972. 477pp.
           In his introduction, Gibbs gives a biographical sketch
       of Davenant's life, as well as a discussion of the songs
       from the plays and masques, and their musical settings.
       Appendix B, edited by Judy Blezzard, is a series of musical
       settings for songs from *The Cruel Brother*; *The Temple of
       Love*; *The Triumphs of the Prince d'Amour*; *Britannia
       Triumphans*; *Luminalia*; and *Salmacida Spolia*. Title and
       incipit indexes are included.

256   DAVIS, JOE LEE. "Richard Brome's Neglected Contribution to
       Comic Theory." *SP*, 40 (1943), 520-28.

Dessen, Alan Charles

Davis' is one of the few sympathetic studies of Brome's *The Antipodes*; he shows "that it incorporates a theory of comic catharsis and what may be termed an *extra*-realistic conception of the relationships between comedy and actuality." In doing this he refers to Thomas Randolph's opinion, stated in *The Muses' Looking-Glass,* that in order for comedy "to carry out its corrective aims, [it] must reflect life with the fidelity of a looking glass."

257   DESSEN, ALAN CHARLES. *Jonson's Moral Comedy.* Evanston: Northwestern University Press, 1971. ix, 256pp.
Chapter 6: "The Decline of Moral Comedy: *The Devil is an Ass* and *The Staple of News,*" and Chapter 7: a general survey of Jonson's moral comedy, are of particular note. "Ideas and techniques implicit in . . . earlier plays, such as the power of money or the modernization of vice, here become explicit, even blatant, thereby helping us to understand what has gone before." The book is indexed by author, subject, and work.

258   DUNCAN, DOUGLAS. "A Guide to *The New Inn.*" *EIC,* 20 (1970), 311-26.
In defense of Jonson's *The New Inn* Duncan stresses the point that the play "is essentially ironic, that it is not the romantic comedy it seems to be; [this opens] the way to the discovery in it of a complex and intelligent, though imperfectly realized design. . . ." About the double title of the play--*The New Inn, or The Light Heart*--Duncan notes "While the second points to a thematic concern of the play, the first may indicate the frame of mind it was written in, an ageing man's comment on his times."

259   DUNN, THOMAS ALEXANDER. *Philip Massinger: The Man and the Playwright.* London: Thomas Nelson and Sons, 1957. x, 284pp.
In the six chapters of his work Dunn covers Massinger's life, as well as his plotting, stagecraft, use of characterization, criticism of life, and style. The work is a general survey of critical materials to 1957, but Dunn attempts to suggest new methods of approach to Massinger's dramas. Appendices include lists of collaborations, of possible associations, and random examples of Massinger's syntax diagrammatically analyzed through examples from *The Roman Actor*; *The Parliament of Love*; and *The Unnatural Combat.* A bibliography is included, as well as a thorough index.

260   DYCE, ALEXANDER. "Some Account of Shirley and His Writings."
        In *Dramatic Works and Poems of James Shirley*. 1867; rept.
        NY: Russell and Russell, 1966, Vol. I. Pp. iii-lxvi.
            Dyce follows his brief biographical note on Shirley's
        ancestry and early education with a chronological statement
        of the majority of Shirley's works beginning with the lost
        poem "Eccho, or The Unfortunate Lovers" (1618). Intermixed
        with the chronology are more biographical notes as they re-
        late to Shirley's literary career. Dyce concludes with
        selected critical evaluations of Shirley, beginning with
        Dryden's classic slur in "MacFlecknoe" and ending with
        Dyce's own magnanimous evaluation.

261   ERICKSON, KENNETH JERROLD. "A Critical Old-Spelling Edition
        of *The Young Admiral* by James Shirley." *DAI*, 28:1783A
        (Rice University), 1967. 177pp.
            Erickson feels that *The Young Admiral* "reveals Shirley's
        affinities with the tragicomedies of Beaumont and Fletcher.
        Although in its use of the love and honor theme this play
        anticipates the heroic plays of the Restoration, it is in
        general much closer to Elizabethan than to Restoration
        drama."

262   EVENHUIS, FRANCIS D. *Massinger's Imagery*. Salzburg:
        Institut für Englische Sprache und Literatur, 1973. 170pp.
            Evenhuis segments his discussion in terms of decorative,
        violent, intensive, exuberant, sunken, expansive, and radi-
        cal images, as well as images of humor. He suggests that
        the subject matter of Massinger's images involves learning,
        which he digests in terms of daily life images, nature,
        animals, body, domestic images, and those related to the
        arts. Both sections of the book are summarized individually
        and in a general summary. The work concludes with a bibli-
        ography; it is not indexed but there are numerous refer-
        ences to *The City Madam* in the study. *See also* the author's
        dissertation: "Massinger's Imagery," *DAI*, 20:1012A
        (University of Iowa), 1958. 198pp.

263   EWING, S. BLAINE. *Burtonian Melancholy in the Plays of John
        Ford*. Princeton: Princeton University Press, 1940. x,
        122pp.
            After reviewing the types of melancholy enumerated by
        Burton, Ewing applies the types to *The Lover's Melancholy;
        The Fancies; The Broken Heart; Love's Sacrifice; 'Tis Pity
        She's a Whore; Perkin Warbeck; The Queen;* and *The Lady's
        Trial*. He then discusses Ford's accuracy in development of
        Burtonian melancholy, and its effect on characterization,
        action, thought, and sympathy in the plays. He contrasts

Faust, Eduard Karl Richard

>
> Ford with Webster and Tourner, and concludes with a dis-
> cussion of the sources of Ford's interests. *See* index for
> references to other Caroline dramatists.

264　FAUST, EDUARD KARL RICHARD. *Richard Brome. Ein Betrag zur
　　　Geschichte der englischen Literatur.* Halle: A. S., 1887.
　　　100pp.
　　　　Faust's dissertation is practically the earliest, reason-
　　ably thorough study of Brome, his works, and his relation-
　　ship with Jonson and other earlier playwrights. He
　　analyzes *The Court Begger; The City Wit; The Northern Lass;
　　The Antipodes; The New Academy; The Damoiselle; The Or-
　　dinary; Covent Garden Weeded; The Sparagus Garden; A Mad
　　Couple Well Match'd; The Love-Sick Court; The Jovial Crew;
　　The Novella; The English Moor;* and *The Queen's Exchange.*
　　He also draws a parallel between *The Antipodes* (III, 244)
　　and Jonson's *Epicoene* (I.iv).

265　FEHRENBACH, ROBERT JULIAN. "A Critical Edition of *The
　　　Polititian* by James Shirley." *DAI,* 29:1206A (University
　　　of Missouri-Columbia), 1968. 535pp.
　　　　Fehrenbach concludes that "Shirley is not a profound
　　thinker, and because his concern is more with the plot than
　　the characters, the play is not successful as a tragedy in
　　spite of the truly tragic potential of Marpisa."

266　FEIL, J. P. "James Shirley's Years of Service." *RES, n.s.,*
　　　8 (1957), 413-16.
　　　　Feil's note sheds light on Shirley's activities between
　　June 1612 and April 1615, based on a deposition of Shirley's
　　made 6 March 1615, concerning a law suit in which Thomas
　　Frith was involved. It substantiates the fact that Shirley
　　was a "servant" to Frith.

267　FIELD, H. "The Early Quartos of Brome's *The Northern Lasse.*"
　　　PBSA, 54 (1960), 179-81.
　　　　Field discusses variant readings in the 1632 and 1663
　　quartos of Brome's play. He is doubtful of Fleay's and
　　Lowndes' claim of a 1635 quarto.

268　FITZGIBBON, G. "An Echo of *Volpone* in *The Broken Heart.*"
　　　N & Q (June 1955), pp. 248-49.
　　　　Fitzgibbon shows parallels between II.i.1 and 7 of
　　Ford's play and II.v.50 in *Volpone.*

269　FLEAY, FREDERICK G. "Annals of the Careers of James and Henry
　　　Shirley." *Anglia,* 8 (1885), 405-14.

Forsythe, Robert Stanley

Fleay gives a chronological listing from September 1596
(Shirley's birth) until October 29, 1666, when James and his
wife Frances succumbed to the effects of the Great Fire.
Fleay also includes chronological lists of Shirley's plays
(including information on publishers, dedications, and
Stationers' Register entries). The article concludes with
a brief statement on Henry Shirley and his four lost plays.

270   FORD, JOHN. *The Chronicle History of Perkin Warbeck: A
       Strange Truth*. Ed. by Peter Ure. London: Methuen, 1968.
       lxxix, 190pp.
           In his commentary on the play, Ure discusses the text,
       its date and authorship, the sources, the play and its
       critics, the themes of majesty and passion in the play, and
       he gives a biographical index to historical characters.
       Following the text are extracts from Gainsford's *True and
       Wonderfull History of Perkin Warbeck,* William Warner's
       Albione England, and brief statements on various enquiries
       on the lost play of *Warbeck; Believe as You List; Believe
       It Is So and It Is So;* and *Perkin Warbeck.* The Commentary
       is indexed.

271   _____. *'Tis Pity She's a Whore*. Ed. by Derek Roper. London:
       Methuen, 1975. lxxi, 146pp.
           In his monograph-length introduction to the play, Roper
       discusses Ford and his works, and the sources and date of
       'Tis Pity; he then gives a critical analysis of the play
       itself, its stage history, and the condition of the text.
       Following the text, in appendices, are extracts from de
       Rosset and Sannazaro, as well as criticisms of the play
       from Pepys through Eliot.

272   FORKER, CHARLES R. "Shirley's *The Cardinal*: Some Problems
       and Cruces." *N & Q* (October 1959), pp. 232-33.
           Forker deals with stage directions related to the comic
       prose scene in the third act of *The Cardinal,* as well as
       the solemn verse scene which follows.

273   FORSYTHE, ROBERT STANLEY. *The Relationship of Shirley's Plays
       to the Elizabethan Drama*. NY: Columbia University Press,
       1914. xiv, 483pp.
           Forsythe attempts "to show that Shirley's true sources
       were, in perhaps the majority of cases, not single plays,
       incidents, or characters, but the aggregate, the sum total,
       of the similar plays, incidents, or characters of earlier
       and contemporary playwrights." In his introductory chap-
       ters Forsythe discusses the English stage 1620-42, Shirley's
       biography, the stage history and chronology of his plays,

Fried, Harvey

general characteristics, stock incidents, and characters in
the plays. The internal chapters are devoted to an individual discussion of the plays and entertainments. The
work concludes with two bibliographies, and two thorough
indices.

274   FRIED, HARVEY. "A Critical Edition of Brome's *The Northern
      Lasse.*" *DAI,* 20:288A (New York University), 1959. 273pp.
      The dissertation includes an introduction, a critical,
      old-spelling edition of the play, and an appendix containing
      the prologue and epilogue for the 1684 edition. Fried dis-
      cusses sources for the play at length.

275   FULLER, DAVID. "The Jonsonian Masque and Its Music." *M & L,*
      54 (1973), 440-52.
      Although Fuller is concerned primarily with Jonson's
      early masques, he points out that Jonson was "very much a
      practical man of the theatre; he was always conscious of
      the conditions of performance for which he was writing and
      must have judged the dramatic balance of his masques with
      these in mind. To see his intentions in this the reader
      too must be aware, especially with so 'occasional' a form
      as the masque, of the part played in the whole by the non-
      literary arts [and] imagine Jonson's masques in action
      displayed, with all their components: design, dances, and
      not least their music."

276   GEBAUER, AUGUST WILLIAM, JR. "Themes and Patterns in the
      Tragedies of John Ford." *DAI,* 37:2842-43A (Tulane
      University), 1975. 207pp.
      Based on the thesis that "John Ford's tragedies dramatize
      the conflict between man's need for a sustaining moral and
      intellectual order, and the importunate demands of his emo-
      tions and appetites," Gebauer analyzes the major characters
      in *Perkin Warbeck; The Broken Heart; Love's Sacrifice;* and
      'Tis Pity She's a Whore in terms of their passions and
      honor.

277   GERBER, RICHARD. *James Shirley: Dramatiker der Decadenz.*
      Bern: A. Franckeag, 1952. 109pp.
      Gerber walks a tightrope between Shirley's "Moral and
      Amoral" idealogy, as exhibited in the characterization, the
      speech and theme of his plays.

278   GIBSON, C. A. "'Behind the Arras' in Massinger's *The
      Renegado.*" *N & Q* (August 1969), pp. 296-97.
      Gibson notes that "the dominant Jacobean and Caroline
      association of the phrase ['behind the arras'] is with

court lechery as well as 'duplicity and sexual immorality.'"
He supports this with references to Jonson, Shirley, Nabbes,
and other works by Massinger, then applies his evidence to
an explication of *The Renegado*, II.vi, 1-7.

279 _____. "The Date of *The Broken Heart*." *N & Q* (December 1971),
p. 458.
Gibson suggests dating Ford's tragedy *c.* 1630-31 because
of a possible borrowing in *The Broken Heart* from Massinger's
The Picture, licensed 8 June 1629, and published in 1630.
He adds that "such a dating would have the further merit
of strengthening the connection with the two other plays
which Ford is known to have written for the King's Men -
The Lover's Melancholy . . . and *Beauty in a Trance*."

280 _____. "Massinger's London Merchant and the Date of *The City
Madam*." *MLR*, 65 (1970), 737-49.
Gibson acknowledges that "though Massinger commonly de-
precated his own industry . . . his scrupulous care to establish a background of authentic detail, even for the most
romantic and improbable of his plots, is coming to be recognized." Gibson then analyzes the realistic details in
Massinger's comedy *The City Madam*. Of particular interest
is his association of the character Sir John Frugal with
the real Sir William Cockayne.

281 GILL, ROMA B. "Collaboration and Revision in Massinger's *A
Very Woman*." *RES*, n.s., 18 (1967), 136-48.
Gill suspects that "behind *A Very Woman* . . . lies a
fairly conventional comedy with a light-hearted treatment
of feminine unreasonableness. . . . Less superficial, less
gay than Fletcher, Massinger struggled to transform the
soufflé into the solid fare of his own tragicomic mode,"
using *The Anatomy of Melancholy* as a guide.

282 GOODMAN, CYNDIA CLEGG. "'Mirth and Sense': A Critical Study
of Richard Brome's Dramatic Art." *DAI*, 36:7436A
(University of California at Los Angeles), 1976. 276pp.
Goodman is concerned with "tracing the evolution of
Brome's dramatic techniques . . . [with a] close examina-
tion of the conventions and formulae." To do this she fo-
cuses on *The City Wit*; *The Queen's Exchange*; *The Love-Sick
Court*; *The Queen and the Concubine*; *The Antipodes*; and *The
Jovial Crew*.

283 GRAY, J. E. "The Source of *The Emperour of the East*." *RES*,
n.s., 1 (1950), 126-35.

Gray, J. E.

> Gray is convinced that the only real source for Massinger's play is a two volume work published in Paris in 1626 entitled *The Holy Court, or The Christian Institution of Men of Quality* written by Sir Thomas Hawkins. Greg cites frequent instances of commonality of idea and diction between the two works. *See also* A. K. McIlwraith's "Did Massinger revise *The Emperor of the East?*," *RES*, 5 (1929), 36-42.

284 _____. "Still More Massinger Corrections." *Library*, 5th ser, 5 (1950), 132-39.

> Gray extends Greg's discussion of the Massinger autograph. *See* W. W. Greg's "More Massinger Corrections," *Library*, 4th ser, 5 (1924), 59-91. For a continuation of the discussion *see* A. K. McIlwraith's "The Manuscript Corrections in Massinger's Plays," *Library*, 5th ser, 6 (1951), 213-16.

285 GRAZIANI, R. I. C. "Ben Jonson's *Chloridia:* Fame and Her Attendants." *RES*, n.s., 7 (1956), 56-58.

> Graziani's note on Jonson's last masque shows the suitability of "the figures representing Poesy, History, Architecture, and Sculpture" as attendants to Fame, and "that there is a certain appropriateness in his celebrating an art which he had successfully practised for more than a quarter of a century."

286 GREG, W. W. "Another Note." *Library*, 4th ser, 12 (1931), 248.

> Greg's note is appended to an article by R. C. Bald in which he discusses "massing of entrances" in Jacobean drama. To Bald's list Greg adds the first scene of Act I of Massinger's *Believe As You List*.

287 GROSS, ALAN GERALD. "Class Structure and Class Conflict in the Plays of Philip Massinger." *DAI*, 23:3375A (Princeton University), 1962. 166pp.

> Gross deals with Massinger's two social comedies, *A New Way to Pay Old Debts*, and *The City Madam* to show "the conflict in early Stuart England between the trading and the upper class."

288 _____. "Contemporary Politics in Massinger." *SEL*, 6 (1966), 279-90.

> Gross examines "not only the dubious nature of the arguments which draw parallels between [Massinger's plays] and contemporary persons and events, but also the ways in which Massinger's commentators misuse historical sources, and

fail to come to terms with official early Stuart censorship." Having done this, he reaffirms the fact that Massinger, as a playwright, showed considerable concern for
politics in his plays.

289   _____. "Social Change and Philip Massinger." *SEL*, 7 (1967),
329-42.
Gross discusses *The City Madam* and *A New Way to Pay Old
Debts* in terms of their commonality. He focuses on "the
care with which Massinger analyzes the increasing power of
the trading class as an outward manifestation of individual
moral perversion." *See also* L. C. Knight's *Drama and Society in the Age of Jonson* (1937), pp. 270-92.

290   HARBAGE, ALFRED. "The Authorship of the Dramatic *Arcadia*."
MP, 35 (1938), 233-37.
Harbage concludes that "it seems probable that Shirley
had nothing to do with [the writing of *Arcadia*] except as
the victim of a bookseller's ruse."

291   _____. "The Mystery of *Perkin Warbeck*." In *Studies in the
English Renaissance Drama in Memory of Karl Julius
Holzknecht*. Ed. by Josephine W. Bennett; Oscar Cargill;
Vernon Hall, Jr. NY: New York University Press, 1959.
Pp. 125-41.
Harbage suggests a possible collaboration between Ford
and Dekker in *Perkin Warbeck*. As evidence, he cites previous collaborations between the two, the fact that "the
chronicle play was obsolete when *Perkin Warbeck* was
written," and information from the title page of the 1634
edition. Harbage's impression is that "Dekker wrote part
of *Perkin Warbeck* and shaped the play as a whole."

292   _____. "Shirley's *The Wedding* and the Marriage of Sir Kenelm
Digby." *PQ*, 16 (1937), 35-40.
Harbage considers the question of date and source for
The Wedding in relation to Shirley's other dramatic works.

293   _____. *Sir William Davenant: Poet Venturer 1606-1668*.
Philadelphia: University of Pennsylvania Press, 1935.
317pp.
The work is a running commentary on the life, times,
product, worth, and imagination of Sir William Davenant;
the book is well-indexed, and includes a bibliography.

294   HART, D. J. "A Critical Edition of John Ford's *The Fancies,
Chaste and Noble*." *DAI*, 32:5739A (University of South
Carolina), 1971. 245pp.

Hart, H. C.

> Hart sees the play as "basically comic, even at times farcical" even "though it does have its serious moments." *See* Nadine Small St. Louis' "A Critical Old-Spelling Edition of John Ford's Comedy Drama *The Fancies, Chaste and Noble*."

295   HART, H. C.   "'The Captain' in Fletcher and Ben Jonson." *N & Q* (September 1904), pp. 184-85.
> Hart makes passing references to *Neptune's Triumph; The Staple of News; Fair Maid of the Inn;* and *Love Tricks,* and is concerned with the various occurrences of the ambiguous "Captain" in Jonson and Fletcher plays. This note is cited as "The Identity of the Captain in *The Fair Maid* and in Jonson's *Staple*" in *CBEL*.

296   HAWKINS, HARRIET.   "The Idea of a Theatre in *The New Inn*." *Ren D*, 9 (1966), 205-26.
> Hawkins, in a sympathetic reappraisal of Jonson's "failure" notes that "throughout *The New Inn* Jonson coaches his audience to consider plot and character in terms of theatrical practice, in relation to conventions which produce dramatic illusion [stressing] the fact that his play, through almost outrageous 'feigning' can teach the audience significant truths about various kinds of illusions within both the world of the theater and the 'theater of the world.'" She concludes that "the play by no means represents a decline in Jonson's 'experimental energy.'"

297   HOBBS, MARY.   "Robert and Thomas Ellice, Friends of Ford and Davenant." *N & Q* (August 1974), pp. 292-93.
> Hobbs is concerned with the friendship which existed between the two Ellice brothers and Ford and Davenant, particularly as exhibited in Ford's dedication to *The Lover's Melancholy* and *'Tis Pity She's a Whore*.

298   HOGAN, ALICE PATRICIA.   "Theme and Structure in Massinger's Plays." *DAI*, 32:3954A (University of Wisconsin), 1971. 368pp.
> Hogan stresses as Massinger's "major thematic concern . . . the destructive power of passion and the fatal tendency of the human ego to embrace irrational self-gratification over voluntary obedience to providential power."

299   HOMAN, SIDNEY P., JR.   "Dekker as Collaborator in Ford's *Perkin Warbeck*." *ELN*, 3 (1965), 104-06.
> Homan states that the chronicle-history of *Perkin Warbeck* "is unlike any of Ford's unaided plays, which are otherwise intense psychological tragedies or courtly romances. Perhaps an early date and the hand of Ford's tutor

in the drama may explain the difference." *See also* Alfred
Harbage's "The Mystery of *Perkin Warbeck*," in *Studies in
the English Renaissance in Memory of Karl Julius Holzknecht*
(1959), pp. 125-41.

300   _____. "Shakespeare and Dekker as Keys to Ford's *'Tis Pity
       She's a Whore*." *SEL*, 7 (1967), 267-76.
           After briefly surveying the peripatetic paths of scholar-
       ship related to *'Tis Pity*, Homan contends "that the danger
       of interpreting *'Tis Pity* solely in terms of the author's
       other unaided plays is that the moral complexity of his
       works will support many readings, some of which may not be
       relevant for this tragedy." Homan then analyzes *'Tis Pity*
       from the perspective of *Romeo and Juliet* (an early source
       for the play), and *The Witch of Edmonton*.

301   HOSKINS, HERBERT WILSON, JR. "A Critical Edition of *Love's
       Sacrifice* by John Ford." *DAI*, 24:2034A (Columbia
       University), 1963. 267pp.
           Hoskins concludes that "Despite surface concessions to
       'Platonick' tastes, the same aristocratic ethic is found to
       be underlying *Love's Sacrifice* that is so strongly asserted
       in Ford's nondramatic works and in his plays most closely
       associated with *Love's Sacrifice*, namely *The Broken Heart*,
       The Queen, and *The Lady's Trial*."

302   HOWARTH, R. G. "John Ford." *N & Q* (June 1957), p. 241.
           Howarth comments on two epigrams, dated 1639 and 1640,
       both of which suggest that Ford was still alive at the time.

303   _____. "A Manuscript of James Shirley's *Court Secret*." *RES*,
       7-8 (1931-32), 302-13.
           Howarth cites an unidentified manuscript in Worchester
       College Library, Oxford (Plays 9.21) titled "Don Manuell"
       and he believes that it is actually "an earlier version
       even than the first sketch" of *The Court Secret*. He sus-
       pects this may be the copy Langbaine mentions existing in
       1691.

304   HOWE, JAMES ROBINSON, IV. "John Ford's Figurative Language:
       Its Dramatic Function in Six Plays." *DAI*, 29:3974-75A
       (New York University), 1968. 640pp.
           Howe states that "In their methods of forming figures of
       speech, John Ford's major characters display their degree
       of credibility and dynamism." He explores this thesis in
       *The Lover's Melancholy; Love's Sacrifice; 'Tis Pity; The
       Broken Heart; Perkin Warbeck;* and *The Lady's Trial*.

Hoy, Cyrus

305   HOY, CYRUS. "'Ignorance and Knowledge': Marlowe's Faustus
       and Ford's Giovanni." *MP*, 57 (1960), 145-54.
           Hoy shows a number of dramatic characteristics in common
       between *Doctor Faustus* and *'Tis Pity She's a Whore*, par-
       ticularly in regards to the scene of incestuous love between
       Giovanni and Annabella in the latter work.

306   _____. "The Shares of Fletcher and His Collaborators in the
       Beaumont and Fletcher Canon, Pt. IV." *SB*, 12 (1959),
       91-116.
           In the latter part of his article, Hoy discusses the
       play *The Night Walker*; he concludes that "there can hardly
       be any doubt that the play was originally a work of
       Fletcher's sole authorship, but it is equally beyond doubt
       that the manuscript behind the only substantive edition -
       the 1640 quarto - represented not the Fletcherian original,
       but Shirley's revision." To Fletcher solely he attributes
       I.vii-viii; to Fletcher and Shirley he attributes I.i-vi;
       II.ii-iv; and III.v.

307   _____. "Verbal Formulae in the Plays of Massinger." *SP*, 56
       (1959), 600-18.
           Hoy says "The current attitude toward parallel passages
       as evidence for authorship being what it is, the interest
       that once attached to Massinger's repetitions as sources of
       authorial evidence is no longer the primary one; though
       when a dramatist repeats himself on the scale of Massinger,
       certain at least of his more distinctive tricks of expres-
       sion . . . must come to possess a corroborative value in
       authorial evidence that it would be sheer obstinancy to
       deny." Having established this premise, Hoy proceeds to
       analyze Massinger's dictional quirks and patterns of
       repetition.

308   HUBERMAN, EDWARD. "Bibliographical Note on James Shirley's
       The Polititian." *Library*, 4th ser, 18 (1937), 104-108.
           Huberman analyzes the similarities between the quarto
       and octavo printings, by Humphrey Moseley, of Shirley's
       The Polititian. He shows that "the two sizes were printed
       from the same type, and without alteration in spacing."

309   HUEBERT, RONALD M. "John Ford: Baroque English Dramatist."
       DAI, 33:4418A (University of Pittsburgh), 1973. 349pp.
           Huebert feels that "Critics who stress historical evolu-
       tion, as well as those who select a great tradition, tend
       to dismiss Ford under the heading of 'decadence.' Two major
       approaches--verbal analysis and archetypal criticism--
       might be more fruitfully applied to Ford's plays in the

future." Huebert discusses *'Tis Pity, The Lover's Melancholy,* and *The Queen* specifically.

310 JONSON, BEN. *The Staple of News.* Ed. by De Winter. NY: Henry Holt, 1905. lix, 273pp.
In his introduction to this edition, Winter discusses the editions of *The Staple of News,* sources, early English journalism, and Nathaniel Butter, as well as the madrigal and Jonson. Following the text is a bibliography and an index.

311 _____. *The Staple of News.* Ed. by Devra Rowland Kifer. Lincoln: University of Nebraska Press, 1974. xxiii, 173pp.
Like most volumes in the Regents Series, Kifer's contains an introduction which covers a critical survey of the play itself, and a note on the date and text. Sources are not discussed. Following the text is a chronology of Jonson's canon and facts related to his life.

312 JORDAN, R. "Calantha's Dance in *The Broken Heart.*" *N & Q* (August 1969), pp. 294-95.
Jordan believes Frederich Burelbach in error when he ascribes the source of Penthe's dance to Castiglione. Jordan discusses Plutarch in this context. *See* Burelbach's "'The Truth' in John Ford's *The Broken Heart* Revisited," *N & Q* (June 1967), pp. 211-12.

313 JUNEJA, RENU. "The Ground of Art: Cosmological Structure in Ben Jonson's Comedies." *DAI,* 35:7869A (Penn State University), 1974. 271pp.
Juneja concludes "In his long career, Jonson experiments with different forms and styles; beginning with something akin to the affirmative New Comedy, he moves to satire, thence to irony, and concludes with plays which have symbolic overtones."

314 KALMAR, ELAINE BUSH. "Miseries of Birth and State. Essays on the Tragedies of James Shirley." *DAI,* 32:5231A (University of New Mexico), 1971. 186pp.
"Chapters III, IV and V analyze Shirley's double theme in the plays *The Maid's Revenge* (1626); *Love's Cruelty* (1631); and *The Cardinal* (1641), in terms of character relationships and dramatic structure."

315 KAUFMANN, RALPH JAMES. "Ford's Waste Land: *The Broken Heart.*" *Ren D, n.s.,* 3 (1970), 167-87.
In an attempt to counter what T. S. Eliot says about Ford, Kaufmann notes that "*The Broken Heart* is imaginatively

Kaufmann, Ralph James

      organic." Through a strict analysis of structure, he con-
cludes "In this beautifully sustained play an unassailable
theory of happiness maintains a fugitive existence within
a format of repression severe and efficacious enough to
make a blighting and blighted Sparta the inevitable symbolic setting of the play's action. This 'tragedy of manners' is the result of these unusual intersections of
beliefs in the divided consciousness of its author."

316   _____. "Richard Brome: Caroline Playwright." *DAI*, 14:1709A
      (Princeton University), 1954. 400pp.
      Kaufmann's dissertation is an early version of the work
that follows. The emphasis here is to show that "Brome
doggedly retained a clear-headed, consistent conservatism
which he employed (at times imaginatively and always compe-
tently) as an intellectual basis for selecting, organizing,
and dramatically rendering his primary social protests
against an emergent set of attitudes which we now recognize
as the basis of the modern world."

317   _____. *Richard Brome: Caroline Playwright*. NY and London:
      Columbia University Press, 1961. 193pp.
      To date, Kaufmann's is the most thorough and sympathetic
estimate of Brome's literary career. Various chapters go
under the titles "On Being a Caroline Playwright," "Biographical Anatomy," "Under the Seal of Ben," "The Caroline
Editorial Page," "Paternalism, Puritanism, and Sociological
Comedy," "Parable and Hageography," "Court Drama and Common-
sense," "Usury and Brotherhood" (particularly thorough),
"Suckling's New Strain of Wit," and "Utopian Epilogue."
There are appendices of undigested records and a chronology
of Brome's plays, as well as a bibliography of Brome criticism. The work is well-indexed.

318   _____. "Suckling and Davenant Satirized by Brome." *MLR*, 55
      (1960), 332-44.
      Using evidence from *The Court Beggar* (1640), the "Pro-
logue" to *The Antipodes* (1638) and *The Damoiselle* (1638),
Kaufmann shows how Brome satirized the pretentiousness and
mediocrity of Suckling and Davenant, in particular, and
"the combination of monopolists, projectors and self-inter-
ested court favorites who used the too uncritical regard
of Charles I as a shield for their profiteering. . . ."
He is also concerned with the role of William Beeston as
he is alluded to in Brome's works.

319   KELLY, MICHAEL J. "The Values of Chronicle and Action in *The
      Broken Heart*." *PLL*, 7 (1971), 150-58.

Kistner, Arthur L.

Kelly suggests that *"The Broken Heart* furnishes an answer to a question every reader of Ford must ask himself:
What is laudable and meaningful in a villainous world and
more specifically, in a kingdom where all are 'turned mad-
caps?'" He is most concerned with the action and interac-
tion of characters as these actions relate to the tone of
the play.

320   KERR, MINA. *Influence of Ben Jonson on English Comedy 1598-*
      1642. NY: D. Appleton, 1912. 132pp.
      Kerr's is an early study of the "sons of Ben." Chapters
      are devoted to the nature of Jonson's comedy, his influence
      on immediate contemporaries, his relation to Nathaniel
      Field, Richard Brome, Thomas May, Robert Davenport, Thomas
      Randolph, Shackerley Marmion, William Cartwright, Jasper
      Mayne, Henry Glapthorne, Thomas Nabbes, and Aston Cockayne.
      She cites frequent similarities of tone, diction, charac-
      terization, and plot between Jonson and other Caroline
      dramatists.

321   KING, T. J. "Shirley's *Coronation* and *Love Will Find Out the*
      Way: Erroneous Title-Pages." *SB*, 18 (1965), 265-69.
      King's major premise is that "Studies relating to print-
      ing house practice have shown that compositors did not al-
      ways distribute title-page type immediately after the
      printing of the forme in which this type was first used;
      sometimes all or part of the title-page was left standing
      for later use in the printing of advertisements or another
      issue of the work." He notes how "this practice may have
      contributed errors in title-page inscriptions" for Shirley's
      plays.

322   KISTNER, ARTHUR L. and M. K. KISTNER. "The Dramatic Function
      of Love in the Tragedies of John Ford." *SP*, 70 (1973),
      62-76.
      The authors note an intrinsic nobility of lovers in
      Ford's tragedies and justify it in terms of his system of
      morality and that of modern critics. They note also that
      all the great tragic figures in Ford's plays "commit im-
      moral or antisocial acts. . . . Although the great passion
      that impels each does not remove the necessity for death
      and expiation, Ford projects it as the overpowering motive
      that makes the acts understandable and the characters
      figures of compassion."

323   _____. "The Fine Balance of Imposture in John Ford's *Perkin*
      Warbeck." *ES*, 52 (1971), 419-23.

Knoll, Robert Edwin

> The authors contradict the commonly held notion that
> Ford "portrays Warbeck's pretensions to the throne as in-
> valid throughout the play."

324 KNOLL, ROBERT EDWIN. *Ben Jonson's Plays: An Introduction.*
Lincoln: University of Nebraska Press, 1964. xvii, 206pp.
The final chapters of Knoll's work are significant here;
they are "*Bartholomew Fair; The Devil Is an Ass;* and *The
Staple of News*" and "The Dotages." In his last chapter
Knoll is concerned with *The New Inn, The Magnetic Lady,* and
the fragmentary "The Sad Shepherd." The work is indexed by
work, author, and subject matter, and is liberally
illustrated.

325 LAIG, FRIEDRICH. *Englische und französische Elemente in Sir
William Davenants dramatischer Kunst* [sic]. Emsdetten:
Anstalt Heine, und J. Lechte, 1934. 133pp.
In pages 1-56 Laig analyzes the French elements in the
following Caroline plays by Davenant: *The Cruel Brother;
The Just Italian; Love and Honor; News from Plymouth; The
Platonic Lovers; The Unfortunate Lovers; The Fair Favorite;
The Distresses;* and *The Siege.* A bibliography is included.

326 LAUREN, BARBARA. "John Ford and Tragic Ritual." *DAI,* 34:
2634A (Yale University), 1973. 198pp.
Focusing on *The Queen* and *The Lover's Melancholy,* Lauren
points out that in his later plays Ford "turns his attention
to an aristocratic code, which, bleakly, offers no cures
but only a poised rigid defiance of circumstances."

327 LAWLESS, DONALD S. "The Parents of Philip Massinger." *N & Q*
(July 1968), pp. 256-58.
Lawless discusses many biographical details, hitherto
undigested, related to the lives of Anne and Arthur
Massinger.

328 _____. *Philip Massinger and His Associates.* Muncie, IN:
Ball State University, 1967. ix, 67pp.
Lawless' monograph is a survey of Massinger's life in
relation to his work and his associates. Chapters include
a biography of Massinger, a discussion of his dramatic
career, his patrons, and his circle. The work is not indexed, but contains references to Shirley, Cockayne, May,
Clavell, Randolph, and others.

329 LEECH, CLIFFORD. "Caroline Echoes of *The Alchemist.*" *RES,* 16
(1940), 432-38.

Levin, Richard

Leech notes verbal echoes in *The Fair Maid of the Inn;*
*The Maid of Honour; The Damoiselle; The City Madam; News
from Plymouth;* and *The Jealous Lovers*. He also notes similarities of scene and situation in Glapthorne's *The Hollander*, Randolph's *Amyntas*, Shirley's *The Young Admiral*, and
Heywood's *The English Traveller*.

330   _____. *John Ford and the Drama of His Time*. London: Chatto
and Windus, 1957.   144pp.
The four internal sections of the work deal with the beginnings of Ford's career, his relationship to Jacobean
authors, his own vision of tragedy, and his treatment of
tragi-comedy in the context of his own time.   The two appendices are a list of Ford's writings, and a brief history
of Ford on the stage after the close of the theatres.   The
book is indexed and notes passing references to other Caroline dramatists.

331   LEMLY, JOHN W.   "'Into Winter Quarters Gone':   The Last Plays
of Jonson and Dryden."   *DAI*, 34:324A (Yale University),
1973.   259pp.
Lemly points out that "the neglected late plays of Jonson
and Dryden represent the efforts of two aging playwrights
to return to the stage under unfavorable conditions."   About
Jonson's Caroline plays, he feels that "For the first time
since his early plays," Jonson used "satiric spokesmen. . . ."

332   LEVIN, LAURENCE L.   "Replication as Dramatic Strategy in the
Comedies of Ben Jonson."   *Ren D, n.s.,* 5 (1972), 37-74.
Levin states that "One of the most striking attempts to
achieve dramatic unity [during the Renaissance] was the de-
ployment of multiple plots which would interact in one way
or another with the main line of action."   He applies an
analysis of the multiple plot structure specifically to the
works of Jonson.   He concludes that "In both *The Devil Is
an Ass* and *The Staple of News*, Jonson carefully weaves in-
terconnected scenes and episodes into a rather complicated
fabric, but the force of the analogous action is dissipated
by a multiplicity of events. . . ."

333   LEVIN, RICHARD.   "The Triple Plot of *Hyde Park*."   *MLR*, 62
(1967), 17-27.
Levin shows that the value of Shirley's play lies not
only in its realism and study of manners.   He contends that
the "tendency to compare [the three plots] is reinforced by
a number of analogous relationships among the plots, im-
bedded in the original conception of the triple-plot structure and repeatedly underscored in the details of its

Lyons, John O.

execution." He also draws parallels between *Hyde Park* and *The Ball,* and *The Gamester* and *The Lady of Pleasure.*

334   LYONS, JOHN O. "Massinger's Imagery." *Ren P,* 2 (1955), 47-54.
      In regards to *The Duke of Milan; The Great Duke of Florence; A New Way to Pay Old Debts;* and *The City Madam,* Lyons is concerned with imagery related to clothes and its dramatic impact on the plays.

335   McCLURE, DONALD STUART. "Richard Brome's *The Weeding of Covent Garden* and *The Sparagus Garden:* A Critical Edition." *DAI,* 31:3512A (Vanderbilt University), 1970. 438pp.
      McClure discusses what little is known of Brome's life and several of his works, including *The Love-Sick Court; The Northern Lass; The Weeding of Covent Garden; The Sparagus Garden;* and *The Antipodes.*

336   McCONNELL, ELIZABETH M. "The Presentation of James Shirley's *St. Patrick for Ireland* at the First Irish Playhouse." *N & Q* (July 1968), pp. 268-69.
      McConnell's note is a rejoinder to Albert Wertheim's in *N & Q* (July 1967), pp. 212-15. She focuses on a clearer explication of the dramatic structure of the play and the impact of the spectacular scenes.

337   McDONALD, CHARLES O. "The Design of John Ford's *The Broken Heart*: A Study in Caroline Sensibility." *SP,* 59 (1962), 141-61.
      For McDonald, and Charles Lamb in *Specimens of English Dramatic Poets* (1808), pp. 264-65, "Calantha is unequivocally [*The Broken Heart's*] tragic heroine and the figure to whom the title primarily refers," despite modern critic elevation of Penthea "to the status of protagonist." In his article, McDonald deals with the moral issues in the play and "the even larger question of precisely how much of his style is due to the 'new sensibility' of the Caroline audience and how much is to the poet's natural bent. . . ."

338   McFARLAND, RONALD E. "Jonson's *Magnetic Lady* and the Reception of Gilbert's *De Magnete.*" *SEL,* 11 (1971), 283-93.
      McFarland's thesis is that "Ben Jonson's *The Magnetic Lady* (1632) illustrates the extent of the popular reception of William Gilbert's *De Magnete* (1600); . . . the comedy is effectively interpreted with references to the magnetic conceit which Jonson likely drew either from Gilbert himself or from Barlow or Ridley. . . ." He concludes that "Without

at least a fundamental knowledge of magnetism, the play is hardly coherent, but when the magnetic conceit is examined, the comedy is seen to be structured as compactly as any that Jonson wrote."

339   McGRATH, JULIET. "James Shirley's Use of *Language*." *SEL*, 6 (1966), 323-39.

McGrath is concerned with the various highly suggestive ways in which the word *language* is used in Shirley's plays. She says "The most general sense in which *language* is used is that of a sustained statement of intention or declaration of feeling made in a single style"; to this she adds "the notion of language which is a special instance of the . . . conception . . . of a profession of love or a verbal declaration of a non-verbal idea or passion." She looks specifically at *Hyde Park; The Lady of Pleasure; The Witty Fair One; The Brothers; The Example; Love Tricks; The Polititian; The Cardinal;* and others.

340   McKINNON, DANA GENE. "*The Ball* by George Chapman and James Shirley: A Critical Edition." *DAI*, 26:7299A (University of Illinois at Urbana-Champaign), 1965. 258pp.

The critical, old-spelling edition is based on the 1639 quarto. The introduction includes a bibliographical study of the quarto, "the stage history of the play, a discussion of the authorship problem, and a critical evaluation of the play."

341   McMANAWAY, JAMES G. "Philip Massinger and The Restoration Drama." *ELH*, 1 (1934), 276-304.

McManaway is concerned with Restoration adaptations of Massinger's plays, and the social criticism they received during this time. Of particular note is his discussion of *The Guardian; The Roman Actor; The City Madam; Believe As You List; The Bashful Lover; A Very Woman;* and others.

342   McMASTER, JULIET. "Love, Lust, and Shame: Structural Patterns in the Plays of John Ford." *Ren D, n.s.*, 2 (1969), 157-166.

McMaster makes a case for considering Ford's plays "as whole units," rather than focusing entirely on the main plots to the utter disregard of subplots "because it is evident that he was consciously using a structural pattern which he intended to have thematic significance." She discusses *The Lover's Melancholy; 'Tis Pity; Love's Sacrifice; The Lady's Trial; The Fancies;* and *The Queen.*

MacMullan, Hugh

343   MacMULLAN, HUGH. "The Sources of Shirley's *St. Patrick for
      Ireland*." *PMLA*, 48 (1933), 806-14.
          MacMullan surveys existing scholarship related to sources
      of *St. Patrick for Ireland* and makes further suggestions for
      possible linkage. He continues the study in "A Note of
      Source-Studies of *St. Patrick for Ireland*," *PMLA*, 51
      (1936), 302.

344   MAKKINK, HENRI JACOB. *Massinger and Fletcher: A Comparison.*
      Rotterdam: Nijgh and Van Ditmer, 1927. v, 206pp.
          In a straight-line comparison, Makkink discusses Massin-
      ger's and Fletcher's likes and dislikes, the features of
      their plays, their attitudes toward women, love and mar-
      riage, religious beliefs and superstitions, patriotism,
      political opinions, habits, customs, knowledge of law terms,
      medicine, and language. Each chapter is followed by a re-
      capitulation; there is no index.

345   MANLY, F. "The Death of Hernando in Shirley's *The Cardinal*."
      N & Q (September 1965), pp. 342-43.
          Manly questions Gifford's and Dyce's stage direction re-
      quiring Hernando to kill himself immediately after he has
      revenged himself on the Cardinal.

346   MARTIN, ROBERT GRANT. "Is *The Late Lancashire Witches* a
      Revision?" *MP*, 13 (1915), 253-65.
          In short, Martin regards "the play as a straight piece
      of collaboration by [Heywood and Brome] done in the summer
      of 1634." Should be read in context with C. E. Andrew's
      "Richard Brome: A Study of His Life and Works." *Yale
      Studies in English*, 46 (1913), 48-53; and Fleay.

347   MASSINGER, PHILIP. *Believe As You List*. Ed. by Charles J.
      Sisson. Oxford: Oxford University Press, for Malone
      Society, 1927. xlviii, 99pp.
          Sisson's transcription is from the BM MS. Egerton 2828;
      his introduction is a detailed discussion of the play, and
      it includes twelve photographic facsimile portions of the
      manuscript.

348   ____. *The Bondman: An Antient Storie*. Ed. by Benjamin
      Townley Spencer. Princeton: Princeton University Press,
      1932. vii, 266pp.
          Spencer discusses the date of composition of *The Bondman*,
      the various editions, its stage history, classical and con-
      temporary sources, the use of classical ideas, and he also
      gives a textual note and an estimation of the play's value.
      Two appendices catalogue influences, publishers and print-
      ers. There is a bibliography.

Massinger, Philip

349   _____. *The City-Madam: A Comedy.* Ed. by Rudolf Kirk.
Princeton: Princeton University Press, 1934. 183pp.
        The introduction to Kirk's edition includes notes on the
date of the play, the condition of the quarto, the printer,
a section entitled "Andrew Pennycruicke and His Patrons,"
commentary on the editions and translations of the play, a
discussion of alterations and adaptations, and one on the
plays influenced by *The City Madam,* particularly Glapthorne's *Wit in a Constable,* and Mayne's *The City Match.*
He also covers stage, time sequences in the play, and its
criticism. There is a bibliography.

350   _____. *The Great Duke of Florence.* Ed. by Johanne M.
Stockholk. Baltimore: J. H. Furst, 1933. xcvi, 231pp.
        The extensive introduction to the critical edition in-
cludes a discussion of the sources, in English drama, for
The Great Duke of Florence, versions before and after 1627
of the Edgar-Alfreda story, the historical and political
elements in the play, its date of composition, stage history, criticism, as well as a note on the texts. There is
an appendix on the references to time, a bibliography, and
a thorough index.

351   _____. *The Maid of Honour.* Ed. by Eva A. W. Bryne. London:
R. C. Lay and Sons, 1927. xcix, 153pp.
        Bryne's introduction is concerned with the literary
sources and analogues of the play, its historical and political elements, date, criticism, and the condition of the
text. Five appendices treat references to time in the play,
verbal parallels between *The Maid of Honour* and Fletcher's
Wit Without Money, classicism in the play, parallels between
The Maid of Honour and other works by Massinger, and those
plays by George Lillo which are an outcome of Massinger's
influence. There is a bibliography and a thorough index.

352   _____. *The Plays of Philip Massinger.* Ed. by William Gifford.
London: Henry Washbourne, 1856. xlvi, 529pp.
        The volume contains a biographical and critical introduc-
tion by Gifford (xi-xxvii) and an "Essay on the Dramatic
Writings of Massinger" by John Ferriar (xxviii-xxxvi), in
which he reviews the plays, gives criticism related to them,
and places Massinger's work in context with Shakespeare,
Jonson, Cartwright, Fletcher and others. The Commendatory
Verse and Glossorial Index conclude the introduction.

353   _____. *The Roman Actor.* Ed. by William Lee Sandedge.
Princeton: Princeton University Press, 1929. 161pp.

Massinger, Philip

Sandedge's introduction to his critical edition includes a discussion of the date, sources and structure of the play. There is a glossary and a bibliography.

354 ____. *The Unnatural Combat*. Ed. by Robert Stockdale Telfer. Princeton: Princeton University Press, 1932. vii, 193pp.
As well as the critical edition of the text, Telfer's work is a lengthy discussion of the sources for the play, its date of composition, and the structure of the work. An appendix treats the printer and the publisher of the quarto; the bibliography is divided by editions of *The Unnatural Combat,* and general entries. A glossary concludes the work.

355 ____ and NATHANIEL FIELD. *The Fatal Dowry*. Ed. by Charles Lacy Lockert, Jr. Lancaster, PA: New Era Press, 1918. iv, 165pp.
The introduction of Lockert's critical edition includes notes on the text and editions, date, sources, collaborations, the critical estimate of the play, stage history, adaptations and derivations. There is a glossary and a bibliography.

356 MILLS, LLOYD LESLIE. "Ben Jonson's Last Plays: A Critical Reconsideration." *DAI*, 26:4635A (University of Washington), 1965. 240pp.
Mills focuses on *The Devil Is an Ass, The Staple of News, The New Inn,* and *The Magnetic Lady*. Each play has a critical chapter devoted to it. "The last chapter describes the typical pattern of Jonson's last plays, and tries to establish a connection between the idea of an organized conceit and Renaissance critical theory."

357 ____. "A Clarification of Broker's Use of 'A Perfect Sanguine' in *The Staple of News*." *N & Q* (June 1967), pp. 208-09.
Mills analyzes money imagery and explicates references to money in Jonson's play.

358 MORILLO, MARVIN. "'Frier Sherley': Shirley and *Mercurius Britanicus*." *N & Q* (September 1960), pp. 338-39.
Morillo fortifies an hypothesis made by Aline Taylor in *N & Q* (January 1960), pp. 31-33, concerning Shirley's Catholicism; he also includes more corroborative evidence.

359 ____. "James Shirley's *The Humorous Courtier*: Edited, with Notes and an Introduction." *DAI*, 19:1389A (University of Michigan), 1958. 225pp.

Nason, Arthur Huntington

In his introduction to the text, Morillo asserts that
The Humorous Courtier represents Shirley's attempt to ex-
press dissatisfaction with the life of the court of Charles
I. . . . In its utilization of the method of comical satire [à la Jonson] in a romantic setting, the play is unlike Shirley's other comedies, which are realistic comedies
of London manners, Fletcherian romantic comedies of love
and intrigue, or combinations of these types."

360 _____. "Shirley's 'Preferment' and the Court of Charles I."
SEL, 1 (1961), 101-17.
In regards to Shirley's statement about his loss of preferment, in the dedication to *The Maid's Revenge*, Morillo
shows that Shirley's loss "refers to a decline of his fortunes at court which began in 1634 and was a result of (a)
his frequent indulgence in satire of court life, (b) the
fad at court of a mode of [morally lax] drama which Shirley
declined to write, and (c) the rapid rise to royal favor
of William Davenant."

361 MORTON, RICHARD. "Deception and Social Dislocation: An
Aspect of Shirley's Drama." *Ren D*, 9 (1966), 227-45.
Morton states that Shirley's plays have elements of both
a "reconciliation of discordant elements" and the "Jonsonian
comedy of manners." Morton further states that Shirley has
many "humors" characters, and "in his best plays he draws
on the fluid and rapidly changing world of Caroline London
to produce a comedy of conflicting social elements which
seems, perhaps because of its source in a world of genuine
social conflict, to have unique urgency and validity." He
analyzes these aspects of Shirley's work in *The Lady of
Pleasure*; *Hyde Park*; *The Ball*; *The Constant Maid*; *The
Traitor*; *The Wedding*; *The Cardinal*; *Love Tricks*; *Love in a
Maze*; *The Gamester*; *The Witty Fair One*; and *The Opportunity*.

362 MUMPER, NIXON. "A Critical Edition of *Love Tricks, or The
School of Compliment*, by James Shirley." *DAI*, 20:300A
(University of Pennsylvania), 1959. 317pp.
The introduction to a critical edition of the 1637 edition of *Love Tricks* contains a biography of Shirley, a history of the production and publication of the play, an
inquiry into the sources of the play, and a discussion of
its realistic background in London life.

363 NASON, ARTHUR HUNTINGTON. *James Shirley, Dramatist: A
Biographical and Critical Study*. NY: Arthur H. Nason,
1915. xv, 471pp.

Neill, Michael

One of the earliest studies of the life and works of
James Shirley, Nason's suffers somewhat from an overlay of
moralism that seems neither sympathetic, perceptive, nor
critically valid in reference to the works themselves. The
first part of the book covers the life of Shirley; the
second covers the plays. He gives particular attention to
*Love Tricks; The Wedding; The Witty Fair One; The Grateful
Servant; The Traitor; The Humerous Courtier; Hyde Park; The
Lady of Pleasure; The Ball; The Young Admiral; The Opportunity; The Doubtful Heir;* and *The Cardinal.* He concludes
that "In short, from Jonsonian and Fletcherian comedy of
manners and humors, Shirley passed to Fletcherian and
Shakespearean romantic comedy, dramatic romance, and romantic tragedy." An annotated bibliography of early works on
Shirley is included, as well as a lengthy alphabetical (by
author) list of works containing references to Shirley.
The book is thoroughly indexed.

364 NEILL, MICHAEL. "Ford and Gainsford: An Unnoticed Borrowing."
N & Q (July 1968), pp. 253–55.
Neill's is yet another note on sources for *Perkin Warbeck.* For antecedents, *see* M. C. Struble's "The Indebtedness of Ford's *Perkin Warbeck* to Gainsford," *Anglia,* 49
(1925), 80–91.

365 _____. "New Light on 'The Truth' in *The Broken Heart.*" *N & Q*
(June 1975), pp. 249–50.
Neill cites a letter of 16 November, 1600, by Philip
Gaudy, related to the death of a Mrs. Ratcliffe, as a pos-
sible source for *The Broken Heart. See also,* Frederick
Burelbach's "'The Truth' in John Ford's *The Broken Heart*
Revisted," *N & Q* (June 1967), pp. 211–12.

366 NETHERCOT, ARTHUR H. *Sir William D'Avenant: Poet Laureate
and Playwright-Manager.* Chicago: University of Chicago
Press, 1938. 488pp.
In his standard life of Davenant, Nethercot tries to
achieve neither the "whitewash" of Harbage, nor the "black-
wash in the school of Edmund Gosse and the other squeamish
older biographers." Five appendices as well as an extensive
index are included.

367 NICHOLSON, B. "R. Brome's *Queene's Exchange,* 1657, and *Royal
Exchange,* 1661." *N & Q* (February 1889), pp. 126–27.
Nicholson states that "the supposed edition of another
play, *The Royal Exchange,* in 1661, was composed of the un-
sold copies of *The Queene's Exchange* of 1657. He notes a

similar fault in Glapthorne's *Albertus Wallenstein* - the editions of 1639 and 1640.

368   NOVARR, DAVID.   "'Gray Dissimulations': Ford and Milton."
      PQ, 41 (1962), 500-04.
      Novarr's brief article shows specific linkage between
      John Ford's *The Broken Heart* (IV.ii.99) and Milton's *Paradise Regained* (I, 497-99), and analyzes the rhetorical,
      stylistic, and tonal similarities.

369   OCHESTER, EDWIN F.   "A Source for Shirley's *The Contention of
      Ajax and Ulysses.*" *N & Q* (April 1970), p. 217.
      Ochester notes that "Both Thomas Heywood's *The Iron Age
      Part I*, Act V, and Shirley's *The Contention of Ajax and
      Ulysses for the Armour of Achilles* are dramatic versions of
      the Ajax-Ulysses conflict in the first section of Book XIII
      of Ovid's *Metamorphoses*.   Shirley followed Ovid in the main
      . . . but also appears to have borrowed from Heywood's
      play."

370   O'CONNOR, JOHN J.   "A Lost Play of *Perkin Warbeck.*" *MLN*, 70
      (1955), 566-68.
      Based on a statement in Thomas Gainsford's *History of
      the Earl of Tyrone* (1619) concerning a play Gainsford had
      seen, O'Connor concludes that an early play entitled *Perkin
      Warbeck* was performed either in the years 1608-10 or in
      1614-18.   He cannot safely conjecture who the author might
      have been or if Ford had a hand in its writing.

371   _____.   "William Warner and Ford's *Perkin Warbeck.*" *N & Q*
      (June 1955), pp. 233-35.
      O'Connor sees William Warner's *Albion's England* as a
      source for the full characterization of Katherine Gordon as
      a faithful and dedicated wife in *Perkin Warbeck*.

372   OLIVER, H. J.   *The Problem of John Ford*.   Melbourne:
      Melbourne University Press, 1955.   vii, 146pp.
      After discussing Ford in his age, his non-dramatic works,
      and those plays written in collaboration, Oliver focuses on
      individual discussions of *The Lover's Melancholy*; *The Broken
      Heart*; *The Queen*; *Love's Sacrifice*; *'Tis Pity*; *Perkin War-
      beck*; *The Fancies*; and *The Lady's Trial*.   In his conclusion,
      Oliver stresses Ford's achievement when compared with pro-
      fessional playwrights such as Massinger and Shirley.   An
      appendix discusses Sir Robert Howard's *Duke of Lerma*.   Check
      index for frequent references to other Caroline dramatists.

Orbison, [Theodore] Tucker

373   ORBISON, [THEODORE] TUCKER.   "The Date of *The Queen*."   *N & Q*
       (July 1968), pp. 255–56.
           Orbison suggests that "Perhaps a dating of *ca*. 1624–33
       for *The Queen* may not be far astray," thus setting a date
       of composition close to two other plays by Ford – *The
       Lover's Melancholy*, and *The Broken Heart*.

374   _____. "The Tragic Vision of John Ford." *DAI*, 24:1620A
       (Boston University Graduate School), 1963. 224pp.
           Orbison "analyzes the changes in the tragic vision" of
       *'Tis Pity She's a Whore; Love's Sacrifice; The Broken
       Heart*; and *Perkin Warbeck*. "The dissertation finds that of
       the four plays only *'Tis Pity* reveals a developed tragic
       vision and that, after narrowing his sense of the tragic in
       Love's Sacrifice, Ford moved to the Stoic and, in part,
       pathetic vision of *Perkin Warbeck*."

375   _____. *The Tragic Vision of John Ford*. Salzburg: Institut
       für Englische Sprache und Literatur, 1974. v, 192pp.
           Orbison's revised dissertation is about "the nature and
       chronology of Ford's tragedies." The first two chapters
       are an overview of criticism, chronology, and Ford's tragic
       vision. The four internal chapters are lengthy critical
       evaluations of *'Tis Pity; Love's Sacrifice; The Broken
       Heart*; and *Perkin Warbeck*. He concludes that "An examina-
       tion of such elements as plot, character, imagery, and
       audience response reveals that Ford's tragic vision varies
       considerably from one play to another . . . until in *Perkin
       Warbeck* it drops out almost entirely."

376   ORGEL, STEPHEN KITAY. *The Jonsonian Masque*. Cambridge, MA:
       Harvard University Press, 1965. viii, 216pp.
           Although Orgel is concerned primarily with the masque
       before 1619, he does discuss, at length, the possible rea-
       sons why Jonson's masques did not appeal to Charles I or
       his court. *See* index for references to latter works.

377   PANEK, LEROY LAD. "Asparagus and Brome's *The Sparagus
       Garden*." *MP*, 68 (1971), 362–63.
           Panek dispels the notion that "Brome and his contempor-
       aries believed asparagus to be an aphrodisiac."

378   _____. "A Critical Old-Spelling Edition of Richard Brome's
       The Sparagus Garden." *DAI*, 29:4465A (Kent State
       University), 1968. 283pp.
           "The secondary aim [of Panek's dissertation] is to pre-
       sent critical materials relevant to the play: a brief ac-
       count of Brome's life, a discussion of the date of the play,

Partridge, Edward B.

a discussion of the sources of the play, a brief critical analysis of the play, and an appendix of explanatory notes to the text."

379 PAPOUSEK, MARILYN DEWEESE. "A Critical Edition of James Shirley's *The Lady of Pleasure*." *DAI*, 32:5195A (University of Iowa), 1971. 285pp.

Papousek includes, with her edition of the play, a thorough analysis of *The Lady of Pleasure*'s "blend of two comic modes, that of comedy of manners, involving the judgment of characters according to social criteria, and that of moral satire, involving the judgment of characters according to moral criteria in social situations." She also discusses the notion that *The Lady of Pleasure* presages Restoration drama.

380 PARLIN, HANSON T. "A Study in Shirley's Comedies of London Life." *Studies in English*, 2 (1914), 1-68.

The work focuses on the life of Shirley, his association with George Chapman, and a critical analysis of Shirley's London comedies, particularly *The Ball*. A text and critical bibliography is included. The bibliography is a good record of sources related to Shirley before 1900.

381 PARSSINEN, CAROL ANN MILLER. "*The Guardian* by Philip Massinger: A Critical, Old-Spelling Edition." *DAI*, 32:928A (Brandeis University), 1971. 191pp.

The introduction to Parssinen's edition of *The Guardian*, based on the 1655 edition, "discusses the date, stage history, sources, and critical reception of the play."

382 PARTRIDGE, EDWARD B. "A Crux in Jonson's *The New Inne*." *MLN*, 71 (1956), 168-70.

Partridge explicates a passage in Jonson's play previously considered confusing and ambiguous, and shows how it is actually the crux of the scene, and how it foreshadows further action. The passage is: "It is a restorative *Pru!* with thy but chafing it,/A barren Hindes grease may worke miracles. . . ." (V.ii.15-16.)

383 _____. "The Symbolism of Clothes in Jonson's Last Plays." *JEGP*, 56 (1957), 396-409.

Partridge traces Jonson's unusual sensitivity "to the symbolic value of clothes from the early plays (particularly *Every Man Out of His Humor* and *Cynthia's Revels*), emphasizing Jonson's concern with this subject in the later plays. He gives particular attention to *The Staple of News* and *The New Inn*. He associates the symbolism of clothes with the

Peel, Donald Frank

theme of decorum and hypocrisy in Jonson's satire, and concludes that for Jonson clothes are "emblematic of pride and
presumption."

384   PEEL, DONALD FRANK. "A Critical Text of *The Emperour of the
East* by Philip Massinger." *DAI*, 31:6583A (University of
Denver), 1970. 328pp.
   Peel collates thirty-two copies of the 1632 quarto for
his edition. His introduction is a discussion of the Folger
autograph of the play, and of "the unity of the play, its
classifications, its sources, and its philosophy."

385   PHELAN, JAMES. *On Philip Massinger*. Halle: E. Karras, 1878.
64pp.
   Phelan is somewhat shakey on Massinger's biography,
having "rolled three Massingers into one" according to
Furnivall and Ewald Flügel. At the conclusion of his work
he lists thirty-one plays which he attributes to Massinger.
See Robert S. Lawless' *Philip Massinger and His Associates*
(1967).

386   PHELPS, WAYNE HOWE. "John Ford's *Perkin Warbeck* and the
Pretender Plays: 1634-1746." *DAI*, 26:3929A (Princeton
University), 1965. 435pp.
   Phelps sees the 1634 *Perkin Warbeck* as "a *speculum* in
which Ford's early seventeenth-century English contemporaries could see both a warning against civil upheaval, un-
restrained passion, and ambitious dissumulators, and a
eulogy of Ford's model of responsible kingship, the Tudor
Henry VII."

387   PHIALAS, PETER GEORGE. "*The Emperor of the East*, by Philip
Massinger. Edited with Introduction and Notes." *DAI*,
31:2887A (Yale University), 1970. 261pp.
   As well as a critical edition based on the 1632 quarto,
Phialas gives a full bibliographical analysis of the play,
its printing history, and sources for the historical plot.

388   _____. "Massinger and the Commedia dell' arte." *MLN*, 65
(1950), 113-14.
   Phialas gives more evidence to affirm Isaac Disraeli's
opinion "that the scene with the empiric in Massinger's
Emperor of the East was modeled on a similar scene of an
Italian burlesque comedy, perhaps a commedia dell' arte,"
in *Curiosities of Literature* (1871), pp. 311-15.

389   _____. "The Sources of Massinger's *Emperour of the East*."
PMLA, 65 (1950), 473-82.

Putt, S. Gorley

Phialas notes "the abundance and variety of historical literature which contains the principal elements of the plot of *Emperour of the East*, and surveys other critics on the subject." The purpose of his study "is to revise [earlier] conclusions and to examine briefly Massinger's use of his sources both in the construction of the plot and the delineation of character."

390 PIERCE, FREDERICK E. "The Collaboration of Dekker and Ford." *Anglia*, 36 (1912), 141-68.
Concerning himself primarily with the authorship and stylistic features of the semi-allegorical play or "moral masque" *The Sun's Darling*, Pierce methodically supports the evidence of the title page--that John Ford and Thomas Dekker are the authors--and by so doing he is in accord with Fleay, Swinburne, Collier, and Ward. The author concludes that "The steady recurrence of parallels from Dekker throughout the play is in harmony with this theory" (e.g., "that Ford recast part of a previous play by the older dramatist.")

391 PRESLEY, HORTON EDWARD. "'O Showes, Showes, Mighty Showes': A Study of the Relationship of the Jones-Jonson Controversy to the Rise of the Illusionistic Staging in Seventeenth-Century British Drama." *DAI*, 28:1056A (University of Kansas), 1966. 308pp.
Presley's dissertation centers around the 1631 controversy and "the continual rise of audience demand for realistic and spectacular elements."

392 PRINCIC, WALTER FRANCIS. "The Tragedies of James Shirley: A Study of Themes and Images." *DAI*, 35:4451A (University of Illinois at Urbana-Champaign), 1974. 235pp.
Princic's "chief purpose is to define Shirleian tragedy and to distinguish it from Shirleian tragicomedy." He discusses *The Maid's Revenge*; *The Traitor*; *Love's Cruelty*; *The Polititian*; and *The Cardinal*. "The approach is to investigate these tragedies in terms of the dramatic themes and poetic images Shirley offers." He concludes that except for *Love's Cruelty*, "Shirleian tragedy is thoroughly romantic."

393 PUTT, S. GORLEY. "The Modernity of Ford." *ES*, 18 (1969), 47-52.
Putt analyzes *'Tis Pity* and *The Broken Heart*, and concludes "That a re-reading of Ford's best plays prompts the suggestion that the literary historians have been too ready to bracket him with his contemporaries in an easy dismissal

Radtke, Stephen John

of 'decadence' in the theatre of the early years of the
reign of Charles I. He is not so much a debased Elizabethan
as a melancholic dramatic poet whose icy passion, strictly
controlled verse, and occasional classical economy look
forward . . . to Corneille and Racine."

394   RADTKE, STEPHEN JOHN. *James Shirley: His Catholic
       Philosophy of Life.* Washington: Catholic University
       Press, 1929. ix, 113pp.
          Father Radtke notes that "biographers invariably have
       referred to [Shirley's] conversion to the Catholic faith in
       a few brief words, or have omitted mention of the fact en-
       tirely." This published dissertation sparked an explosion
       of articles, centered around the controversial conversion.
       Radtke's work also includes chapters on Shirley criticism
       from 1675-1922, on Shirley's life and "Catholic Philos-
       ophy," and on his dramatic works.

395   READ, FORREST GODFREY. "Audience, Poet, and Structure in Ben
       Jonson's Plays." *DAI*, 22:3187-88A (Cornell University),
       1962. 444pp.
          Read's thesis is "To understand fully the structures and
       techniques of Jonson's plays, one must try to see them in
       their theatre, presented before certain kinds of audiences,
       for distinctly calculated purposes." To this intent, he
       analyzes Jonson's manipulation and understanding of his
       audiences, and the structure of his plays in terms of a
       particular audience.

396   REED, ROBERT RENTOUL, JR. "James Shirley and the Sentimental
       Comedy." *Anglia*, 73 (1955), 149-70.
          Reed defines sentimentality as "the elaboration of the
       pronounced and generally selfless moral goodness that was
       believed to stem from man's inner nature," and applies his
       definition to Shirley's realistic comedies, particularly
       *The Witty Fair One; Love in a Maze; Hyde Park; The Gamester;
       The Example;* and *The Lady of Pleasure.* It is Reed's con-
       tention that "Shirley's presentation of a moral thesis in-
       evitably offsets the coarseness so essential to the taste
       of the contemporary audience" and in his didactic moralizing
       produces sentimental comedy or elements of sentimentality
       that "far from being the result of accident . . . are so
       consistent in pattern as to be the deliberate effects of a
       deeply rooted moral consciousness." He attributes Shirley's
       popularity during the Restoration to just these elements.

397   REIMER, A. P. "Shirley's Revisions and the Date of *The
       Constant Maid.*" *RES, n.s.*, 17 (1966), 145-48.

Sackton, Alexander H.

Reimer feels that *Love Will Find Out the Way* (1661) "is not a revision by another hand of *The Constant Maid,* but that additions and changes were made by Shirley himself. This enables Reimer to date *The Constant Maid* at 1636.

398 _____. "A Source for Shirley's *The Traitor.*" *RES,* n.s., 14 (1963), 380-83.
In contradiction to Swinburne's "James Shirley" in *Fortnightly Review,* 47 (1890), 467, Reimer states that the subplot of *The Traitor* is "based closely on an account of Buondelmonte's murder [Florence 1215] which Shirley found in Thomas Bedingfield's translation of Machiavelli's *Le Istorie Fiorentine.*

399 REQUA, KENNETH A. "'Music in the Ear': Giovanni as Tragic Hero in Ford's *'Tis Pity She's a Whore.*" *PLL,* 7 (1971), 13-25.
The article explores "Giovanni's causal relationship to the tragedy by focusing on Giovanni alone; second, on Giovanni and Annabella and the incest theme; and third, on how the relationships of Parmesan society, of Putana, and of the Friar to the tragedy differ from Giovanni's essential relationship."

400 ROBERTS, JEANNE ADDISON. "John Ford's Passionate Abstractions." *SHR,* 7 (1973), 322-32.
In her discussion of *'Tis Pity She's a Whore; The Broken Heart;* and *Love's Sacrifice,* Roberts notes that "John Ford's plays strike a modern audience as possessing a strange urgency and an almost nightmarish clarity of vision." She deals with "the relation of the individual 'conscience' to the 'conscience' of the group." She concludes that "there is typically something clean and cool about Ford's drama, even at its most passionate and most violent, a remote, dream-like quality, and enforced symbolic distance; [and] to the receptive interpreter of allegorical abstractions, the moral involvement becomes intense and unforgettable."

401 SACKTON, ALEXANDER H. *Rhetoric as a Dramatic Language in Ben Jonson.* NY: Columbia University Press, 1948. viii, 175pp.
In a discussion of his overall approach to Jonson's plays, Sackton includes a study of the traditional rhetoric in Jonson's time, the uses of rhetoric in literature, the nature of jargon as dramatic speech in Jonson's maturity, and hyperbole in Jonson's latter plays. There is a bibliography of works cited, and an index to authors, works, and subjects.

St. Louis, Nadine Small

402   ST. LOUIS, NADINE SMALL. "A Critical Old-Spelling Edition of
John Ford's Comedy Drama *The Fancies, Chaste and Noble*."
DAI, 33:285A (University of California--Los Angeles), 1972.
581pp.
    "This edition consists of the text of Ford's play, with
a critical and textual introduction, extensive Commentary,
and Textual Notes." The introduction is a thorough cover-
age of the themes, plot, structure, language, and date for
the play.

403   SALMON, VIVIAN. "James Shirley and Some Problems of
Seventeenth Century Grammar." *Archiv*, 197 (1961), 287-96.
    Salmon examines the material contained in the two gram-
mars Shirley wrote; the information is loosely applicable
to the diction of his plays.

404   SARGEAUNT, MARGARET JOAN. *John Ford*. Oxford: Blackwell,
1935. v, 232pp.
    Sargeaunt discusses Ford's early life, the canon and
chronology of his plays post-1620, his work as a collaborator and as independent dramatist, the setting for his plays,
and his use and development of dramatic verse. She concludes with a discussion of his literary reputation, and
two appendices on *The Queen*. There is a bibliography, and
the work is indexed.

405   SCHELLING, FELIX E. "Shirley and the Last of the Old Drama."
In his *English Drama*. London: J. M. Dent, 1914.
Pp. 204-33.
    Schelling touches on the salons surrounding Henrietta
Maria, the learned ladies, the Platonic love tradition, and
makes passing reference to almost all Caroline playwrights
and plays in an attempt to catalogue both, neatly.

406   SCHERRER, GEBHARD JOSEPH. *James Shirleys Nachruhm*. Zurich:
Juris-Verlag, 1951. 102pp.
    Scherrer is concerned primarily with the critical and
dramatic reception of Shirley's work following the close of
the theatres through Swinburne.

407   SCHIPPER, J. *James Shirley: Sein Leben und seine Werke;
nebst einer Übersetzung seines Dramas "The Royal Master*."
Vienna and Leipzig: Wilhelm Braumüller, 1911. xiii,
447pp.
    Schipper treats Shirley's life and career by periods:
from 1596-1624; from 1625-1636; from 1636-1640; from 1640-
1641; and from 1642-1666. The table of contents is a
thorough introduction to the topics and issues discussed
in the work.

408   SENSABAUGH, GEORGE F. "Another Play by John Ford." *MLQ*, 3
       (1942), 595-601.
           Sensabaugh confirms Harbage who, "in a recent disclosure
       of Restoration pilfering, assigns to John Ford Sir Robert
       Howard's *The Great Favourite, or The Duke of Lerma.* . . ."
       [In "Elizabethan-Restoration Palimpsest," *MLR*, 35 (1940),
       287-319.] Sensabaugh analyzes the play critically, alines
       it with other works by Ford, and concludes that "Ford's in-
       tense genius seems to glow through most of *The Great Favor-
       ite,* fusing Burton's medical realism and oblique court
       idealism to produce situations truly unique."

409   _____. "John Ford and Platonic Love in the Court." *SP*, 36
       (1939), 206-26.
           Sensabaugh refutes the criticism that Ford had "twisted
       ethics and perverted idealism" by pointing out that the
       morals in his plays are appropriate, both to his setting,
       his characters, and his audience. He cites similar ap-
       proaches in *Love's Sacrifice; The Northern Lasse; The Broken
       Heart; The New Inn; The Shepherd's Paradise; The Temple of
       Love; Lady Alimony; The Platonic Lovers;* and others. *See
       also* Sensabaugh's "Platonic Love in Shirley's *The Lady of
       Pleasure,*" in *A Tribute to G. C. Taylor,* ed. by Arnold
       Williams (1952), pp. 168-77.

410   _____. "John Ford Revisited." *SEL*, 4 (1964), 195-216.
           Sensabaugh explores "why Ford has been so esteemed among
       a growing number of modern critics. . . ." Cited as reasons
       are "his quiet blank verse [and] tableau-like scenes [which]
       enhance his dramatic effects" as well as how he handled con-
       temporary artistic problems. Sensabaugh proceeds to analyze
       Ford's tragic fables in terms of the effects they achieve.
       Among others, he considers *The Broken Heart* and *'Tis Pity
       She's a Whore.*

411   _____. "John Ford's Tragedy of Love-Melancholy." *E Studien,*
       83 (1939), 212-19.
           Sensabaugh analyzes *The Lover's Melancholy* and *Love's
       Sacrifice* in terms of Burton's *Anatomy of Melancholy.*

412   _____. *The Tragic Muse of John Ford.* Stanford: Stanford
       University Press, 1944. ix, 196pp.
           Sensabaugh notes that "The chief reason why Ford remains
       in [an] uncertain position is that few critics have tried
       to discover what his plays have to say about man." There-
       fore "The present study . . . undertakes the . . . task of
       trying to discover, through an examination of Ford's im-
       mediate *milieu,* what his serious plays attempted to say and

Sharp, Robert Boies

why what they say, as critics have often suggested, sounds
familiar to modern Man." He does this in four major chapters entitled "Fame and Confusion," "Scientific Determin-
ism," "Unbridled Individualism," and "The Tragic Muse."
The work is indexed and cites numerous references to contemporary playwrights, notably Brome, Carlell, Cartwright,
Davenant, Goffe, Shirley, and others. *See* the index for
individual plays by title.

413   SHARP, ROBERT BOIES. "The Sources of Richard Brome's *The
      Novella*." *SP*, 30 (1933), 69-85.
         Sharp concludes that *The Novella* is indebted to a careful
      compression of contemporary travel literature; the majority
      of the article, however, is devoted to explication of the
      play. He does not show similarities of approach between
      The Novella and *The Antipodes*.

414   SHAVER, CHESTER LINN. "The Date of *Revenge for Honour*." *MLN*,
      53 (1938), 96-98.
         Shaver's note is a reply to Fredson Bowers' "The Date of
      Revenge for Honour," *MLN*, 52 (1937), 192-96, in which
      Bowers asserts that the play was produced in 1619/20.
      Shaver feels, as do many critics, that *Revenge* is by Henry
      Glapthorne who would have been nine at the time Bowers sug-
      gests for production. For numerous reasons Shaver sets
      outside dates of composition between 1627 and 1641. Neither
      Bowers nor Shaver attribute *Revenge for Honour* to Chapman,
      as do Parrott in his edition of Chapman's tragedies, and
      Gilbert Cosulich in "*Revenge for Honour* and *Othello*," *MLN*,
      29 (1914), 194-95.

415   SHAW, CATHERINE M. "The Masque of Ben Jonson: Editions and
      Editorial Criticism." *Genre*, 3 (1970), 272-88.
         Shaw discusses the critical reception of Jonson's
      masques, the various editions and the editing of them, as
      well as major works of criticism related to the masques.

416   SHERMAN, STUART P. "A New Play by Ford." *MLN*, 23 (1909),
      245-49.
         Sherman re-affirms earlier critics who attribute the
      anonymous play *The Queen, or The Excellency of Her Sex* to
      John Ford. He analyzes the dramatic structure of the play,
      and draws parallels between it and other works by Ford. He
      concludes that the "tragi-comedy exhibits Ford's character-
      istic merits and defects; it occasionally rises to the
      tragic pitch of *'Tis Pity* and *The Broken Heart*, but it sinks
      still more frequently to the flatness of *The Fancies*. . . ."

Simonds, Peggy Muñoz

417 _____. "Stella and *The Broken Heart*." *PMLA*, 24 (1909),
274-85.
Sherman looks for early sources of *The Broken Heart*.
Based on information in the prologue, he associates Stella
with Lady Penelope, Countess of Devonshire.

418 SHIRLEY, JAMES. *The Best Plays of the Old Dramatists: James
Shirley*. Ed. by Edmund Gosse. London: Vizetelly and
Company, 1888. xxx, 466pp.
Gosse's introduction is a brief analysis of the dating
of Shirley's plays, and their respective places in the de-
velopment of his career.

419 _____. *The Cardinal*. Ed. by Charles R. Forker. Bloomington:
Indiana University Press, 1964. lxxi, 143pp.
Before his edition of the 1652 text of *The Cardinal*,
Forker gives a lengthy introduction to the play in which he
discusses textual matters, previous and recent editions of
Shirley, the date and topical significance of the play,
sources and influences, stage history, and the critical
estimate of the play.

420 _____. *The Dramatic Works and Poems*. Ed. by William Gifford,
with additional notes by Alexander Dyce. London: John
Murray, 1833. 5 vols.
Gifford's introduction, "Some Account of Shirley and His
Writings" (pp. iii-lxvi), traces Shirley's life and sets
the works in the context of his life. The commendatory
verse precedes the edited work of Volume I.

421 _____. *The Traitor*. Ed. by John Stewart Carter. London:
Edward Arnold, 1965. xviii, 111pp.
In his brief introduction to *The Traitor*, Carter dis-
cusses sources, stage history, textual problems, and the
relative merits of the play in the context of the rest of
Shirley's career.

422 SIMONDS, PEGGY MUÑOZ. "Iconography and Iconology in John
Ford's *'Tis Pity She's a Whore*." *DAI*, 36:1537A (American
University), 1975. 64pp.
Simonds' dissertation "is a study of the main incest
plot as a metaphorical dramatization of that transcendent
but incestuous love between spirit and matter, heaven and
earth, that lies at the heart of the Christian myth."
Through an iconographic study of major issues, she links
the play specifically to tenets and ideas of the Roman
Catholic Church.

423   SIMPSON, PERCY.   "Ben Jonson and the Devil Tavern."   *MLR*, 34
        (1939), 367-73.
              Simpson is concerned primarily with a series of rules
        set up by Ben Jonson and his "tribe" in "The Apollo" - a
        room in Simon Wadloe's Devil Tavern.   He then illustrates
        and annotates the rules from contemporary literature.

424   SIRLUCK, ERNEST.   "Shakespeare and Jonson among the
        Pamphleteers of the First Civil War: Some Unreported
        Seventeenth-Century Allusions."   *MP*, 52 (1955), 88-99.
              The author notes that "the Puritans used Shakespeare and
        Jonson approximately twice as often in political propaganda
        as the royalists did," which leads him to question Louis
        Wright's contention that it was the Puritans who closed
        the theatres.

425   SMITH, G. GREGORY.   *Ben Jonson*.   London: Macmillan, 1919.
        vi, 310pp.
              Of particular interest are Smith's Chapters one through
        five in which he discusses Jonson's life, his literary con-
        science, the comedies and masques, and Chapter nine, which
        is a discussion of Jonson's influence on his contemporaries
        and his followers.   The work is indexed by author and title.

426   SOUTH, MALCOLM HUDSON.   "Animal Imagery in Ben Jonson's
        Plays."   *DAI*, 29:4505A (University of Georgia), 1968.
        169pp.
              South centers on "the way in which animal references
        contribute to the theme, plot, and characterization" of
        Jonson's plays from *The Case Is Altered* through *The Magnetic
        Lady*.   He is particularly concerned with animal references
        in *The New Inn* which "elucidate the subject of romantic
        love," and in *The Staple of News* and *The Magnetic Lady*.   He
        notes that "the effects of avarice and greed, and animal
        references in these plays help bring out Jonson's treatment
        of greed."

427   SQUIER, CHARLES LA BARGE.   "The Comic Spirit of Sir William
        Davenant: A Critical Study of His Caroline Comedies."
        DAI, 24:2488-89A (University of Michigan), 1963.   176pp.
              Squier focuses on *The Just Italian*; *News from Plymouth*;
        The Wits; *The Platonic Lovers*; and the "devastating paro-
        dies of *précieuse* dialogue."

428   _____.   "Davenant's Comic Assault on Préciosité: *The Platonic
        Lovers*."   *Univ of Colorado Stud, Ser in Lang & Lit*, 10
        (1966), 57-72.

Stevenson, Allan H.

Squier suggests that Davenant's early works, particularly *The Temple of Love*; *Love and Honour*; *The Platonic Lovers*; *The Fair Favourite*; *The Distresses*; and *The Unfortunate Lovers*, "in varying degrees . . . reflect the fashionable love philosophy of the court." However, he feels that in *The Platonic Lovers*, Davenant "has concocted a clever and telling burlesque of court Platonism and its dramatic expression."

429 STAVIG, MARK LUTHER. *John Ford and the Traditional Moral Order*. Madison: University of Wisconsin Press, 1968. xx, 225pp.
In his introduction, Stavig gives a brief history of Ford's life and scholarship related to his works. He discusses Ford's early ethical thought, his work in the context of the drama of his time, his tragi-comedies as a genre, the "concord in discord" theme within the plays, and, in Chapters four through seven, gives a lengthy critical analysis of the plot, structure, characterization and multiple themes in *'Tis Pity She's a Whore*; *Love's Sacrifice*; *The Broken Heart*; and *Perkin Warbeck*. A bibliography and index are included.

430 _____. "Traditional Morality in the Drama of John Ford." *DAI*, 23:227A (Princeton University), 1961. 359pp.
Stavig deals with traditional theatrical conventions viewed in an "historical perspective" as they relate to *Honor Triumphant*; *The Lover's Melancholy*; *The Queen*; *'Tis Pity She's a Whore*; *Love's Sacrifice*; *The Broken Heart*; and *Perkin Warbeck*. He concludes "that the scholars who have argued that Ford was sympathetic to people in conflict with the moral order and that he was interested mainly in creating effective theatre are wrong."

431 STEINER, ARPAD. "Massinger's *The Picture*, Bandello, and Hungary." *MLN*, 46 (1931), 401-03.
Steiner points out that Massinger called his play *The Picture* a "true Hungarian History" because he based his plot on what he assumed was an authentic anecdote from Bandello's *novella*. "By changing the historic characters of the plot, however, he unwittingly forfeited the only Hungarian element of his drama." *See also* C. R. Baskerville's "Bandello and *The Broken Heart*," *MLN*, 28 (1913), 51-52.

432 STEVENSON, ALLAN H. "Shirley and the Actors of the First Irish Theatre." *MP*, 40 (1942), 147-60.

Stevenson, Allan H.

        Stevenson analyzes the position of native Irish actors
c. 1637, and concludes that "the Londoners of Dublin would
prefer to import not only a dramatist and plays but some
good professional actors from London." He then discusses
what actors might be considered to appear in Dublin, what
their numbers were, and what plays they performed. He con-
jectures that Thomas Jordan, the future playwright, "may
still have been young enough to play women's roles." At
any rate, Stevenson includes him in the Dublin troupe.

433   ____. "Shirley's Dedication and the Date of His Return to
England." *MLN*, 61 (1946), 79–83.
        Stevenson sets the date of Shirley's return from Ireland
on or about April 20, 1639; this "is of aid in conjecturing
the publication dates of the 1639-40 plays." *See also* 434.

434   ____. "Shirley's Years in Ireland." *RES*, 20 (1944), 19–28.
        Stevenson points out "a reasonable probability that
Shirley went to Ireland in November 1636, and satisfactory
evidence that he returned to England in mid-April 1640."

435   STONE, CARL WARREN. "John Ford's Women: The Moral Center of
His Drama." *DAI*, 37:341A (Kent State University), 1975.
240pp.
        Stone sees the role and dominance of women as a theme of
continuity in virtually all of Ford's dramatic works. He
states that "the ability of Ford's women to resist and on
occasion actually oppose for as long as they do the interference generated by the disordered society's misconceived
notions of their value allows them to dominate the majority
of [Ford's] plays." This "pattern of interference" is an
enlargement of Alan Brissenden's thesis in "Impediments to
Love: A Theme in John Ford," *Ren D*, 7 (1964), 95–102.

436   STRUBLE, MILDRED CLARA. "The Indebtedness of Ford's *Perkin
Warbeck* to Gainsford." *Anglia*, 49 (1926), 80–91.
        Struble takes J. LeGay Brereton's study of the origins
of *Perkin Warbeck* in *Anglia*, 34 (1911), 194-234, and extends it. Brereton concluded that Ford's major source for
Perkin Warbeck was Bacon's *History of King Henry the Seventh*; to that Struble would add Gainsford's *True and Wonderful History of Perkin Warbeck*, a little known work appearing
variously in the *Harleian Miscellany*. She feels that "Ford
would seem to have had before him as he wrote, the histories
of both Bacon and Gainsford, and to have drawn therefrom
about equally." The majority of the article is concerned
with the textual parallels, and to "Ford's judicious selection from the accounts of several historians, his skillful

intermingling of varied source materials into a composite, harmonious adaptation, and, in the last act, his vigorous rejection of the limitations of the historian. . . ." *See also* John O'Connor's "William Warner and Ford's *Perkin Warbeck*," *N & Q* (June 1955), pp. 233-35; Michael Neill's "Ford and Gainsford: An Unnoticed Borrowing," *N & Q* (July 1968), pp. 253-55; and Struble's introduction to *A Critical Edition of Ford's* Perkin Warbeck, Seattle: University of Washington Press, 1924.

437   SUTTON, JULIET. "Ford's Use of Burton's Imagery." *N & Q* (September 1963), p. 415.
      Sutton notes an additional use of Burton's *Anatomy* in Ford's *The Lover's Melancholy* (III.i.).

438   _____. "Platonic Love in Ford's *The Fancies Chaste and Noble*." *SEL*, 7 (1967), 299-309.
      Sutton, having admitted that most Ford critics dismiss *The Fancies* as dismal, tries to show that there is a "plan and moral purpose" to it. She sees the moral of the play as *"honi soit qui mal y pense."*

439   SWINBURNE, ALGERNON CHARLES. *Contemporaries of Shakespeare.* Ed. by Edmund Gosse and Thomas Wise. London: W. Henmann, 1919. xii, 308pp.
      This work includes individual studies of the canon of Philip Massinger, John Day, Robert Davenport, Thomas Nabbes, Richard Brome, and James Shirley, as well as others. About Swinburne as critic, Gosse states "No one who ever lived, not Charles Lamb himself, approached [Swinburne] in worship of the Elizabethans and Jacobeans or in textual familiarity with their writings. He had read and reread them all, even the obscurest; not one 'dim watchfire of some darkling hour' but he had measured what faint light and heat it had to give." What Gosse neglects to mention is the perceptive nature of Swinburne's criticism.

440   _____. *A Study of Ben Jonson.* London: Chatto and Windus, 1889. 181pp.
      The first part of Swinburne's study--"Comedies, Tragedies, and Masques"--is of particular interest because of the recent swing toward evaluating Jonson's late plays as Swinburne did. He states that *The Magnetic Lady*, in relation to the "higher genius of Ben Jonson as a comic poet was yet once more to show itself before its approaching sunset."

Targan, Barry Donald

441 TARGAN, BARRY DONALD. "Two Comic Worlds: An Analysis of the
Structure of Thirteen of Ben Jonson's Comedies." *DAI*,
24:2465A (Brandeis University), 1962. 243pp.
　　The first chapters of Targan's dissertation analyze the
structure of the comedies in terms of their didactic and
mimetic effect; subsequent chapters elaborate on the structure of the plays. Targan is particularly concerned with
demonstrating that Jonson "was experimental throughout his
dramatic career."

442 TAYLOR, ALINE MACKENZIE. "James Shirley and 'Mr. Vincent
Cane' the Franciscan." *N & Q* (January 1960), pp. 31-33.
　　Taylor identifies Mr. Vincent Cane (as he is noted in
Shirley's will) as Vincent Canes, a learned Franciscan.
From evidence and inference, she concludes that Shirley
had converted to Catholicism before his death. For con-
firmation and more evidence *see* Marvin Morillo's "'Frier
Shirley': James Shirley and *Mercurius Britanicus*," *N & Q*
(September 1960), pp. 338-39.

443 THALER, ALWIN. "Thomas Heywood, Davenant and *The Seige of
Rhodes*." *PMLA*, 39 (1924), 624-41.
　　Thaler gives a sometimes confusing discussion of Davenant's *Seige of Rhodes*, resting much of his discussion on
similarities to *The Fair Maid* which is "a far more hearty
more honest thing than any D'Avenant ever achieved."

444 THAYER, CALVIN GRAHAM. *Ben Jonson: Studies in The Plays*.
Norman: University of Oklahoma Press, 1963. xii, 280pp.
　　In Chapter V, "*Bartholomew Fair* and the Late Comedies,"
Thayer discusses *The Staple of News*; *The New Inn*; and *The
Magnetic Lady*. There is a selected bibliography and an
index.

445 THOMAS, D. L. "Authorship of *Revenge for Honour*." *MP*, 5
(1908), 617-36.
　　The play, because of information on the title page of
the first edition in 1654, has been attributed to Chapman.
Using internal and external evidence, Thomas attributes it
to Glapthorne.

446 TOMLINSON, T. B. "Decadence: The Hollowness of Chapman and
Ford." In his *A Study of Elizabethan and Jacobean Tragedy*.
Cambridge: The University Press, 1964. Pp. 256-76.
　　Tomlinson's thesis is that "the seriousness and solemnity
of tone in Chapman and Ford is much more worrying than any-
thing in the highly irresponsible Beaumont and Fletcher.
Indeed, the dangers of taking minor Jacobean drama at face

value are well illustrated by . . . Chapman and Ford . . . [who] appear to be making a serious point when in fact they are only making a sentimental one. [For them] controls have so broken down that the drama is struggling to make any point at all."

447   URE, PETER. "Cult and Initiates in Ford's *Love's Sacrifice*." *MLQ,* 11 (1950), 298–306.
      Ure discusses the plot and its structure in *Love's Sacrifice,* which he dates between 1625 and 1628, then shows similarities of theme between it, *'Tis Pity She's a Whore* and *The Broken Heart.* He analyzes the roles of Fernando and Bianca in terms of the Platonic love theme, and concludes that the play, like other works by Ford, "preserves in the separate fates of the main protagonist a consistent ethical scheme, although it is not one so complete or so complex as many found in the true court drama of the metaphysic of love."

448   _____. "Marriage and the Domestic Drama in Heywood and Ford." *ES,* 32 (1951), 200–16.
      Ure is concerned with a specific and qualified definition of domestic drama, and one particular to a subgroup which he calls "marriage plays." Ingredients of these plays are citizen class characters, "the sensibility of ordinary people in ordinary life" [Eliot in *Selected Essays* (1934), p. 175], a common man as hero, and a primary concern with relationships between husbands and wives. Ure gives particular attention to *The Broken Heart* in the latter part of his essay.

449   _____. "A Pointer to the Date of *Perkin Warbeck*." *N & Q* (June 1970), pp. 215–17.
      Ure discusses internal and external evidence leading to dating *Perkin Warbeck* late in 1632 or early 1633, based on the fact that "throughout the play Ford for his history normally sticks very closely to the *known* historical sources; the most insignificant-seeming details are almost invariably grounded on them."

450   WAITH, EUGENE M. "Things As They Are and the World of Absolutes in Jonson's Plays and Masques." In *The Elizabethan Theatre,* Vol. IV. Ed. by G. B. Hibbard and Don Mills. Ontario: Macmillan of Canada (1974), pp. 106–26.
      Among other things, Waith gives attention to *The Staple of News* and the inherent phenomenological existentialism in Jonson's dramatic works.

Walter, J. H.

451   WALTER, J. H. "*Revenge for Honour*: Date, Authorship and
        Sources." *RES*, 13 (1937), 425-37.
            Based on internal and external evidence, Walter concludes
        that *Revenge for Honour* was written by Glapthorne, alone,
        about 1640, and that "He based his plot on *The Life and
        Death of Mahomet*, but borrowed dramatic situations from
        *Cupid's Revenge; Albertus Wallenstein; Osmond, The Great
        Turk;* as well as others. Walter also shows considerable
        commonality between *The Revenge for Honour* and other works
        by Glapthorne. *See* Fredson Bowers' reply in *RES*, 14 (1938),
        329-30.

452   WARD, C. E. "Massinger and Dryden." *ELH*, 2 (1935), 263-66.
            Supplementing James McManaway's "Philip Massinger and
        the Restoration Drama," *ELH*, 1 (1934), 276-304, Ward notes
        that Dryden must have known Massinger's *The Virgin Martyr*,
        "and that it was fresh in his mind when he wrote *Tyrannic
        Love*--that indeed *The Virgin Martyr* provided the starting
        point of [Dryden's] play."

453   W[ARNER], G. F. "An Autograph Play of Massinger." *Athenaem*,
        19 (1901), 90-91.
            Warner traces the history of a copy of Massinger's *Be-
        lieve As You List* which he is certain is an autograph, and
        says, "As an autograph play by an early English dramatist
        of almost the first rank, *Believe As You List* is, so far
        as I know, unique."

454   WEATHERS, WINSTON. "*Perkin Warbeck*: A Seventeenth-Century
        Psychological Play." *SEL*, 4 (1964), 217-26.
            Weathers agrees with Havelock Ellis in *Five Plays* (1957),
        p. xi, that "John Ford 'is the most modern of the tribe to
        whom he belonged' because of his obvious 'interest in psy-
        chological problems.'" He applies this judgment to an
        analysis of *Perkin Warbeck* and concludes that "Ford spoke
        to his times; he acted out before them the psychological
        drama that carried its own message--delusion fails, reason
        conquers; the kingdom of reason and the kingdom of emotion
        must coexist in peace--and by anchoring his psychological
        myth in English history, he anchored it in a reality that
        none of his audience could deny."

455   WEBB, MARGARET ANDREWS KAHIM. "Richard Brome, Caroline
        Dramatist: A Study of Brome's Development as a Playwright."
        DAI, 33:2348A (University of California-Berkeley), 1972.
        208pp.
            Webb is particularly interested in the "social vision"
        of "middle-class English life" reflected in Brome's plays.

Wertheim, Albert

She gives specific attention to *The Novella*; *The English Moor*; *The City Wit*; *The Antipodes*; and *The Jovial Crew*.

456 WERTHEIM, ALBERT. "The Dramatic Art of James Shirley." *DAI*, 26:6702A (Yale University), 1966. 282pp.
Wertheim feels that the range of Shirley's drama "is extraordinary, for he wrote in practically every popular dramatic form." His approach to the comedies, tragicomedies, and tragedies is critical rather than summary.

457 _____. "Games and Courtship in James Shirley's *Hyde Park*." *Anglia*, 90 (1972), 71-91.
Wertheim gives a structural and thematic analysis of *Hyde Park*, focusing on the parallel themes of games and courtship. He also notes "that [while] a significant number of Caroline plays . . . make mention of a particular London *lokal*, Shirley's use of the actual park in Acts III and IV is structurally interwoven into the rest of the play. *See also* Theodore Miles' "Place-Realism in a Group of Caroline Plays," *RES*, 18 (1942), 436.

458 _____. "James Shirley and the Caroline Masque of Ben Jonson." *TN*, 27 (1973), 157-61.
Wertheim notes that Ben Jonson's "first two plays to appear before the Caroline court, *Love's Triumph through Callipolis* and *Chloridia* may have been performed there at Shirley's instigation." As evidence he notes "the extended praise of the Jonsonian masque in Shirley's tragedy *Love's Cruelty*, licensed on November 14, 1631, less than nine months after the production of *Chloridia*. . . . Shirley, it would seem, is reminding the sovereigns with whom he had found favour to recall how artfully and lavishly they have been celebrated by Jonson, and is encouraging them through the public adulation once more to employ the aging poet."

459 _____. "The Presentation of *St. Patrick for Ireland* at the First Irish Playhouse." *N & Q* (June 1967), pp. 212-15.
Wertheim traces the early history of the Werburgh Street plays in Dublin and James Shirley's involvement with it. He particularly notes Shirley's disappointment in the Irish audience as exhibited in the prologues he wrote to the plays performed between 1637-39. Wertheim focuses, however, on a critical evaluation of *St. Patrick for Ireland*. For a continuation of this discussion *see* Elizabeth M. McConnell's "The Presentation of James Shirley's *St. Patrick for Ireland* at the First Irish Playhouse," *N & Q* (July 1968), pp. 268-69.

Wheeler, Charles F.

460   WHEELER, CHARLES F. *Classical Mythology in the Plays, Masques and Poems of Ben Jonson*. Princeton: Princeton University Press, 1938. vi, 212pp.

        In the introduction to his study, Wheeler generally discusses classical influences. The major portion of the work contains about 700 classical sources for Jonson's canon.

461   WINSTON, FLORENCE T. "The Significance of Women in the Plays of Philip Massinger." *DAI*, 33:2909A (University of Kansas), 1972. 192pp.

        Winston looks at the moral tone of Massinger's plays through the window of women's roles "as related to current opinions in Stuart England." She discusses *A New Way to Pay Old Debts; The City Madam; The Maid of Honour; The Picture; The Bondman; The Emperor of the East; The Unnatural Combat; The Roman Actor;* and *The Renegado*.

462   WITT, ROBERT W. *"Mirror Within a Mirror": Ben Jonson and the Play-Within*. Salzburg: Institut für Englische Sprache und Literatur, 1975. 154pp.

        Witt states that "although Jonson employs only a few . . . examples of the formal play-within, a close examination of his plays reveals that variations of the device appear frequently and, furthermore, that they serve the same purposes as the formal plays-within in the work of earlier and contemporary dramatists." As well as the early plays, Witt discusses *The Staple of News; The New Inn;* and *The Magnetic Lady*.

463   ZIMMER, RUTH KACHEL. "A Study of the Heroines in the Dramatic Pieces of James Shirley." *DAI*, 33:736-37A (University of Kentucky), 1971. 255pp.

        Chapter I surveys the Elizabethan and Jacobean woman and her role in society and literature; subsequent chapters discuss Shirley's "Caroline girl" in her social and literary *milieu*.

Lesser Caroline Dramatists

464 ACKERMAN, CATHERINE A. "Fashionable Platonism and Sir Kenelm Digby's Private Memoirs." *Coll Lang Assoc J*, 5 (1961), 136-41.

Ackerman discusses the idea of "Platonic" love at Charles I's court, and its fashionable portrayal in the literature of the time. She notes that "the clearest description of the nature of . . . 'platonized' love appears in Sir Kenelm Digby's *Private Memoirs*," or *Loose Fancies*. It is regrettable that Digby's two plays have not survived because it would be interesting to apply his theory to his practice.

465 ADAMS, JOSEPH QUINCY, JR. "Some Notes on Henry Glapthorne's *Wit in a Constable*." *JEGP*, 13 (1914), 299-304.

By comparing the first edition of Glapthorne's *Wit in a Constable* with Pearson's reprint (1874), Adams derives a considerable list of textual and miscellaneous emendations for the latter. For a continuation of this list *see* D. L. Thomas' "Concerning Glapthorne's *Wit in a Constable*," *JEGP*, 14 (1915), 299-304. About the play itself, Adams states that the first edition has been corrected in a contemporary hand, that the notes and corrections show the type of accuracy that would lead one to believe "they were made by someone who was familiar with the lines," that the date of authorship is fixed as 1639, rather than in the year of publication, as well as other textual matters.

466 BALD, R. C. "Arthur Wilson's *The Inconstant Lady*." *Library*, 4th ser, 18 (1938), 287-313.

Bald is concerned with dating *The Inconstant Lady*; setting outside dates of between 1622/23 and 1632, he narrows the time to a possible acting date of 1630, at which time Wilson probably made final revisions of the play.

467 _____. "Middleton's Civic Employments." *MP*, 31 (1933), 65-78.

Bald brings Middleton's career as a writer of civic pageants up to 1626, when his popularity was practically depleted.

Bald, R. C.

468 _____. "Sir William Berkeley's *The Lost Lady*." *Library*,
4th ser, 17 (1937), 395-426.
After a brief biography of Berkeley, Bald traces the
stage and literary history of *The Lost Lady* (1637), particularly its renewed popularity during the Restoration.
Finally, he analyzes bibliographical details in the surviving texts of the play.

469 BARNARD, DEAN STANTON, JR. *"Hollands Leaguer* by Nicholas
Goodman: A Critical Edition." *DAI*, 24:737A (University
of Michigan), 1962. 149pp.
Barnard suggests, among other things, that Mrs. Holland's
brothel is a satire of the Church of England.

470 BARRY, J. W. "Thomas May's *Cleopatra*." *Discourse*, 11 (1968),
67-75.
Barry notes that "May's drama has strong points which
should distinguish it as a significant contribution to the
dramatic literature on the Cleopatra theme. Particularly
impressive to the modern reader is May's considerable
knowledge of psychology, his emphasis on the righteousness
of Anthony's war against Octavius, and his perceptive delineation of wily Cleopatra."

471 BECKINGHAM, C. F. *"Othello* and *Revenge for Honour*." *RES*, 11
(1935), 198-202.
Beckingham notes that "the worthless play, *Revenge for
Honour*, was entered in the Stationer's Register in 1653 as
the work of Glapthorne, and published in the following year
with Chapman's name on the title-page." Although he does
not concern himself with authorship in his note, Beckingham
sees numerous similarities between *The Revenge for Honour*
and *Othello*.

472 BERGERON, DAVID. "Two Compositors in Heywood's *Londoni Ius
Honorarium*, 1631." *SB*, 22 (1969), 223-26.
By examining the "peculiarities of spelling and running-
titles" in Heywood's civic pageant, Bergeron is able to
determine that two compositors set the type.

473 BERRY, JOE WILKES, JR. "A Critical Old-Spelling Edition of
The Tragedy of Cleopatra, Queen of Aegypt by Thomas May."
DAI, 25:1888A (Rice University). 275pp.
The introduction to Berry's work "contains a short biographical sketch of Thomas May, a survey of his other dramatic works, a bibliographical description of *Cleopatra*, and
an examination of May's use of both classical and contemporary sources in the play, with special attention to the

relationship between Plutarch and May, Shakespeare and May. *See also* Denzell Stewart Smith's dissertation (561) on the same play.

474   BLANSHARD, RUFUS A.   "Carew and Jonson." *SP*, 52 (1955), 195-211.
      Blanshard traces Carew's attitude toward Jonson, and concludes that "If we went by what Carew tells us, we should never know that Jonson was a non-dramatic poet, let alone the 'father' of the Cavaliers." In passing, he mentions Carew's single masque, *Coelum Britannicum*, and its indebtedness to masque conventions which Jonson had established, *e.g.*, "the antimasque, song, allegorical figures, and ethical, social, and celestial themes."

475   BOAS, F. S.   "Killigrew's *Claracilla*." *TLS* (18 March 1944), p. 44.
      Boas gives a brief account of the recently found MS of Thomas Killigrew's *Claracilla* (1639); he compares and contrasts it with the printed editions of 1641 and 1664.

476   _____. *Thomas Heywood*. London: Williams and Norgate, 1950. 159pp.
      Boas' final chapter, "Pleasant Dialogues and Dramas-- London Mayoral Dramas--Lost Plays," is of general interest to the student of Heywood's final output. Boas surveys and categorizes the late canon.

477   BOWERS, FREDSON THAYER.   "The Date of *Revenge for Honour*." *MLN*, 52 (1937), 192-96.
      Bowers infers, from a letter by Girolamo Lando, Venetian Ambassador to England, as well as other pieces of evidence, that there was a production of *The Revenge for Honour* in 1619/20. *See* Chester Linn Shaver's reply, *MLN*, 53 (1968), 96-98, for a divergent point of view.

478   _____. "Jonson, Thomas Randolph, and *The Drinking Academy*." *N & Q* (September 1937), pp. 166-68.
      Bowers discusses Thomas Randolph's association with Jonson in the Apollo room of the Devil Tavern. He also discusses Randolph's *The Drinking Academy* and (?) *The Fairy Knight*, Shirley's *Love in a Maze*, and Jonson's *The Staple of News* and *The Devil Is an Ass*.

479   CAREW, THOMAS.   "The Poetical Works." In *The Poetical Works of Michael Drayton*. Edinburgh: Mundell and Son, 1793. Pp. 671-723.

Cartwright, William

       A brief life of Carew is prefaced to the poetical works
and the text of *Coelum Britannicum*; there are copious notes
but the editor is unidentified. The Table of Contents for
the works of Carew is on p. 753.

480   CARTWRIGHT, WILLIAM. *The Plays and Poems of William
       Cartwright*. Ed. by G. Blakemore Evans. Madison:
       University of Wisconsin Press, 1951. 861pp.
       In his introduction to the edition, Evans discusses the
author's life, his plays and poems, his influence and later
reputation, and the various texts. The appendix includes
a bibliography of Cartwright's publications, and a list of
manuscripts. The work is indexed by author, title, subject,
character and first lines.

481   CHESTER, ALLAN GRIFFITH. *Thomas May: Man of Letters 1595-
       1650*. Philadelphia: University of Pennsylvania Press,
       1932. 204pp.
       Chester's analysis of May's life and work includes a
discussion of his early life and financial disappointments,
May as a man of letters and poet laureate, his comedies,
tragedies, and translations, his narrative poetry, and his
political writing. A bibliography and index conclude the
work.

482   CLARK, ARTHUR MELVILLE. *Thomas Heywood: Playwright and
       Miscellanist*. Oxford: Basil Blackwell, 1931. xii, 356pp.
       Clark is most concerned with correcting old errors re-
lated to "biographical, historical [and] literary-histori-
cal" aspects of Heywood's life and works. Chapter V,
"Retirement from the Stage," Chapter VI, "Pageants and
Masques: Last Plays," Chapter VII, "Miscellanies and Compilations," and Chapter VIII, "Politics and Puritanism:
Heywood's Death," are of particular note. Check the index
for references to individual Caroline plays and authors.

483   COPE, JACKSON I. "Marmion and Pope's *Rape of the Lock*." *MLN*,
       72 (1957), 265-67.
       Cope feels that "the high serious attendance of the
sylphs to the preparations at their mistresses' dressing-
table may not have sprung quite as full-blown from Pope's
imagination as [some] evaluations suggest. . . ; the scene
had been anticipated in detail and in tone by the episode
of Venus at Paphos in Shackerley Marmion's *Cupid and Psyche*
(1637)."

484   CROMWELL, OTELIA. *Thomas Heywood: A Study in Elizabethan
       Drama of Everyday Life*. New Haven: Yale University Press,
       1928. viii, 227pp.

Davies, H. Neville

Cromwell contends that of Heywood's seventeen plays, fourteen are written deliberately to portray contemporary manners. She surveys his dramatic career, discusses his use of realism and other dramatic techniques, and gives a long examination of the problems of authorship. The book focuses on plays prior to 1626, but includes a thorough survey of scholarship on the dating and authorship of *The Late Lancashire Witches*.

485 CUTTS, J. P. "Nabbes' *Hannibal and Scipio*." *Eng Miscellany* [Rome], 14 (1963), 73-81.

Cutts reviews Nabbes' reputation regarding *The Bride; Microcosmus; The Unfortunate Mother; Tottenham Court; Covent Garden;* and *Hannibal and Scipio,* particularly in the light of Nabbes' use of music. He focuses on *Hannibal and Scipio,* and gives a transcription for "On, on, Bravely on."

486 _____. "Some Jacobean and Caroline Dramatic Lyrics." *N & Q* (March 1955), pp. 107-109.

Cutts refers to Peter Hausted's comedy *The Rival Friends,* Suckling's *The Tragedy of Brennoralt,* and *The Goblins.* He also takes a stand on the issue of dramatic lyrics being more than decorative in Jacobean and Caroline drama. He is supported earlier by William Bowden in *The English Dramatic Lyric, 1603-42* (1951), and later by Frederick Sternfeld, in *Songs in Shakespearean Tragedies* (1961).

487 DANTON, J. PERIAM. "William Cartwright and His *Comedies, Tragi-Comedies, with Other Poems . . . 1651*." *Lib Q,* 12 (1942), 438-56.

Danton comments on the high regard Cartwright had during his lifetime and gives a summary outline of his life with a resumé of the fifty-odd contemporary sources referring to him. He justifies the tastes of the Jacobean and Caroline audiences to those of a modern audience, then moves on to a bibliographical description of *The Royal Slave* (1639), and the incumbant problems of the later printings. Included is a reproduction of the cancelled index to Cartwright's *Comedies,* and a table of "The Nature of the Principal Signature Variants in Institutionally Owned Copies of Cartwright's *Comedies, Tragi-Comedies . . . 1651*." He concludes by noting "that at least twenty-eight of [the known copies] are in one way or another imperfect" and that "the complexity of the preliminary signatures and the various changes . . . must be blamed."

488 DAVIES, H. NEVILLE. "Dryden's *All for Love* and May's *Cleopatra*." *N & Q* (April 1965), pp. 139-44.

97

Davis, Richard Beale

>Davies gives many reasons for seeing Thomas May's *The Tragedie of Cleopatra Queen of Aegypt* (1626), as one source for Dryden's *All for Love*, and draws parallels between the two plays.

489   DAVIS, RICHARD BEALE. *George Sandys: Poet-Adventurer.*
      London: The Bodley Head Press, 1955. 320pp.
      Davis gives an extensive biography of Sandys from his heritage through his involvement with the Virginia Company. Although the critical matter in the book is slanted toward the poetry, the biography is useful for those interested in working on the translations from Grotius' *Christ's Passion*. There is a comprehensive bibliography and the work is indexed.

490   DAY, CYRUS L. "Thomas Randolph and *The Drinking Academy*."
      PMLA, 43 (1928), 800-809.
      Day, like others, feels that *The Drinking Academy* "is in all probability the work of Thomas Randolph." He gives extensive evidence for his assumption, and compares the play with other works by Randolph, especially *The Jealous Lovers*. Day concludes that "in the case of *The Drinking Academy*, the borrowings are too numerous and too widely scattered throughout Randolph's poems and plays to support the hypothesis of theft."

491   _____. "Thomas Randolph's Part in the Authorship of *Hey for Honesty*." *PMLA*, 41 (1926), 325-34.
      Day gives new evidence to support the fact that Randolph, along with F. J., was the author of *Hey for Honesty*, and that Randolph was probably its original translator from Aristophanes' *Plutus*, as well as its adaptor. In the process, he dates the play pre-1635, and notes the many contemporary allusions in the work.

492   DEAN, J. S. "Borrowings from *Philomela* in *The City Night-Cap*."
      N & Q (August 1966), pp. 302-03.
      Dean's study "lists verbal borrowings not mentioned by [John C.] Jordan, and shows the great extent to which Davenport drew upon Green's romance." *See* Jordan's "Davenport's *The City Nightcap* and Green's *Philomela*," in *MLN*, 36 (1921), 281-84. Dean lists twenty-seven new citations of borrowings.

493   EAGLE, R. L. "Thomas Randolph and Francis Bacon." *Baconiana*, 25 (1941), 149-50.
      Eagle notes Randolph's probable acquaintance with Francis Bacon, and his esteem for him as a poet.

Gates, William Bryan

494 ECKHARDT, EDUARD. "Davenports Lustspiel *A New Trick to Cheat the Devil.*" *Anglia,* 59 (1935), 394-403.
Eckhardt surveys the dramatic origins of theme and technique in Robert Davenport's *A New Trick to Cheat the Devil,* as well as influences it may have had on subsequent plays.

495 EWTON, GENE STEPHENSON. "A Critical Edition of *The Passionate Lovers* by Lodowick Carlell." *DAI,* 24:3322A (Rice University), 1963. 241pp.
Ewton sees *The Passionate Lovers* as "a typical Cavalier romance." Along with the critical old-spelling text he supplies "A Short Historical and Critical Introduction."

496 FORDYCE, RACHEL POOLE. "A Diplomatic Edition of Robert Chamberlaine's Comedy *The Swaggering Damsell* 1640: The Man and the Play." *DAI,* 34:2557A (University of Pittsburgh), 1972. 233pp.
The study surveys Chamberlaine's life and work, his associations with Brome, Nabbes, Rawlins, Tatham, Jordan, Gerbier, and Benlowes, and his heavy use of comic irony in terms of the themes of usury, Platonism, cavalierism, male and female roles, and parent-child relationships. The edition concludes with a glossary and a bibliography.

497 FREEHAFER, JOHN. "*The Italian Night Piece* and Suckling's *Aglaura.*" *JEGP,* 67 (1968), 249-65.
Freehafer surveys the scholarship related to the unidentified play *The Italian Night Piece* (or *Italian Night Masque* as it is variously referred to), and dismisses previous associations of it with Massinger, Davenant, Fletcher, Cartwright, Habington, and Henry Killigrew. He then gives considerable evidence for associating it with Sir John Suckling's *Aglaura.*

498 GABRIELI, VITTORIO. *Sir Kenelm Digby: Inglese Italianato nell' età della contiriforma.* Rome: Edizioni de storia e letteratura, 1957. 302pp.
Of general interest is the material surveyed in Chapter I, "L'educazione d'un cortigiano Stuardo." Check the index for passing references to Digby's contemporaries, particularly Beeston and Thomas May.

499 GATES, WILLIAM BRYAN. *The Dramatic Works and Translations of Sir William Lower: With a Reprint of* The Enchanted Lovers. Philadelphia: University of Pennsylvania Press, 1932. 166pp.
In his discussion of *The Enchanted Lovers,* Gates notes its similarity to other non-Italianate pastorals such as

Glapthorne, Henry

> Walter Montague's *Shepherd's Paradise*, Knevet's *Rhodon and Iris*, Cowley's *Love's Riddle*, and others. Gates also discusses Lower's other play, *The Phoenix in Her Flames* (1639). Information he includes and speculations he makes lead one to question the assumption that *The Enchanted Lovers* was written outside the Caroline period; however Gates does not take his discussion that far.

500   GLAPTHORNE, HENRY. *The Plays and Poems*. London: John Pearson, 1874. 2 vols.
    Volume I contains a "Memoir of Henry Glapthorne," which briefly surveys his poems, his masque, and two plays; Volume II contains two plays and the poems.

501   GOURLAY, J. J. "A Caroline Play, *The Wasp*." *TLS* (5 June 1943), p. 271.
    Concerning an anonymous play entitled *The Wasp*, listed by Bentley as being written around 1630, Gourlay suggests that the author is Thomas Jordan: that it was "presumably acted by the amalgamated King's Revels-Queen Henrietta's Company at Salisbury Court in Fleet Street"; that the "Ambrose" mentioned in the manuscript "may indicate that Ambrose Byland, formerly of the King's Company, had found his way into the troup by 1638"; and Gourley would add to Bentley's list of actors the name "Noble."

502   GRAY, CHARLES H. *Lodowick Carlell: His Life, a Discussion of His Plays and* The Deserving Favourite, *a Tragi-Comedy*. Chicago: University of Chicago Press, 1905. 177pp.
    In his monograph-length introduction to an edition of Carlell's *The Deserving Favourite*, Gray gives a biography of Carlell, a list of his plays, a discussion of the sources for the play, and a comment on the two editions of 1629 and 1659. Appendices include copies of Carlell's will, that of his wife Jean, and three copies of contemporary materials related to Carlell's life.

503   GRIVELET, MICHEL. "Note sur Thomas Heywood et le Théâtre sous Charles 1er." *EA*, 7 (1954), 101-106.
    Grivelet recognizes the role of Heywood, Carew, Davenant, and others in judging the widely-divergent Caroline audience. *See also* Georges Bas' "James Shirley et 'th' Untun'd Kennell': Une petite Guerre de Théâtre vers 1630," *EA*, 16 (1923), 11-22.

504   HARBAGE, ALFRED. *Thomas Killigrew, Cavalier Dramatist, 1612-83*. Philadelphia: University of Pennsylvania Press, 1930. ix, 247pp.

Heywood, Thomas

Approximately one half of Harbage's study is devoted to an analysis of Killigrew's life and career as a courtier, a younger son, a playwright in exile, and finally, as a royal favorite; he also shows how Killigrew's biography affects the material of his plays and an interpretation of them. Harbage includes sections on the amateur plays, on semi-professional plays, and on closet drama, as well as a bibliography and complete index. About *The Parson's Wedding*, he feels that it "was not designed for a special coterie, but for a popular audience, the dramatist apparently having his eye upon the lucrative possibilities of the public theatres. The comedy is in the manner of its time in that its plot is a mosaic of themes and situations tested by older dramatists, but the general tone foreshadows the comedy of the Restoration. . . ."

505   _____. "An Unnoted Caroline Dramatist." *SP*, 31 (1934), 28-36.
Harbage adds, to the long list of English dramatists, the name of Mildman Fane, Earl of Westmoreland, "author of at least seven plays, several of which were actually presented, albeit privately, and by amateurs. . . ." He notes the whereabouts of the seven plays and briefly analyzes them as to content, intent, and structure.

506   "Henry Glapthorne's Plays." *The Retrospective Review*, 10 (1824), 122-59.
The author focuses on *Argalus and Parthenia; The Hollander*, a scene from *Egers; Wit in a Constable; The Ladies Privilege;* and *Albertus Wallenstein*, with liberal quotations from the latter. The author states that "Glapthorne belongs to an inferior order of genius: not being able to lay open the springs of passion, he covers them with flowers, in order that, as he cannot gratify us with their refreshing waters, he must, at least, hide their existence." He denigrates Glapthorne's "rhetorical flourishes, poetical images and dazzling metaphors." From that point on the article becomes more negative and the author, finally, dismisses Glapthorne's book of verse and four unpublished plays.

507   HEYWOOD, THOMAS. *Love's Mistress; or, The Queen's Masque*. London: Charles Baldwyn, 1924. xxii, 82pp.
The introduction to this anonymous edition places Heywood's masque in context with his earlier works, especially *The Apology for Actors*.

Holaday, Allan

508   HOLADAY, ALLAN. "Thomas Heywood and the Puritans." *JEGP*, 45 (1950), 192-203.

        Holaday's point of attack is Arthur M. Clark's assumption, in *Thomas Heywood, Playwright and Miscellanist* (1931), pp. 191ff., that Heywood became an ardent Puritan, *cum* Scottish Presbyterianism, shortly before his death in 1641. Clark's assumption is based primarily on two Puritanly sympathetic and anonymous pamphlets, *A Revelation of Mr. Brightman's Revelation* and *Machiavel as He Lately Appeared* (both 1641), which he attributes to Heywood. Holaday's contention, which he substantiates, is that Heywood's "conjectured authorship of these pamphlets is highly dubious, and that he did not become a Puritan of any kind, particularly not a Presbyterian." Holaday bases his discussion on the similarity of tone, diction and attitude between Heywood's early *signed* pamphlets, and his late ones.

509   JORDAN, JOHN CLARK. "*The City Night-Cap* and Green's *Philomela*." *MLN*, 36 (1921), 281-84.

        Jordan attempts to show "the exact relations" between Davenport's *The City Nightcap, or, Crede Quod Habes et Habes* and Robert Greene's early novel *Philomela*. He concludes that the "treatment of the play is much more condensed than that of the novel" and that "Davenport was indebted to Greene for more than the plot of his play," *e.g.*, for "turns of expression and euphuistic mannerisms."

510   JUMP, J. D. "The Anonymous Masque in MS. Egerton 1994." *RES*, 11 (1935), 186-91.

        Because of internal evidence and similarities between the *Masque* and *Byron's Revenge*, Jump sets the date of composition between 1641 and 1643, which precludes the possibility of Chapman being the author as he died in 1634. *See also* Jump's "The Anonymous Masque in MS. Egerton 1994," *RES*, 12 (1936), 455, for further corroboration, and John Cutts' "The Anonymous Masque-Like Entertainment in Egerton MS. 1994," *Comp D*, 1 (1967).

511   KAUFMAN, HELEN A. "*Trappolin Supposed a Prince* and *Measure for Measure*." *MLQ*, 18 (1957), 113-24.

        Kaufman shows "undeniable similarities" between Cockayne's farce and Shakespeare's tragi-comedy, notably similarities of structure, theme and source.

512   KEAST, WILLIAM R. "Killigrew's Use of Donne in *The Parson's Wedding*." *MLR*, 45 (1950), 512-15.

        Keast says that "In view of the recognized importance of the play as a prototype of the new comedy--and especially

as an early instance of worldly and witty conversation
about love--it is worth noting that Killigrew derived some
of the materials of his wit in dialogue from poems of John
Donne," specifically, "A Lecture Upon the Shadow," "Breake
of Day," and "Loves Alchymie."

513 _____. "Some Seventeenth-Century Allusions to Shakespeare
and Jonson." *N & Q* (October 1949), pp. 468-69.
Keast cites allusions to Shakespeare and Jonson in
William Sampson's *The Vow-Breaker, or, The Faire Maide of
Clifton*, in Killigrew's *The Parson's Wedding*, and his
Tomaso, or, The Wanderer, Part II.

514 KNEVET, RALPH. *A Gallery to the Temple.* Ed. by Giuliano
Pellegrini. Pisa: Libreria Goliardica, 1954. 171pp.
In his introduction to the poems, Pellegrini gives a
brief history of Knevet and criticism of his literary works.
The text of the book is in English; the introduction is in
Italian. A Table of Contents concludes the work.

515 _____. *The Shorter Poems of Ralph Knevet.* Ed. by Amy M.
Charles. Athens, OH: Ohio State University Press, 1966.
426pp.
The first eighty-six pages of this work are a running
account of Knevet's life, and his published and manuscript
works. Primary critical attention is given to Knevet's
poems. The work is well-indexed.

516 KNIGHT, WILLIAM STANLEY MacBEAN. *The Life and Works of Hugo
Grotius.* NY: Oceana Publishing Company, 1962. xiv,
304pp.
Knight, in his analysis of Grotius' work, refers to
George Sandys' translation of *Christ's Passion* (1640).

517 KOCH, J. "Thomas Nabbes, ein zu wenig beachteter Dichter."
Anglia, 47 (1923), 332-82.
Koch devotes much of his article to the defence of
Nabbes' dramatic work and places him in context with Jon-
son, Marston, Heywood, Jordan and Tatham.

518 KOTTAS, KARL. *Thomas Randolph: sein Leben und seine Werke.*
Vienna and Leipzig: W. Braumüller, 1909. vii, 105pp.
Chapter I of Kottas' study is devoted to Randolph's
life; the midsection of the work concerns Randolph's drama-
tic works, particularly *The Jealous Lovers; The Muses'
Looking-Glass; Amyntas;* and *Hey for Honesty.*

Lautner, Edward John

519   LAUTNER, EDWARD JOHN. "A Modern-Spelling Edition of Thomas
       May's *The Tragedy of Antigone, The Theban Princesse*." *DAI*,
       32:923A (Case Western Reserve University), 1970. 247pp.
           Lautner dates the play between 1627 and 1631, and dis-
       cusses May's indebtedness to Sophocles, Seneca, Statius,
       Lucan, and Shakespeare. He concludes that "May's play is
       too diffuse to be effective dramatically."

520   LAWLESS, DONALD S. and J. H. P. PAFFORD. "John Clavell, 1603-
       42: Highwayman, Author and Quack Doctor." *N & Q* (January
       1957), p. 9.
           The authors definitely ascribe *The Soddered Citizen* to
       John Clavell (rather than Shackerley Marmion), and date it
       ca. 1631.

521   LAWRENCE, W. J. "Early Substantive Masques." *TLS* (8 December
       1921), p. 814.
           Of Nabbes' moral masque *Microcosmus*, Lawrence says "If
       we could be sure that Nabbes' scenic arrangements were re-
       ligiously carried out, the production of the masque would
       rank as the first employment of moveable scenery in the
       English theatre."

522   _____. "John Kirke: The Caroline Actor-Dramatist." *SP*, 21
       (1924), 586-93.
           Lawrence, in a sympathetic appraisal of John Kirke, at-
       tributes the work *The Seven Champions of Christendom* to him
       and shows his involvement with the Red Bull Theatre and its
       very mixed audience. He says "Judging . . . by the quality
       of *The Seven Champions of Christendom*, Kirke was of the
       school of Heywood and Will Rowley . . . and had glibly
       learnt his lesson."

523   LEA, KATHLEEN M. "Cokayne and the Commedia dell' Arte." *MLR*,
       23 (1928), 47-51.
           Lea sees Sir Aston Cokayne's *Trappolin, creduto Principe,*
       or *Trappolin Suppos'd a Prince* as "an undisputed instance
       of the connection between Caroline drama and *commedia dell'
       arte*. Refer to P. G. Phialas' "Massinger and the *Commedia
       dell' Arte*," *MLN*, 65 (1950), 113-14.

524   LEECH, CLIFFORD. "A 'Dram of Ease.'" *TLS* (11 January 1936),
       p. 35.
           Leech discusses Mildman Fane's *Candy Restored*, a part of
       which may be "an example of a Shakespearean reminiscence
       . . . peculiar in that it seems to echo a corruption of
       Shakespeare's text" of *Hamlet*. Leech is most concerned
       with correcting the 1604-05 text reading "dram of eale" to
       "dram of ease."

Magoun, F. P., Jr.

525 _____. *The John Fletcher Plays*. Cambridge, MA: Harvard
University Press, 1962. ix, 180pp.
Leech discusses the problem of evaluating Fletcher as an
individual dramatist, his "dramatic mode," the comedies,
tragedies, and tragicomedies, and Fletcher's relationship
to the work of Shakespeare. Check the index for references
to the last plays.

526 LEVER, J. W. "*The Wasp*: A Trial Flight." In *The Elizabethan
Theatre IV*. Ed. by G. B. Hibbard. Don Mills, Ontario:
Macmillan of Canada, 1974. Pp. 57-59.
Lever discusses the sketchy history of criticism and
analysis of *The Wasp*, and includes a photocopy of two pages
of the original manuscript. From internal evidence, he suggests that the date of composition lies between May 1636
and October 1637, and that the play was intended to be performed at Salisbury Court.

527 *The Life of Sir Kenelm Digby, By One of His Descendants*.
London: Longmans, Green, 1896. 310pp.
The table of contents, in which individual chapters are
highly glossed, is the best guide to information within the
book. The work is primarily a biography with passing references to Jonson, Randolph, and other Caroline dramatists.
Amyntas is considered briefly.

528 LOISEAU, JEAN. *Abraham Cowley's Reputation in England*.
Paris: Henri Didier, 1931. viii, 221pp.
The author treats Cowley's critical reception from his
lifetime through the nineteenth century. Chapter VII,
"Cowley Redivivus," gives an overview of objective, appre-
ciative, and sentimental criticism of Cowley.

529 LURIE, DONA JEAN BARRY. "A Critical Edition of Thomas Nabbes'
The Bride." *DAI*, 35:4437A (University of Michigan), 1974.
304pp.
Besides the edition, Lurie's dissertation contains an
introduction which "deals with Thomas Nabbes and his work
in relation to the dramatic and social environment of Caroline England, focusing on *The Bride* as the union of the
best of Nabbes' dramatic impulses and his individual world
view."

530 MAGOUN, F. P., JR. "Hermus *vs*. Hormuz." *PMLA*, 42 (1927),
670-72.
Magoun gives a note for an allusion in the "anonymous"
play *The Drinking Academy*.

Marmion, Shackerley

531   MARMION, SHACKERLEY. *The Soddered Citizen*. Ed. by John
      Henry Pyle Pafford. Oxford: University Press, 1935-36.
      112pp.
          The introduction to the edition is a collaboration be-
      tween Pafford and Greg, and contains much analytical ma-
      terial related to the registering, dating, and editing of
      the play, as well as a note on the authorship of the pro-
      logue and one passage in the play which they attribute to
      John Clavell. A brief biography of Clavell, a famous
      seventeenth-century highwayman but not so famous author,
      is included by the editor.

532   MAXWELL, J. C. "Notes on *King John and Matilda*." *N & Q*
      (June 1967), pp. 215-17.
          Maxwell makes many corrections of W. A. Armstrong's
      edition of the Davenport play.

533   MAXWELL, SUE. "A Misprint in *Holland's Leaguer*." *MLR*, 39
      (1944), 179-80.
          Maxwell notes that Marmion's "printer mistook the trans-
      lation of *castor* for *bezer* instead of *bever* [beaver] in
      V.iii. of *Holland's Leaguer*." She then traces the history
      of faulty emendations of the word.

534   MAY, THOMAS. *The Old Couple*. Ed. by M. Simplicia
      Fitzgibbons. Washington, D. C.: Catholic University
      Press, 1943. lxxviii, 140pp.
          In her preface, Fitzgibbons notes that the play "is an
      interesting exception to the anti-Puritan type of play
      which was popular with the Commonwealth presses." She
      goes on to discuss May's biography, the dating of the play,
      its criticism, and the special topics of marriage in *The
      Old Couple*, usury, and Commonwealth play productions; and
      she gives textual comments. There is a lengthy bibliog-
      raphy.

535   _____. The Tragedy of Julia Agrippina: Empresse of Rome,
      nebst einem Anhang die Tragoedie "Nero." Ed. by F. Ernst
      Schmid. Louvain: A. Uystrunst, 1914. 304pp.
          Schmidt's lengthy introduction contains a life of May,
      the sources for *Agrippina*, and a critical analysis of the
      structure, meter, stylistics, and characterization in the
      play. Following the edition and its notes is a discussion
      of May's tragedy *Nero*, pp. 155-217.

536   MAYNE, JASPER. *The Amorous War*. Ed. by Mary Helen Burriss.
      Ithaca, NY: Cornell University Press, 1928. xxxiii, 134pp.

Neale, Thomas

Before the critical edition of Mayne's play, Burriss
discusses his life, the relationships between *The City
Match* and *The Amorous War*, and a variety of subjects, such
as editions, production, sources, dramatic form, plotting,
style, characterization, parallel passages, and Mayne as a
dramatist. There is a bibliography.

537   MEAD, ROBERT. *The Combat of Love and Friendship*. Ed. by
       Margaret Cabell Boles. Ithaca, NY: Cornell University
       Press, 1930. xxxviii, 119pp.
          In her introduction to the edition, Boles discusses
       Mead's life, the date of composition, the text of the first
       edition, and stage performances; she gives a synopsis of
       the plot, showing distinct parallels between *The Combat of
       Love and Friendship* and Cartwright's *The Royal Slave*, and
       gives a critical analysis of the play. A bibliography is
       included.

538   MILLS, LAURENS J. *Peter Hausted: Playwright, Poet, and
       Preacher*. Bloomington: Indiana University Press, 1940.
       63pp.
          Chapter II, "Playwright--Hausted *vs.* Randolph," is of
       particular note, although the monograph is essentially a
       biography rather than a critical work. It concludes with
       Anthony à Wood's entry about Hausted in *Fasti Oxonienses*,
       and "notes from the Register of Baptisms, Marriages, and
       Burials, 1559-1682, Much Hadham."

539   MONTFORT, MONTAGUE. *The Launching of the Mary*. Ed. by John
       Henry Walter. London: Oxford University Press, 1933.
       xxiv, 125pp.
          Greg's transcription with notes of *The Launching of the
       Mary, or, The Seaman's Honest Wife* is prefaced by a discus-
       sion of the only surviving manuscript of the play. Walter
       discusses literary parallels, dating, the identification of
       the author, and other matters. *See also* J. Q. Adams' "The
       Authorship of Two Seventeenth-Century Plays," *MLN*, 22
       (1907), 135-37, and Frederick S. Boas' *Shakespeare and the
       Universities* (1923), which includes three essays on the
       play.

540   NEALE, THOMAS. *The Warde*. Ed. by John Arthur Mitchell.
       Philadelphia: University of Pennsylvania Press, 1937.
       100pp.
          In a long and well-documented introduction, the editor
       discusses Neale's biography and his works. The text of the
       edition is from the Bodleian collection. The manuscript is
       in one hand and Mitchell gives supportive evidence to

Nethercot, Arthur H.

suggest that the hand is Neale's. A glossary and an extended bibliography of works related to Neale are included.

541 NETHERCOT, ARTHUR H. "Abraham Cowley as Dramatist." *RES*, 4
(1928), 1-24.
Nethercot acknowledges Cowley as author or part-author
of five plays: *Love's Riddle*; *Naufragium Joculare*; *The
Guardian*; *The Cutter of Coleman Street*; and *The Rehearsal*.

542 OLIVE, W. J. "Shakespeare Parody in Davenport's *A New Tricke
to Cheat the Divell*." *MLN*, 66 (1951), 478-80.
Olive traces Shakespearean allusions in Davenport's play,
especially those to Falstaff, and shows how Davenport paro-
dies Falstaff's monologue in *I Henry IV*, V.i.

543 PESTELL, THOMAS. *The Poems of Thomas Pestell*. Ed. by Hannah
Buckan. Oxford: Blackwell, 1940. 146pp.
The forty-one page introduction is an analysis of Pestell's country and literary lives, primarily as they
affected his poetic output.

544 POWELL, WOODROW W. "A Critical Edition of Thomas Heywood's
A Challenge for Beautie, with Introduction and Notes."
DAI, 19:525-26A (Duke University), 1958. 345pp.
Powell sets 1625 as the date for *A Challenge*, showing
parallels between it, *The Guardian*, and other plays, placing
it in context with other works by Heywood. Powell also discusses the main and subplots, as well as their themes, and
gives a bibliographical analysis of the play.

545 R., W. "Arthur Wilson's Play *The Swisser*." *Athenaeum*
(14 February 1903), pp. 219-20.
The author comments on a recently discovered MS of Wilson's *The Swisser*, which had been performed at Blackfriars
in 1631. He notes that there is a *dramatis personae* with
what was probably the original cast list; he comments on a
three-stanza'd aubade in the third act, the incipit of which
is "So doth the early lark salute the day," and concludes
with the suggestion that the Earl of Warwich might have the
early drafts or manuscripts of Wilson's play.

546 RANDOLPH, THOMAS. *The Drinking Academy*. Ed. by Samuel A.
Tannenbaum and Hyder E. Rollins. Cambridge, MA: Harvard
University Press, 1930. xxiv, 64pp.
Rollins' introduction to *The Drinking Academy, or, The
Cheaters' Holiday* reviews previous scholarship on Randolph,
especially C. L. Day's "Thomas Randolph and *The Drinking
Academy*," *PMLA*, 43 (1928), 800-09, and gives a critical

108

analysis of the structure, style, and plot of the play. He particularly points out Randolph's indebtedness to Jonson.

547 _____. *The Fairy Knight, or, Oberon the Second.* Ed. by Fredson Thayer Bowers. Chapel Hill: University of North Carolina Press, 1942. xlii, 87pp.

In his introduction to the play, Bowers discusses the text of the Randolph MS, its date, the transcriber of the MS and his methods, sources and analogues for the play, authorship, the date of the original play, and the signs of revision and augmentation. Bowers notes the similarities between *The Fairy Knight* and *The Drinking Academy*; *The Jealous Lovers*; *The Muses' Looking-Glass*; and *Amyntas*.

548 _____. *Poetical and Dramatic Works.* Ed. by W. Carew Hazlitt. 1875; rept. NY: Benjamin Blom, 1968. 2 vols.

In his introduction, "Some Account of Thomas Randolph," Hazlitt gives a fuller biography of Randolph than that in the *DNB*, and includes some contemporary allusions to him.

549 RICE, WARNER G. "Source of William Cartwright's *The Royall Slave.*" *MLN*, 45 (1930), 515-18.

Rice discusses the early popularity of Cartwright's *The Royall Slave* (1636), the similarities of plot between it and Massinger's *The Bondman*, and also relationships with Dion's *De Regno* (1604).

550 RICHARDS, KENNETH. "The Source of Sir Ralph Freeman's *Imperiale.*" *SN*, 40 (1968), 185-96.

Richards is concerned with Freeman's "Senecan tragedy" *Imperiale*, published in 1639, which Bentley labels a "closet drama" in *The Jacobean and Caroline Stage IV* (1956), p. 470. Richards analyzes the plot, structure and Latinate style of the play, and suggests possible sources for the plot.

551 RICHARDS, NATHANAEL. *Tragedy of Messallina: The Roman Emperesse.* Ed. by A. R. Skemp. Louvain: A. Uystpruyst, 1910. 160pp.

Prefatory material includes a brief bibliography of sources consulted, and a sixty-three-page introduction containing a life of Richards, critical evaluations of his works other than *Messallina*, and an extended textual analysis of the play with particular attention given to Roman sources.

552 ROLLINS, HYDER. "*The Drinking Academy, or The Cheater's Holiday.*" *PMLA*, 39 (1924), 837-71. [Pp. 838-42 are misbound.]

109

Rollins, Hyder

Rollins gives a description and transcription of *The Drinking Academy*, although he does not attribute to it an author nor give it a date.

553 _____. "Thomas Randolph, Robert Bacon, and *The Drinking Academy*." *PMLA*, 46 (1931), 786-801.
Rollins refutes the authorship of Bacon in regards to this play.

554 RUOFF, JAMES E. "Cartwright's Human Sacrifice Scene in *The Royal Slave*." *N & Q* (July 1957), pp. 295-96.
Ruoff traces the history of "the human sacrifice scene" through Carlell's *Arviragus and Philicia* (1636); Cartwright's *The Royal Slave* (1636); William Chamberlaine's *Love's Victory* (1658); Dryden's *Indian Emperour*, and other scattered sources.

555 _____. "A Critical Edition of *Arviragus and Philicia* by Lodowick Carlell: With an Account of the Author's Life and Plays." *DAI*, 14:1421A (University of Pennsylvania), 1954. 563pp.
Ruoff defines Carlell's play as a "Cavalier romance," and he places it in a social, historical, and literary context. The edition is based on the printed edition of 1639, and two earlier manuscripts.

556 _____. "The Dating of Carlell's *Passionate Lovers*." *N & Q* (February 1956), pp. 68-70.
Ruoff disputes 1637 as the date of composition for *The Passionate Lovers*, feeling that it may have been performed as early as 1634. He makes reference to Carlell's *Deserving Favorite*, and *Arviragus and Philicia*, as well as to *The Lover's Melancholy*; *The Picture*; *The Soddered Citizen*; and Arthur Wilson's *The Swisser*.

557 _____. "A 'Lost' Manuscript of Carlell's *Arviragus and Philicia*." *N & Q* (January 1955), pp. 21-22.
Ruoff traces the history of Carlell's "lost" play and concludes that "the Countess of Carlisle, one of the leading patronesses of Henrietta Maria's Platonic coterie at the Stuart court and a woman whose notorious predilection for preciosity may well have inspired the torturous eloquence of Carlell's romantic play." For support and reply *see* Margaret Toynbee and Sir Gyles Isham. "Lodowick Carlell," *N & Q* (May 1955), p. 204.

558 SABOL, A. J. "New Documents on *The Triumph of Peace*." *M & L*, 47 (1966), 10-26.

Sabol acknowledges that *The Triumph of Peace* (1634), was "one of the most spectacular of Caroline masques," and it is certainly one of the best documented. Sabol adds to the documentation with nineteen new items. A list of actors is included.

559 SANDYS, GEORGE. *The Poetical Works I*. Ed. and rev. by Richard Hooper. London: John Russell Smith, 1872. 195 + 16pp.
Although both volumes of Hooper's edition are devoted solely to the poetry of George Sandys, in his forty-page introduction Hooper gives a biography of Sandys and a survey evaluation of *Christ's Passion*.

560 SCHOENBAUM, SAMUEL. *"Wit's Triumvirate*: A Caroline Comedy Recovered." *SEL*, 4 (1964), 227-37.
In his treatment of the anonymous comedy *Wit's Triumvirate, or, The Philosopher* (1635), Schoenbaum makes a case for the value of further investigation of this comedy which did not come to light until 1942. He gives a brief physical description of the play, and likens it to *The Alchemist*.

561 SMITH, DENZELL STEWART. *"The Tragoedy of Cleopatra, Queene of Aegypt,* by Thomas May: A Critical Edition." *DAI*, 26:1029A (University of Minnesota), 1965. 328pp.
Smith investigates the traditional interpretations of Cleopatra's character and May's departure from tradition, his classical sources, "the intellectual climate in which he lived," and his skepticism about the human condition.

562 SMITH, G. C. MOORE. "The Canon of Randolph's Dramatic Works." *RES*, 1 (1925), 309-23.
Smith is particularly concerned with the authorship of the epilogue to *The Careless Shepherdess*, although he gives some attention to *The Jealous Lovers; Hey for Honesty*; and *Cornelianum Dolium*. Smith also reviews and evaluates some contemporary Randolph criticism.

563 _____. "Nathanael Richards, Dramatist." *N & Q* (June 1909), pp. 461-62.
Smith shows conclusively that the biography given for Richards (dramatist) in the *DNB* is not his.

564 _____. "Thomas Randolph." *Proc Br Academy*, 13 (1927), 79-121.
Moore Smith, in his printed lecture, gives a biography of Randolph and an evaluation of his short literary career. He concludes that "It was no small achievement in his brief span of years to produce four plays so brilliant in their

Sonnenshein, Richard Adolph

different kinds as *Aristippus*; *The Muses' Looking-Glass*; *Amyntas*; and *The Jealous Lovers*, not to speak of his grave and weighty *Echlogues*." Smith does not discuss *The Fary Knight*, which Bowers attributes to Randolph, nor *The Drinking Academy*.

565 SONNENSHEIN, RICHARD ADOLPH. "*A Fine Companion* by Shackerley Marmion (1633)--A Critical, Old Spelling Edition." *DAI*, 29:2725-26A (Northwestern University), 1968. 317pp.
In his critical introduction to the text, Sonnenshein discusses Marmion's life and works, especially *Holland's Leaguer*; *A Fine Companion*; and *The Antiquary*, as well as Marmion's debt to Jonson's coterie at the Devil Tavern, and other contemporaries of Marmion.

566 STEVENSON, ALLAN H. "The Case of the Decapitated Cast: Or *The Night-Walker* at Smock Alley." *SQ*, 6 (1955), 275-96.
Stevenson concerns himself with reconstructing one of the casts for Fletcher's *The Night-Walker* from a seventeenth-century copy of the play housed at the Folger. Apparently "A stupid, blundering binder had cut off the beginning of every name, except perhaps one; had, in fact, decapitated the cast." A photographic reproduction of this misdeed is included. Stevenson shows that the cast for this Caroline play could not have been a contemporary one and suggests it redates to a production at Smock Alley in the winter of 1677-78. Considerable evidence is given to support this supposition and, in addition, Stevenson identifies twelve of the sixteen or seventeen names of the cast.

567 STOYE, J. W. "The Whereabouts of Thomas Killigrew 1639-41." *RES*, 25 (1949), 245-48.
Based on correspondence included in the *Lismore Papers*, edited by A. B. Grosart (1886, 1888), Stoye concludes that Killigrew spent part of the three-year period on the continent, specifically in Paris, Geneva, and Basel, and returned to England about June 1640. Stoye shows the sometimes vexing and always peripatetic nature of Killigrew, and links the writing of *The Parson's Wedding*, as well as the themes included in it, with Killigrew's stay on the continent.

568 STRODE, WILLIAM. *The Poetical Works*. Ed. by Bertram Dobell. London: By the Author, 1907. lvi, 270pp.
Dobell discusses the early reception of *The Floating Island* (1636), and gives a resumé of its plot and structure.

Toback, Phyllis Brooks

569   SWINBURNE, ALGERNON CHARLES. *Letters on the Elizabethan Dramatists.* London: By the Author, 1910. 48pp.
         Of particular note are Swinburne's references to Nabbes, to *Captain Underwit* [*The Country Captain*] which Swinburne and Bullen both attribute to Shirley, and Harbage attributes to William Cavendish, and to *The Launcheinge of the May* [*sic.*] which he styles "a quasi-historical document, and a 'good jest for fever.'"

570   SYKES, H. DUGDALE. "Glapthorne's Play: *The Lady Mother.*" *N & Q* (December 1923), pp. 503–05.
         To establish Glapthorne once and for all as the author of *The Lady Mother,* Sykes gives the reader "an idea not only of the manner in which *The Lady Mother* echoes the language of plays whose title-pages bear Glapthorne's name, but of the extent of [his] repetitions. . . . This [serves] the double purpose of confirming his ascription and of demonstrating how easily Glapthorne's work may be recognized."

571   ____. "*Revenge for Honour*: Glapthorne's Play Attributed to Chapman." *N & Q* (May 1916), pp. 401–04.
         Sykes takes Fleay's assumption--that *Revenge for Honour*'s author is Henry Glapthorne--one step further. He discounts Schelling's assertion that it is "of a general excellence beyond the reach of Glapthorne."

572   THOMAS, D. L. "Concerning Glapthorne's *Wit in a Constable.*" *JEGP,* 14 (1915), 89–92.
         Thomas corrects some emendations which J. Q. Adams, Jr. made of Pearson's reprint of Glapthorne's play. *See* Adams' "Some Notes on Henry Glapthorne's *Wit in a Constable,*" *JEGP,* 13 (1914), 299–304.

573   THORN-DRURY, G. "Jordan's *Money Is an Asse*, 1668." *RES,* 1 (1925), 219–20.
         Thorn-Drury comments on Jordan's cavalier and opportunistic treatment of his 1668 publication of *Money Is an Asse.*

574   TIKRITI, KHALID MAHIR. "A Critical Old-Spelling Edition of Thomas Heywood's *A Mayden-Head Well Lost.*" *DAI,* 32:4581A (St. Louis University), 1971. 138pp.
         The second section of the introduction to the play deals briefly with "the literary and dramatic qualities of the play with special emphasis on its love versus honor theme."

575   TOBACK, PHYLLIS BROOKS. "Thomas Randolph's *Hey for Honesty, Down with Knavery:* A Critical Edition." *DAI,* 32:3967-68A (New York University), 1971. 445pp.

113

Velte, Mowbray

> Toback comments at length on Randolph's dramatic style
> and technique, and his tendency to draw heavily on his own
> works as sources for other works. She also emphasizes the
> strong link with Aristophanes in the play. The play is
> dated between 1626-28.

576   VELTE, MOWBRAY. *The Bourgeois Elements in the Dramas of
      Thomas Heywood.* Mysore: Wesleyan Mission Press, 1922.
      156pp.
> Velte's study includes a discussion of Heywood's life,
> his chronicle histories, his dramatization of classical
> themes, his romantic dramas, those concerning land and sea
> adventures, the dramas of contemporary life, and an analy-
> sis of the bourgeois elements in the plays. There is a
> selected bibliography.

577   VINCE, R. W. "Morality and Masque: The Context for Thomas
      Nabbes' *Microcosmus*." *ES*, 53 (1972), 328-34.
> Vince's article is an analysis of Ford and Dekker's *The
> Sun's Darling* (1624), and Nabbes' *Microcosmus* (1636) as
> "moral masks." He is concerned with dramatic structure, as
> well as theme in the two plays.

578   _____. "Nabbes' *Hannibal and Scipio*: Sources and Theme."
      SEL, 11 (1971), 327-43.
> Vince says "the question of the sources for *Hannibal and
> Scipio* is intimately related to the question of the play's
> theme. Nabbes' reference to 'a former play' has proved
> barren. . . . A comparison of the possible non-dramatic
> sources with the play suggests that [they might be] Livy
> . . . North's Plutarch . . . [or] Petrarch." Vince shows
> that both Nabbes and Petrarch "maintain the Ciceronian dis-
> tinction between political and contemplative virtues" and
> in so doing, Nabbes attempted to make his play a type of
> "epic-tragedy."

579   _____. "Thomas Nabbes and the Professional Drama 1630-1642."
      DAI, 29:2286-87A (Northwestern University), 1968. 247pp.
> After a biography of Nabbes, Vince gives "a formal analy-
> sis of the dramatist's six plays written for the profes-
> sional stage within their literary and theatrical contexts."
> Specifically, he treats *Covent Garden*; *Tottenham Court*; *The
> Bride*; *Microcosmus*; *Hannibal and Scipio*; and *The Unfortunate
> Mother*.

580   WAGNER, BERNARD M. "Manuscript Plays of the Seventeenth
      Century." *TLS* (4 October 1934), p. 675.

Ward, John Woodruff

Wagner offers notes on manuscripts attributed to Henry
Birkhead ("The Female Rebellion"), Brome ("The English
Moor"), Carlell ("The Fool Would Be a Favorite," "Osmond
the Great," and "Arviragus and Philicia"), Cosmo Manuche
("The Just General," "The Lost Lover," "The Bastard," and
"The Banished Shepherdesse"), Randolph ("Conceited Peddler"
and "Wine, Beer, Ale"), and Arthur Wilson ("The Swisser").
For a rejoinder to the note on Cosmo Manuche *see* A. Watkins-
Jones' "Seventeenth-Century Plays," *TLS* (15 November 1934),
p. 795.

581   WALLERSTEIN, RUTH C. "Suckling's Imitation of Shakespeare:
      A Caroline View of His Art." *RES*, 19 (1943), 290-95.
         Wallerstein feels that "Sir John Suckling's *Goblins*,
      written with Shakespeare's *Tempest* in mind, but written for
      an audience in whom sentimental and heroic concepts of psy-
      chology and of drama had begun to prevail, is a play almost
      chaotically disunified in tone and method." Yet "*The Gob-
      lins* is of immense interest in showing how, in the midst of
      the rising triumph of the drama of heroic sentiment, men of
      the mid-century actually experienced Shakespeare."

582   WALTER, J. H. "Henry Glapthorne." *TLS* (19 September 1936),
      p. 748.
         Walter gives recently discovered facts about Glapthorne's
      life, from Baptismal, Marriage and Burial Registers. He
      also makes several biographical and literary connections.

583   _____. "*Wit in a Constable*: Censorship and Revision." *MLR*,
      34 (1939), 9-20.
         Walter's thesis is that "There are many plays of the
      early seventeenth century which bear traces of censorship
      and revision, and many more in which censorship and revi-
      sion are suspected; but few plays contain in their printed
      texts such extensive evidence of both as Glapthorne's *Wit
      in a Constable*. Indeed, it is not unreasonable to suggest
      on a cursory reading that Glapthorne has substituted the
      ending of one play for that of another and entirely differ-
      ent play."

584   WARD, JOHN WOODRUFF. "A Critical Old Spelling Edition of
      Jasper Mayne's *The Citye Match*." *DAI*, 35:7275A (University
      of Delaware), 1975. 221pp.
         As well as the edition, Ward's work includes a biographi-
      cal introduction and a critical introduction which "asserts
      that *The Citye Match* . . . repays close reading because it
      treats a significant theme--the impact of 'modern' economic
      values on human relationships--responsibly and not

Watkins-Jones, A.

unskillfully, in addition to satirizing both court Platonism and Puritanism." Ward places Mayne in the tradition of
Jonson, Middleton and Massinger, as a comic writer.

585   WATKINS-JONES, A. "Seventeenth-Century Plays." *TLS*
      (15 November 1934), p. 795.
          The author gives additional information on, and additions
      to, B. M. Wagner's note on Cosmo Manuche and others in
      "Manuscript Plays of the Seventeenth Century," *TLS*
      (4 October 1934), p. 675.

586   WERTHEIM, ALBERT. "A New Light on the Dramatic Works of
      Thomas Killigrew." *SB*, 24 (1971), 149-52.
          Wertheim contends that all eight of Killigrew's plays
      were written before or during the Interregnum. He deter-
      mines this based on internal evidence from the 1664 folio
      of Killigrew's *Comedies and Tragedies*.

587   WILDE, GEORGE. *Eumorphus sive Cupido Adultus*. Ed. and
      trans. by Heinz J. Vienken. Munich: Wilhelm Fink, 1973.
      364pp.
          Vienken's introduction before his translation and edi-
      tion of the Wilde academic comedy contains a lengthy state-
      ment on academic drama at Oxford, 1603-1642, and a comment
      on the author. About the play itself, he summarizes the
      plot, discussing *Eumorphus* and the Narcissus theme, devices
      of disguise, language, mythology, and the play in the con-
      text of its own time. He concludes with a note on editing
      and translating the work.

588   _____. *Love's Hospital*. Ed. by Jay Louis Funston. Salzburg:
      Institut für Englische Sprache und Literatur, 1973. lxix,
      144pp.
          Funston's introduction includes a biography of George
      Wilde, commentary on his plays, the literary tradition of
      Love's Hospital, its production, and a discussion of the
      various manuscripts. Appendices include a transcription of
      Folger MS. 1487.2, and a glossary of terms. There is a
      bibliography as well as a reconstruction of the stage and
      auditorium for the production of the play in the hall of
      St. John's College, Oxford, August 30, 1936.

589   WILEY, AUDREY NELL. "The Prologue and Epilogue to *The
      Guardian*." *RES*, 10 (1934), 443-47.
          Wiley notes the appearance of the name Francis Cole as
      author on the title page of *The Guardian*. However, she
      definitely attributes the play to Abraham Cowley, for in-
      ternal as well as external reasons.

590   WILKINSON, C. H. "A Note on May." *RES*, 11 (1935), 195-98.
       Based on May's pamphleteer activity, Wilkinson can con-
       clude that Thomas May was much concerned with the side of
       Parliament during the Civil War.

591   WILSON, ARTHUR. *The Inconstant Lady*. Oxford: S.
       Collingwood, 1814. viii, 178pp.
       Following this anonymous edition of *The Inconstant Lady*
       are the title page and *dramatis personae* for a play called
       The Corporal, some observations about Arthur Wilson, by
       himself, the "author's picture, in verse, of himself," his
       will and its codicil, and Bathurst's and Wood's accounts
       of Wilson's character.

592   _____. *The Swisser*. Ed. by Albert Feuillerat. Paris:
       Librairie Feschbacher, 1904. cxxii, 112pp.
       Feuillerat's introduction, in French, traces the multi-
       leveled life of Arthur Wilson and his literary career. The
       editor is most concerned with Wilson's comedies and gives
       particular attention to the dramatic impact of *The Swisser*.
       There is an appendix of biographical materials, and of
       Wilson's poems on John Donne and himself. There is also a
       bibliography of works cited. The text of the play is in
       English.

593   WRIGHT, LOUIS B. "Notes on Thomas Heywood's Later Reputation."
       RES, 4 (1928), 135-44.
       Wright includes notes on information he has collected
       relating to Heywood's regard after his death, through 1920.

Individual Studies and Comprehensive Works

594   ADAMS, HENRY HITCH. *English Domestic or, Homiletic Tragedy,*
      1575 to 1642: Being an Account of the Development of the
      Tragedy of the Common Man Showing His Great Dependence on
      Religious Morality. . . . NY: Columbia University Press,
      1943. 228pp.
         Of particular interest are Chapters VII and IX on seven-
      teenth-century murder plays and on the decline of domestic
      tragedies, and Chapter X, the conclusion. Appendix B dis-
      cusses Heywood and Brome and their authorship of *The Late*
      Lancashire Witches. The book is indexed.

595   ANDERSON, DONALD K. "The Banquet of Love in English Drama
      (1595-1642)." *JEGP,* 63 (1964), 422-32.
         Anderson analyzes two types of love banquets in Eliza-
      bethan, Jacobean and Caroline drama: the scene "in which
      an assignation takes place and a seduction is attempted,"
      and dramatic occasions when the banquet "serves as a meta-
      phor, becoming the language of love." Of particular inter-
      est is his discussion of Jonson's *The New Inn* with its
      "banquet of sense, like that of Ovid"; Massinger's *The*
      Roman Actor, the anonymous *Bloodie Banquet,* Ford's *The*
      Broken Heart and *'Tis Pity She's a Whore,* and Suckling's
      Aglaura. He stresses the versatility of the Caroline
      dramatist to "exploit the possibilities of the love banquet."

596   _____. "The Mirror Concept and Its Relation to the Drama of
      the Renaissance." *Northwestern Missouri State Teachers*
      Coll St, 3 (1939), 1-30.
         In his discussion of the mirror concept as it is used in
      Renaissance drama, Anderson pays particular attention to
      the work of Thomas Randolph.

597   ASHLEY, MAURICE. "Love and Marriage in Seventeenth Century
      English." *History To-Day,* 8 (1958), 667-76.
         Ashley contends that "Church and State stood foursquare
      behind the superiority of man. . . . It was only when a
      lady became a widow that a glorious opportunity for

Aydelotte, Frank

> authority and freedom suddenly flooded in upon her." The
> article is liberally sprinkled with relevant plates.

598   AYDELOTTE, FRANK. *Elizabethan Rogues and Vagabonds*. London:
       Oxford University Press, 1913. x, 187pp.
>   Aydelotte's work cuts off at approximately 1600, but it
> is an excellent background and history for the study of
> vagabonds, gypsies, beggars, rufflers, hookers, counter-
> feiters, pedlars, tinkers, minstrels, jugglers, spies, and
> rogues of all descriptions.

599   BABB, LAWRENCE. *The Elizabethan Malady: A Study of
       Melancholia in English Literature from 1580-1642*. East
       Lansing: Michigan State College, 1951. xi, 206pp.
>   Babb's contention is that melancholy was "a fashionable
> psychic malady . . . much in vogue in the England of Eliza-
> beth and the early Stuarts, especially among the intellec-
> tuals and would-be intellectuals." Since Babb's study is
> thorough and well-documented, it is worthwhile to focus his
> hypothesis on the Caroline period, particularly the comedy
> where the malady was becoming less fashionable and hence a
> subject for ridicule. Many references to and discussions
> of Caroline playwrights are included in the work, particu-
> larly some related to Brome, Ford, Glapthorne, Massinger
> and Shirley. Note Bibliography II: "Selected List of
> Modern Studies" and the index.

600   BARBER, CHARLES L. *The Idea of Honour in English Drama,
       1591-1700*. Stockholm and Göteborg: Elanders Boytrycheri
       Aktiebolag, 1957. 364pp.
>   Barber's is an exhaustive statistical study of the use
> of the word and concept of honor, and its corrolary terms
> of reputation, virtue, and chastity as they appear in the
> seventeenth century. Check the index and two appendices of
> chronological and alphabetical lists of plays used as
> sources for the study. For a discussion of the methodology
> of the book *see* Chapter I, "Aims, Methods, and Materials."

601   BASKERVILL, CHARLES READ. *The Elizabethan Jig and Related
       Song Drama*. Chicago: University of Chicago Press, 1929.
       642pp.
>   Part I of this work contains the history of the jig;
> Part II, the texts for many jigs used in dramatic produc-
> tions. Check the index for numerous references to Caroline
> drama-references to Caroline dramatists, particularly
> Shirley and Davenant.

602   BASTIAENEN, JOHANNES ADAM. *The Moral Tone of Jacobean and Caroline Drama*. Amsterdam: H. J. Paris, 1930. 198pp.
      About Caroline drama, Bastiaenen feels "Much of the scurrilous matter, many objectionable situations and a great portion of the shameless display of sensational crime and vice, are, without any doubt, due to the putrid cravings of [a] gradually decreasing audience." He feels also that "the decadence of the drama, with regard to its moral tone, was, therefore, no less a gradual process than the decline of its poetic and artistic worth." For a divergent point of view *see* Harriet Hawkins' *Likeness and Truth in Elizabethan and Jacobean Drama* (1972).

603   BECK, ERVIN, JR. "Prodigal Son Comedy: The Continuity of a Paradigm in English Drama, 1500-1642." *DAI*, 33:6339A (Indiana University), 1973. 344pp.
      Of the many subjects discussed in the work, only Massinger's treatment of Luke Frugal in *The City Madam* is of major importance to the Caroline period.

604   BENNETT, A. L. "The Moral Tone of Massinger's Dramas." *PLL*, 2 (1966), 207-16.
      Bennett refers frequently to Massinger's *A New Way to Pay Old Debts* and his latter plays, but in effect his article is an indictment of the Caroline period in general.

605   BENNETT, H. S. *English Books and Readers 1603-1640*. Cambridge: Cambridge University Press, 1970. xiv, 253pp.
      The purpose of the work is "to investigate the different kinds of audiences the books hoped to interest." He also analyzes the front material of books, regulations related to the book trade, and the subject matter of the books themselves. *See also* Charles Mish's "Comparative Popularity of Early Fiction and Drama," *N & Q* (June 1952), pp. 269-70, and Louis B. Wright's *Middle Class Culture in Elizabethan England* (1935).

606   BERNBAUM, ERNEST. *The Drama of Sensibility*. 1915; rept. Gloucester, MA: Peter Smith, 1958. ix, 288pp.
      Of particular interest is Bernbaum's Chapter IV on the inhibition of sentimentalism from plays of domestic life from 1660-1695 in which he discusses Cowley's *The Guardian* and his *Cutter of Coleman Street*, as well as Shirley's *The Example*. Check the earlier chapters for references to Heywood, Brome and Fletcher.

607   BLACK, A. BRUCE and ROBERT METCALF SMITH. *Shakespeare Allusions and Parallels*. 1931; rept. NY: AMS, 1971. viii, 59pp.

Blaney, Glenn H.

> Passages are included that show the similarities of text between Shakespeare and Massinger, Fletcher, Shirley, Ford, Heywood, Jonson, Mayne, Randolph and Arthur Wilson.

608   BLANEY, GLENN H. "The Enforcement of Marriage in English Drama 1600-1650." *PQ,* 38 (1959), 459-72.

> Blaney's thesis is that "only after the notion of romantic love within marriage had gained some acceptance in the Renaissance would protests in literature against the enforcement of marriage by parents and others grow strong and frequent." He cites numerous examples of Renaissance plays to support frequency; among others is his discussion of *The Broken Heart. See also* his "Convention, Plot, and Structure in *The Broken Heart, MP,* 56 (1958), 1-9.

609   BOAS, FREDERICK S. *An Introduction to Stuart Drama.* Oxford: Oxford University Press, 1946. 443pp.

> Boas gives many sturdy critical sketches on Jonson, Heywood, Fletcher, Massinger, Ford, Shirley, Brome, Davenant, masques and university plays. The book is well-indexed.

610   _____. *Shakespeare and the Universities: And Other Studies in Elizabethan Drama.* Oxford: The Shakespeare Head Press, 1923. 272pp.

> Of interest is Chapter V on Egerton MS. 1994, and examples of censorship in it, and Chapters VIII through X on Walter Mountford's play *The Launching of the Mary* which "exhibits all the stages through which the 'copy' of the play passed before (if ever) it was sent to the printer." This study explicitly demonstrates the nature of stage censorship as practiced by Sir Henry Herbert under Charles I.

611   BODE, ROBERT F. "A Study of the Development of the Theme of Love and Duty in English Comedy from Charles I to George I." *DAI,* 31:5351A (University of South Carolina), 1971. 149pp.

> The only Caroline dramatist Bode is concerned with is William Davenant, and he analyzes Davenant's contribution to the conventional theme of love and honor.

612   BOWDEN, WILLIAM R. *The English Dramatic Lyric, 1603-42.* New Haven: Yale University Press, 1951. xii, 219pp.

> Bowden's work is a two-part evaluation of dramatic lyrics after 1602. The first part discusses the meaning of song in the seventeenth century, its psychological and nonpsychological functions in terms of structure, characterization, convention, dramatic and realistic effects, and its effects on audiences. He deals with the question of song

as extraneous entertainment, and categorizes the various
songs in plays by types. The concluding chapter of the
first part is entitled "The Human Element and the Dramatic
Lyric," and it is concerned with the dramatists, the actors,
the acting companies, and the changing times. The second
half of the book, the Appendix (pp. 133-209), is a list of
songs in 479 plays, by author. To interpret the terminology
in the appendix, one must read the first part of the book.
A bibliography of works cited is included. Although there
is no index, there are frequent references to Caroline
plays in the work.

613   B[OWEN], G[EORGE] S[PENCER]. *A Study of the Prologue and
      Epilogue in English Literature from Shakespeare to Dryden.*
      1884; rept. Folcroft, PA: Folcroft Press, 1969. xi,
      187pp.
         Bowen discusses prologues and epilogues in, among other
      works, those of Jonson, Mayne, Massinger, Brome, Shirley,
      as well as the authors' attitudes toward them. The work
      analyzes the development of the various uses of the prologue
      and epilogue, information related to stage usage, and stage
      conventions.

614   BOWERS, FREDSON THAYER. *Elizabethan Revenge Tragedy 1587-
      1642.* 1936; rept. Gloucester, MA: Peter Smith, 1959.
      288pp.
         Beginning with a discussion of Davenant's *Albovine*
      (1626), p. 202, the remainder of Bowers' book is primarily
      devoted to Caroline drama. In his last three chapters he
      stresses the "disapproval" of the revenge tradition and its
      decadence in the Caroline period.

615   BRADBROOK, MURIEL CLARA. *Growth and Structure of Elizabethan
      Comedy.* London: Chatto and Windus, 1955. ix, 245pp.
         Bradbrook's is an excellent study of comedy pre-1625 and,
      as such, serves as background material for the study of
      comedy after 1625.

616   _____. *Themes and Conventions of Elizabethan Tragedy.*
      Cambridge: Cambridge University Press, 1935. vii, 275pp.
         Although Bradbrook's study precedes the period of this
      work, the final chapter on "The Decadence" treats the work
      of many Caroline dramatists. It is also useful as a study
      of Tudor and Stuart antecedents in theatrical convention,
      particularly convention related to presentation, acting
      and speech. Bradbrook also comments on Elizabethan habits
      of reading, writing and listening. The work is indexed by
      author.

Bridenbaugh, Carl

617   BRIDENBAUGH, CARL. *Vexed and Troubled English Men: 1590-
        1642.* NY: Oxford University Press, 1968. 487pp.
             Bridenbaugh's is a well-documented, Anglo-American his-
        tory of country, town-citizen, and court life in Renais-
        sance England. The author traces influences and shows
        connections between the various strata of culture in Eng-
        land during the period. Check the index for citations on
        amusements, architecture, education, manners, music, women,
        and individual authors and works.

618   BROEKER, HARRIET DURKEE. "The Influence of *Othello* on
        Jacobean and Caroline Drama." *DAI*, 17:2006A (University
        of Minnesota), 1957. 349pp.
             Broeker discusses Massinger's *The Duke of Milan*, Ford's
        The Queen, *Love's Sacrifice*, and *'Tis Pity*, Davenant's
        Albovine; *The Platonic Lovers*; and *The Cruel Brother*, and
        Shirley's general indebtedness to the Shakespearean play.
        "Of the minor Caroline playwrights, Carlell borrows the
        villain and the temptation in *The Deserving Favorite*;
        J. D. in *The Knave in Grane* uses these elements and borrows
        a number of lines, parts of the temptation, and passages
        from the final scene; Rider in *The Twins* combines eaves-
        dropping and temptation somewhat as Davenant had done;
        Glapthorne in *Revenge for Honour* borrows lines, the appar-
        ently honest villain, and the temptation."

619   CAMDEN, CARROLL. *The Elizabethan Woman.* Houston: Elsevier
        Press, 1952. 333pp.
             Camden's work is a narrative on Tudor and Stuart women,
        their education, domestic, legal and personal relationships,
        marriage customs, clothing, and controversies surrounding
        any discussion of women, particularly in the post-Eliza-
        bethan period. The index and bibliography of primary
        sources are comprehensive.

620   CAWLEY, ROBERT RALSTON. *Unpathed Waters: Studies in the
        Influence of the Voyagers in Elizabethan Literature.*
        Princeton: Princeton University Press, 1940. viii, 285pp.
             In his discussion of voyage literature and its uses in
        Renaissance literature, Cawley gives an historical back-
        ground for the usages in Caroline literature and at one
        point focuses on Davenant's plays after 1640. Check the
        index for frequent references to Killigrew, Brome, May,
        Randolph, Massinger, Heywood, Shirley, Nabbes, Sandys, and
        Mayne.

621   _____. *The Voyagers and Elizabethan Drama.* Boston: Oxford
        University Press, 1938. 428pp.

Cawley's work is a well-indexed, and well-documented source for the study of Renaissance travel as it relates to dramatic works, primarily in the reigns of Elizabeth and James, although much Caroline source material of a prose-essay nature is cited. Check index for references to Brome, Nabbes, Benlowes, Carew, Carell, Glapthorne, Randolph, Cartwright, Heywood, Mayne, Sandys, Quarles, Shirley, and many others, as well as to individual plays.

622 CAZAMIAN, LOUIS. *The Development of English Drama*. Durham: Duke University Press, 1952. 421pp.
Chapter XIII, sections 8-11, are devoted to the comedy of Heywood, Massinger, Ford, and Shirley. Randolph, Brome, and others are mentioned in passing.

623 CHANDLER, FRANK WADLEIGH. *The Literature of Roguery*. Boston: Houghton Mifflin, 1907. 2 vols.
"In the broadest sense, this history follows the fortunes of the anti-hero in literature." Volume I treats roguery in drama, particularly that of Shakespeare, Jonson, and Fletcher, as well as the rogue in fiction, criminal biographies, jest books, popular tales, satires, beggar-books, pamphlets and prison tracts. As a survey, the book gives a thorough contemporary picture of the rogue through the literature in which he appears. There are frequent references to Caroline dramatists. The index and bibliography are in Volume II.

624 CHEW, SAMUEL C. *The Crescent and the Rose: Islam and England during the Renaissance*. NY: Oxford University Press, 1937. xviii, 583pp.
In Chapter X, "Festivals alla Turchesca and alla Moresca," Chew discusses Heywood's *Porta Pietatis* (1638), his *Londini Status Pacatus* (1639), and other lord mayors' shows, as well as water shows and revels at court. In Chapter XI, "Moslems on the London Stage," there is an extended discussion of Massinger's *The Renegado*. Check the thorough index for other references to Massinger, Fletcher, Ford, Suckling, Shirley, and other Caroline writers.

625 COLLIER, JOHN PAYNE. *History of English Dramatic Poetry, to the Time of Shakespeare: And Annals of the Stage to the Restoration*. London: John Murray, 1831. 3 vols.
Collier's work is an attempt to rectify the neglect received by Renaissance dramatic poetry, with the possible exception of editorial work on Shakespeare. Volume II includes his annals of the stage "from the accession of Charles I . . . to the close of the theatres." Volume III,

Cope, Jackson Irving

> following p. 263, treats "old theatres, their appurtenances
> . . . , [an] account of the old theatres of London [and]
> details connected with the performance of plays."

626   COPE, JACKSON IRVING. *The Theatre and the Drama: From Metaphor to Form in Renaissance Drama.* Baltimore: Johns Hopkins University Press, 1973. ix, 331pp.

    Three sections of the book are of particular significance in relation to theatrical activity and the background for it. These are the prologue, "The Rediscovery of Anti-Form in Renaissance Drama," Chapter V, "Seventeenth-Century English Commedia Improvvisa: Art over Nature," and Chapter VI, "Seventeenth-Century English Commedia Improvvisa: Nature over Art." The book is supplied with copious annotated notes and a thorough index listing frequent references to Caroline plays.

627   CRAIG, HARDIN. *The Enchanted Glass: The Elizabethan Mind in Literature.* 1936; rept. Westport, CT: Greenwood Press, 1975. ix, 273pp.

    The author is concerned with "the characteristic reaction of the Elizabethan mind as compared to our contemporary mind." Through this contrast, he gives an historical basis for the evolution of ideas in the Caroline period.

628   CURRY, JOHN V. *Deception in Elizabethan Comedy.* Chicago: Loyola University Press, 1955. 197pp.

    The value of Curry's book, to a Caroline critic, is his definition, by delineation, of the term deception. The works surveyed, for the most part, are prelude to the comic intrigues and deception scenes in Caroline drama. Refer to index as well as Bibliography B, "Historical and Critical Works."

629   CUTTS, JOHN P. "Seventeenth-Century Songs and Lyrics in Edinburgh University Library Music MS Dc. I.69." *Musica Disciplina,* 13 (1959), 169-94.

    In his discussion of the seventeenth-century collection of songs and lyrics, Cutts notes a single voice part for song #7, from *The Triumph of Peace.* He gives a list of contents for the MS's 129 songs. Check the "Commentary" for references to other Caroline works.

630   _____. "William Lawes' Writing for the Theatre and the Court." *Library,* 5th ser, 7 (1952), 83-96.

    A setting of BM additional MS 31,432, for a song from *The Lost Lady,* is given; its incipit is "Where did you borrow that last sigh." Settings are also given for songs from *The Triumph of Peace* and *The Cardinal.*

631   DAVIS, JOE LEE.   "The Case for Comedy in Caroline Theatrical Apologetics."   *PMLA,* 58 (1943), 353-71.
       Davis dispels, somewhat, the contemporary notion that "Caroline dramatists were responsible . . . for the inequities of Caroline society." In doing so, he cites information from Massinger's *The Roman Actor,* Randolph's *The Muses' Looking Glass,* and tracts like Prynne's *Histrio-Mastix,* Richard Rawlidge's *A Monster Late Found Out and Discovered,* and *A Short Treatise against Stage-Players.* He concludes that "on the basis of the evidence . . . the . . . claim may be made that there was a Caroline foreshadowing of the Collier controversy."

632   _____.   *The Sons of Ben: Jonsonian Comedy in Caroline England.*   Detroit: Wayne State University Press, 1967. 252pp.
       Davis gives particular attention to Jonsonian comic themes and dramatic techniques as they affected the work of Brome, Cartwright, Cavendish, Davenant, Glapthorne, Hausted, Nabbes, and Randolph. Implicit to his point of view is the attitude that "the twentieth century has not restored Jonson to the place above Shakespeare where the later seventeenth and early eighteenth centuries seemed to have wrongly elevated him as a consequence of their neoclassical prejudices." The book is well-indexed and gives extensive "Notes and References."

633   DEIERKAUF-HOLSBOER, S. WILMA.   *L'histoire de la mise en scène dans le théâtre français à Paris de 1600 à 1673.*   Paris: Librairie A. Nizet, 1960.   165pp.
       This work is useful for comparative purposes, particularly in terms of types of theatres, stage dressings, costumes, performances, and audience.   A bibliography and Table of Contents conclude the work.

634   DONALDSON, IAN.   *The World Upside-Down. Comedy from Jonson to Fielding.*   Oxford: Clarendon Press, 1970.   211pp.
       Chapter IV of Donaldson's study, "'Living Backward': *The Antipodes,*" (pp. 78-98), is a sympathetic treatment of Brome's play in the context of its own time. This chapter should be read in conjunction with Chapter I, "Justice in the Stocks," which gives an overview of the whole work. Donaldson sets Brome solidly in the Jonsonian tradition; although his feelings about Brome's literary abilities are mixed, he does not dismiss *The Antipodes* as a structurally

Ellehauge, Martin

flawed play as most critics do, and he quite logically puts
it into the tradition of absurdist drama.

635   ELLEHAUGE, MARTIN. *English Restoration Drama: Its Relation
to Past English and Past and Contemporary French Drama.*
Copenhagen: Levin and Munksgaard, 1933. 322pp.
Part I, "English Drama from Elizabethan to the Restoration Period" is concerned with dramatic form, types of
characters, and general subject matter in the plays. It
is of note because of the correlations between Renaissance,
Restoration and contemporary French works, particularly
those of Molière.

636   ELLIS-FERMOR, UNA MARY. *The Jacobean Drama.* 1936; rept.
NY: Vintage Books, 1961. xvi, 348pp.
Fermor extends her discussion of Jacobean drama through
1634 to include Ford. She acknowledges that he "stands
some distance from his Jacobean predecessors"; what is of
particular note, however, is the similarity in pattern and
subject matter which Fermor attributes to Ford's Caroline
drama and such Jacobean dramatists as Beaumont, Fletcher,
Middleton, and especially Webster.

637   EVANS, HERBERT ARTHUR, ed. *English Masques.* 1897; rept.
Freeport, NY: Books for Library Presses, 1971. lxiii,
245pp.
In his early, monograph-length introduction to the
masques, Evans sets out many of the critical issues and
problems inherent to the analysis of a masque. There is
also some discussion of Shirley's *Triumph of Peace,* and
Davenant's *Salmacida Spolia.* He concludes his essay with
a discussion of the popularity of the antimasque and its
ultimate degeneration during the Caroline period.

638   EWBANK, INGA-STINA. "The Eloquence of Masques." *Ren D, n.s.,*
1 (1968), 307-27.
Ewbank gives a survey and evaluation of the better-known,
recent scholarship on masques.

639   FEIL, DORIS. "The Female Page in Renaissance Drama." *DAI,*
31:6007A (Arizona State University), 1971. 312pp.
"This work investigates a total of fifty-one plays containing fifty-nine female pages. Each of the first six
chapters is devoted to a decade or part of a decade, from
1592-1642, giving as succinctly as possible the action in
which the female page is involved. Twenty-nine authors
are represented, including two anonymous authors."

Fletcher, Ivan Kyrle

640   FEIL, J. P. "Dramatic References from the Scudamore Papers."
      Shak Sur, 11 (1958), 107-16.
      After a brief history of those members of the Scudamore
      family noted in this article, Feil lists, in chronological
      order, references to plays from the papers for the years
      1610/11 through 1638.

641   FIELD, BRADFORD S., JR. "The Use of Prose Fiction in English
      Drama, 1616-1642." *DAI*, 25:1910-11A (University of
      Maryland), 1963. 513pp.
      Field surveys approximately sixty plays of the period
      "that are based upon prose fiction . . . to see what can
      be established about the use of prose fiction pieces on the
      stage. . . ." His conclusions "are valid for the period as
      a whole, independent of relative dates within the period
      and of individual authorship as well."

642   FINNEY, GRETCHEN LUDKE. *Musical Backgrounds for English
      Literature 1580-1650*. New Brunswick, NJ: Rutgers
      University Press, 1962. 202pp.
      Finney is concerned generally with the *ethos* of music,
      with *musica theorica*, and the perception of these in the
      Renaissance mind. Specifically, through references to con-
      temporary literature, she discusses neo-Platonic and human-
      istic attitudes toward music. The book is indexed by
      author, subject, and work.

643   FISCH, HAROLD. "The Puritans and the Reform of Prose Style."
      J of ELH, 19 (1952), 229-48.
      Fisch deals with a Puritan concern for "simple and
      plaine speech" and shows the ramifications of this concept
      on prose style in the mid-seventeenth century.

644   FLANAGAN, JAMES DONALD. "The Satirist-Intriguer in
      Elizabethan and Jacobean Comedy." *DAI*, 34:2557A
      (University of Minnesota), 1973. 250pp.
      Flanagan is concerned with Renaissance satiric comedies
      in which there is "a character who is both a satiric com-
      mentator and an important participant in the play." Among
      their works, Flanagan discusses Jonson's "undervalued"
      play, *The Magnetic Lady*.

645   FLETCHER, IVAN KYRLE. "Italian Comedians in England in the
      Seventeenth Century." *TN*, 8 (1954), 86-91.
      Fletcher says, as far as recorded information is con-
      cerned, "on 18 February 1630, Francis Nicoline, an Italian,
      was granted a warrant by the Master of the Revels for his
      troupe to dance on the ropes, to use interludes and masques,

Fletcher, Jefferson Butler

and to sell powders and balsams. Then there is a gap of
thirty years, until 22 October 1660," before another such
patent is granted.

646   FLETCHER, JEFFERSON BUTLER. *The Religion of Beauty in Women,
and Other Essays on Platonic Love in Poetry and Society.*
NY: Haskell House, 1911. xi, 205pp.
Fletcher's final chapter, "Precieuses at the Court of
Charles I" is of particular note. He takes a severe look
at the grosser elements of the court and notes how it,
under the influence of Henrietta Maria, and the writings
of Davenant and others, was countered. He also gives some
attention to the parody of Platonic love in Caroline plays.

647   FOWELL, FRANK and FRANK PALMER. *Censorship in England.*
London: Frank Palmer, 1913. xii, 390pp.
One third of the book is devoted to a discussion of the
origins of censorship regulations, the attitudes and fees
of Henry Herbert and other Renaissance censors, and the
problems of suppression and reaction which characterize
Puritan attitudes and actions. The work is well-indexed.

648   FREEBURG, VICTOR OSCAR. *Disguise Plots in Elizabethan Drama:
A Study in Stage Tradition.* NY: Columbia University
Press, 1915. 241pp.
Freeburg's is a comprehensive and highly-suggestive
analysis of the techniques and varieties of disguises in
Renaissance dramatic literature. General topics that are
covered are "the origins and extent of dramatic disguise,
female pages, boy brides, rogues, spies and lovers in disguise." A wide variety of literature is covered. The index should be consulted for references to Caroline works.

649   FROST, D. L. *School of Shakespeare: The Influence of
Shakespeare on English Drama 1600-42.* Cambridge:
Cambridge University Press, 1968. xi, 304pp.
Frost devotes lengthy chapters of his work to Massinger
and Ford (as anti-Shakespearean), and to a discussion of
the impact of *Hamlet* on revenge traditions. In the latter
context, he treats Suckling's *Aglaura*, Brome's *The Antipodes*, Shirley's *The Cardinal*, and others.

650   GAGEN, JEAN ELIZABETH. *The New Woman: Her Emergence in
English Drama 1600-1730.* NY: Twayne, 1954. 193pp.
Gagen's book is an invaluable work, as much for the
scope of the study as for its critical focus; the scholarship is tied closely to primary sources and she draws on

dramatic sources as well as contemporary essays, discussions, letters, and studies of manners.

651   GAIR, W. R.   "The Politics of Scholarship: A Dramatic Comment on the Autocracy of Charles I." In *The Elizabethan Theatre III*. Ed. by David Galloway. Hamden, CT: Shoestring Press, 1973. Pp. 100-18.
        Based on a dramatic incident in Marmion's *The Antiquary* and one in *Holland's Leaguer*, and on information garnered from the Society of Antiquaries, Gair discusses Charles I's autocratic plays for suppression. He questions whether or not *The Antiquary*, like Chapman's *Old Joiner of Algate*, might not be "an attempt to influence a judicial decision of the Star Chamber."

652   GOLDING, AMY M.   "The London Background of English Comedy, 1600-1642." *DAI*, 21:3450 (New York University), 1960. 398pp.
        The second half of Golding's dissertation is a consideration of the effect of comedy of manners on English drama post-1628. She focuses on *The City Madam*; *The Guardian*; and others, and feels that in "external details consisted all the novelty of Caroline comedy, and by 1640 the plays and London life, like the London theatre, were trivial, parasitic, and devoid of vitality."

653   GOLDSTEIN, LEONARD.   "Three Significant Dramatists and Their Relation to the Moral Decadence of Jacobean and Caroline Drama: A Study of George Chapman, John Ford, and John Webster." *DAI*, 15:1386-87A (Brown University), 1955. 223pp.
        Goldstein discusses the literary antecedents of Platonic love, and the phenomenon itself in terms of Caroline drama. He feels that the "expression of this decadence varies to the degree that the dramatists transcend their natal social group."

654   GRAVES, THORNTON S.   "Notes on Puritanism and the Stage." *SP*, 18 (1921), 141-69.
        Focusing on Prynne's *Histrio-Mastix*, Graves also includes "a few minor contributions to the struggle between the Puritans and the theatres which have not been indicated in the recent discussions on the subject," *e.g.*, R. Junius' *Complete Armour against Civill Society*, and his *The Drunkard's Character*, Francis Lenton's *The Young Gallants Whirligig*, and Ralph Knevet's "epistle to the Society of Florists," prefixed to his *Rhodon and Iris*. Admitting that the Puritan controversy was almost ended with the close of the

Graves, Thornton S.

        theatres, Graves notes that not all pamphleteering or ser-
monizing had stopped.

655   ____. "Women on the Pre-Restoration Stage." *SP*, 22 (1925),
        184-97.
        Citing material from many contemporary sources, Graves
comes to the conclusion "that it is almost inconceivable
that females were totally excluded from appearance on the
stage during the Elizabethan period." He allows, especially,
that female curiosities and freaks may have been "sometimes
introduced into the regular theatres of London. . . ."

656   GREEN, A. WIGFALL. *The Inns of Court and Early English Drama.*
        1931; rept. NY: Benjamin Blom, 1965, 1968. xii, 190pp.
        Green's work includes an evaluation of James Shirley's
masque *The Triumph of Peace*, and Davenant's *The Triumphs
of the Prince D'Amour*, as well as a representative bibliography.

657   GREG, W. W. *Pastoral Poetry and Pastoral Drama.* 1906; rept.
        NY: Russell and Russell, 1959. xii, 464pp.
        Greg's work is "A literary inquiry, with special refer-
ence to the pre-Restoration stage in England." Chapter V,
section ii, contains an analysis and criticism of Randolph's
The Faithful Shepherdess; Chapters VI and VII are concerned
with other English pastoral dramas, including Milton's
Comus.

658   HAAKER, ANN. "The Plague, the Theatre, and The Poet."
        Ren D, n.s., 1 (1968), 283-306.
        In her examination of the plague of 1636/37, Haaker
cites many examples of its effect on Caroline dramatists.
She focuses on two 1640 documents that give the "most de-
tailed evidence to date of the relationship between an
early theatre [Salisbury Court] and its playwright [Richard
Brome]." Transcripts of two documents, Heaton *vs.* Brome
(Bill), and Heaton *vs.* Brome (Answer) are given.

659   HARBAGE, ALFRED. *Cavalier Drama: An Historical and Critical
Supplement to the Study of the Elizabethan and Restoration
Stage.* NY: MLA, 1936. ix, 302pp.
        Harbage's work is a systematic review of amateur, pro-
fessional, court, and university dramatic works from 1626
through 1669. Part One is concerned with trends and patterns in Caroline, Interregnum and early Restoration drama,
on the subjects of the court invasion of drama, the cavalier
mood, cavalier drama and the Restoration heroic play, and
the trends in comedy. Part Two is a survey of the plays.

Hill, Christopher

Representative divisions of the work are the courtier playwrights, the amateurs of town and university, the professional playwrights, plays on the civil war, Caroline and
commonwealth private theatricals, closet drama of the commonwealth, and the last of the cavalier playwrights. There
is a conclusion, a chronological list of plays with pertinent information, and an addenda related to MS plays that
may belong to the period. The work is thorough and well-
indexed.

660   HARRIS, VICTOR. "The Arts of Discourse in England, 1500-1700."
       PQ, 37 (1958), 484-94.
       This article, while not directly related to drama, is
       interesting in association with the highly stylized and
       satirical use of "Platonic" dialogue which it discusses in
       regards to the late Caroline period.

661   HAWKINS, HARRIET. *Likeness of Truth in Elizabethan and
       Restoration Drama*. Oxford: Clarendon Press, 1972. 174pp.
       The author feels that "some very influential modern
       criticism has substituted moral criteria for dramatic cri-
       teria in its evaluation of characters, and thus imposed a
       relatively easy moral idealism upon the dramatic presenta-
       tion of certain hard facts about human experience." She
       counters this by analyzing eight Elizabethan and Jacobean
       plays, and three from the Restoration period, showing their
       "likeness in truth" or aspects of that concept in each of
       the plays. Compare with Bastiaenen's *Moral Tone of Jacobean
       and Caroline Drama* (1930).

662   HELTZEL, VIRGIL B. "The Dedication of Tudor and Stuart Plays."
       SEL, 65 (1957), 74-86.
       Heltzel is concerned primarily with plays up to 1625;
       however, his thesis and generalizations are background for
       a study of Caroline dedications.

663   HERRICK, MARVIN T. *Tragicomedy: Its Origins and Development
       in Italy, France and England*. Urbana: University of
       Illinois Press, 1955. vii, 329pp.
       The first seven chapters of Herrick's work are devoted
       to an analysis of the classical background and development
       of tragicomedy through Beaumont and Fletcher. Of particular
       interest are the final two chapters: "English Tragicomedy
       from Fletcher through Davenant," and "The Aftermath of
       Tragicomedy." There is a bibliography, as well as an index.

664   HILL, CHRISTOPHER. *Society and Puritanism in Pre-Revolutionary
       England*. London: Secker and Warburg, 1964. 520pp.

133

Holden, William P.

Hill's is a thorough study of the Puritan influence on social, economic, religious, and political matters from the late 1500's to the end of the 1640's. Check the index for *passim* references to Caroline authors.

665   HOLDEN, WILLIAM P. *Anti-Puritan Satire 1572-1642*. New Haven: Yale University Press, 1954. 165pp.
Chapter I, "The Evolving Pattern of Religious Dispute," and more specifically, Chapter II, "The Puritans and the Stage," are of use. Holden sees Jonson and Massinger as close "to the central points of the polemical and philosophical defenders of Anglicanism." He is weak in his evaluation of Brome and Shirley.

666   HOY, CYRUS. "Renaissance and Restoration Dramatic Plotting." *Ren D,* 9 (1966), 247-64.
Hoy points out that the action, in all the Jacobean and Caroline plays he discusses, "turns on frustrated passion, and frustrated passion is the mainspring of the action in the typical Restoration heroic play." He concludes that "to evoke admiration is to evoke wonder, and to arouse a sense of wonder is the whole endeavor of the drama of the late Jacobean, Caroline and Restoration periods."

667   HUGHES, LEO. *A Century of English Farce*. Princeton: Princeton University Press, 1956. 307pp.
The "century" referred to in the title is primarily from 1660-1750. Hughes' study is witty and urbane, and although he gives only a passing nod to Caroline dramatists, two chapters, "A Problem in Definition," and "Structure and Devices" are theoretically useful to a Caroline researcher.

668   JENKINS, HAROLD. *Edward Benlowes: Biography of a Minor Poet*. London: Athlone Press, 1952. 371pp.
Benlowes is noted here not because of his poetry, but because he was a spiritual and financial supporter or patron of several Caroline playwrights, and a contributor of Commendatory Verse.

669   JONES, F. L. "Echoes of Shakspere [*sic.*] in Later Elizabethan Drama." *PMLA,* 45 (1930), 791-803.
Jones gives much attention to the abundant Shakespearean allusions in Shakerley Marmion's *The Antiquary,* particularly its similarity to *Romeo and Juliet* (II.ii). He touches on Thomas Rawlins' tragedy *The Rebellion* as well.

670   JONES, RICHARD F. "Science and Language in England of the Mid-Seventeenth Century." *JEGP,* 31 (1932), 315-31.

Jones is concerned here with showing the origin of the "influence which science exerted upon the style of English prose, both secular and religious, in the early Restoration." The work is valuable when applied to rhetoric in late Caroline drama.

671   KAUFMANN, RALPH J., ed. *Elizabethan Drama: Modern Essays in Criticism*. NY: Oxford University Press, 1961. 372pp.
      Of particular note are the following essays: T. S. Eliot's "Philip Massinger," for his concern with *The City Madam*, and Kaufmann's "Ford's Tragic Perspective" for its treatment of *Love's Sacrifice* and *The Broken Heart*.

672   KERNAN, ALVIN. *The Cankered Muse: Satire of the English Renaissance*. New Haven: Yale University Press, 1959. 261pp.
      In Chapter IV, "The Satirist in the Theatre," Kernan is strong on early Jonson; however, the book is of most value here because of his "Theory of Satire" in Chapter I.

673   KLEIN, DAVID. *The Elizabethan Dramatists as Critics*. Westport, CT: Greenwood Press, 1963. 420pp.
      Klein makes frequent references to the works of Fletcher, Brome, Shirley, Jonson, Ford, Massinger, Randolph, Cartwright, Carew, Davenport, Heywood, Glapthorne, Thomas Killigrew, May, Mayne, Marmion, and other Caroline dramatists.

674   KNIGHT, G. WILSON. *The Golden Labyrinth*. London: Phoenix House Press, 1962. xiv, 402pp.
      Knight surveys drama from Greek to Georgian times; however pp. 110-123 are devoted to Caroline plays, especially those of John Ford.

675   KNIGHTS, L. C. *Drama and Society in the Age of Jonson*. London: Chatto and Windus, 1937. 347pp.
      A superb study of economic effects on the content of dramatic productions: Knight traces economic order from pre-Elizabethan times through Charles I as "Background"; the second section of the book deals with "The Dramatists," particularly Jonson, Dekker, Heywood, Middleton, and Massinger. There are frequent references to Brome, Shirley, and other Caroline dramatists, but the real worth of the book is the economic analysis that Knight establishes, and its application to Caroline drama.

676   KNOX, NORMAN. *The Word Irony and Its Context: 1500-1755*. Durham: Duke University Press, 1961. 258pp.

Koch, J.

>   Knox's work is an invaluable, contextual definition and
> etymological study of the word *irony* as well as its corol-
> lary terms, such as *raillery* and *banter*. The "dictionary"
> is segmented as to methods of ironic writing, such as irony
> as pretense and deception, irony as limited deception, as
> blame-by-praise and praise-by-blame, as contrariness through
> emphasis, as understatement, as indirection, as elaboration,
> and as derisive attack. There is an extensive bibliography
> and an index.

677   KOCH, J. "Echte und 'unechte' Masken." *E Studien,* 58 (1924),
>   179-212.
>   Although Koch is concerned primarily with masques of the
> early seventeenth century, he does discuss *Mercury Vindi-*
> *cated; The Fortunate Isles; Chloridia; Love's Triumph*
> *through Callipolis; Salmacida Spolia; Cupid and Death; The*
> *Sun's Darling;* and *Love's Mistress.*

678   LAIDLER, JOSEPHINE. "A History of Pastoral Drama in England
>   until 1700." *E Studien,* 35 (1905), 193-259.
>   Of note is Laidler's discussion of Jonson's *Sad Shepherd,*
> Shirley's *Love Tricks,* Knevet's *Rhodon and Iris,* Rutter's
> *Shepherds' Holiday,* Heywood's *Pleasant Dialogues* , Wilde's
> *Converted Robber,* Cowley's *Love's Riddle,* and Randolph's
> *Amyntas.* She also traces the critical reception of the
> pastoral drama.

679   LAWRENCE, T. E. *The French Stage in the XVIIth Century: A*
>   *Study in the Advent of the Italian Order.* Manchester:
>   Manchester University Press, 1957. 209pp.
>   Lawrence's is an extensive study of influence on the
> seventeenth-century French stage, and is useful for compari-
> son with the contemporary English stage. Included is an
> excellent bibliography of printed sources, manuscripts, and
> engravings.

680   LAWRENCE, WILLIAM J. *Pre-Restoration Stage Studies.*
>   Cambridge, MA: Harvard University Press, 1927. 435pp.
>   A series of sixteen interrelated essays, twelve of which
> apply directly to Caroline drama: Lawrence's suggestions
> and speculations on the origin of "the substantive theatre
> Masque," on collaboration and promptbooks, and other special
> topics are highly suggestive for further research in the
> field. The book is indexed primarily by author and work.

681   _____. *Those Nut-Cracking Elizabethans: Studies in the Early*
>   *Theatre and Drama.* London: Argonaut, 1935. 212pp.

Lawrence gives essays on a great mixture of topics, many of which are directly and indirectly related to Caroline drama, such as the use of animals in dramatic productions, stage furniture and its removers as well as removers of the dead, and on wedding songs. Check the index for references to Brome, Shirley, Davenant and others. There is a small section on Massinger's punctuation.

682 LEECH, CLIFFORD. *Shakespeare's Tragedies, and Other Studies in Seventeenth Century Drama*. London: Chatto and Windus, 1950. vii, 232pp.
Two chapters in Part II of this work are of particular note: "The Caroline Audience," and "Love as a Dramatic Theme." He notes "that Caroline audiences are often courtly, but it should be far more generally recognized that many Caroline plays were written for an entirely different public from the popular Elizabethan one." He pursues this discussion in the first chapter cited. Later, in his discussion of the theme of love, he is concerned with *'Tis Pity She's a Whore; The Antiquary; The Tragedy of Albertus Wallenstein; The Emperor of the East; The City Wit; The Guardian; Holland's Leaguer; The Witty Fair One; Love's Cruelty; The Distresses; The Hollander; The Gamester; News from Plymouth;* and others. Leech is also interested in "Catholic and Protestant Drama," and the theme of escape as it is associated with the theme of love in Caroline drama.

683 LEVIN, RICHARD. *The Multiple Plot in English Renaissance Drama*. Chicago: University of Chicago Press, 1971. xiv, 277pp.
Levin, in a work devoted primarily to Tudor and early Stuart plays, sets the groundwork for further analysis of the multiple plot structure.

684 LONG, JOHN, ed. *Music in English Renaissance Drama*. Lexington: University of Kentucky Press, 1968. xvi, 184pp.
Long's edition is a potpourri of essays by various hands on subjects loosely related to English plays and masques prior to 1642.

685 LOUGH, JOHN. *Paris Theatre Audiences in the Seventeenth and Eighteenth Centuries*. London: Oxford University Press, 1957. 293pp.
Chapters I, "The Age of Alexander Hardy," and II, "From Corneille to Lesage" are a good historical survey of French drama during the English Caroline period, and useful for comparative purposes. The size of the audience, its economic and social stratification, and the geographic

Lynch, Kathleen M.

location of theatres for special segments of the audience
are all focused on. A bibliography of primary and secondary
sources is included.

686　LYNCH, KATHLEEN M. *The Social Mode of Restoration Drama.*
NY: Macmillan, 1926. xii, 242pp.
　　Despite the title, approximately one half of Dr. Lynch's
book is devoted specifically to Caroline drama, and ultimately, its influence on the précieuse tradition from 1642-
1664. Of particular note are Chapters II, "The Trend of
Realistic Comedy from Jonson to Shirley"; III, "Court Influences on Serious Drama in the Reign of Charles I"; and
IV, "Court Influences on Comedy in the Reign of Charles I."
Lynch's book is a well-balanced discussion of dramatic
trends in Caroline and Restoration drama; the bibliography
and index are extensive.

687　LYONS, BRIDGET GELLERT. *Voices of Melancholy: Studies in
Literary Treatments of Melancholy in Renaissance England.*
London: Routledge and Kegan Paul, 1971. xvii, 189pp.
　　Lyons acknowledges that "the medical idea of the four
humors governing the human temperment is now entirely obsolete; it was in the process of becoming so at the very
time that English writers of the Renaissance were creating
literary masterpieces based upon it." Yet she notes that
"scientific propositions become especially susceptible to
literary treatment at the point where they lose their validity as science; their transformation into imagery involves
the blurring of those categories that make them applicable
only to one particular system of ideas." Upon this premise
she bases a thorough study of the treatment of melancholy
in Jacobean, and occasionally, Caroline literature. The
book is of more value as theory than as a study of a particular Caroline work. It is indexed and a bibliography is
included.

688　McCAULLEY, MARTHA GAUSE. "Function and Content of the
Prologue, Chorus, and Other Non-Dramatic Elements in
English Drama, from the Beginnings to 1642." In *Studies
in English Drama,* 1st ser. Ed. by Allison Gaw.
Philadelphia: University of Pennsylvania Press, 1917.
Pp. 161-258.
　　McCaulley discusses dramatic conventions related to what
are, essentially, non-dramatic elements in plays; consider-
able attention is given to Caroline prologues. The work is
indexed.

689 McDONALD, CHARLES OSBOURNE. *Rhetoric of Tragedy: Form in
Stuart Drama.* Amherst: University of Massachusetts Press,
1966. vii, 360pp.
The subject of this work "is an examination of the influences of the modes of rhetorical instruction used in
fifth century B.C. Greece, first century A.D. Rome," and
the English sixteenth and seventeenth centuries, "upon the
form of tragic drama in these three times and places."
McDonald's attack is both historical and critical, and in
the final chapter entitled "Stuart Tragedy in Decline," he
gives a comprehensive application of his thesis to John
Ford's *The Broken Heart. See also* the author's "The Design
of John Ford's *The Broken Heart*: A Study in the Development
of Caroline Sensibility," *SP,* 59 (1962), 141-61.

690 McEUEN, KATHERINE ANDERSON. *Classical Influences on the Tribe
of Ben.* Iowa: Columbia University Torch Books, 1939. xix,
316pp.
After defining "the tribe of Ben," McEuen discusses the
classical influences of Martial, Juvenal, Persius, Horace,
the Latin elegists, Virgil, Anacreon, and the general Greek
tradition. She concludes that the influence is general and
widespread. Check the index for references to Caroline
dramatists, particularly to Nathaniel Field, Cartwright,
Suckling, and Randolph. There is a rich bibliography of
sources related to the subject.

691 MACKIE, JOHN DUNCAN. *Cavalier and Puritans, 1603-49.* London:
Thomas Nelson and Sons, 1936. 270pp.
Mackie's book is a general discussion of the causes for
abrasion between puritans and cavaliers.

692 McPEEK, JAMES A. S. *The Black Book of Knaves and Unthrifts
in Shakespeare and Other Renaissance Authors.* Storrs:
University of Connecticut Press, 1969. xiii, 298pp.
McPeek's work is primarily a study of gypsies, vagabonds,
unthrifts, and such types as they appear in Tudor and Jacobean literature, but because of its thoroughness and its
theoretical analysis, it is included here: it should be
looked at in relation to works on the dissolution of householding, and in relation to the latter ironic treatments of
vagabonds, particularly Brome's *The Jovial Crew.* Check the
index for references to Ford, Brome, Massinger and others.

693 MANIFOLD, JOHN STREETER. *The Music in English Drama from
Shakespeare to Purcell.* London: Rockliff, 1956. 208pp.
The first half of Manifold's book is a discussion of
musical instruments, the musicians and ensemble, and types

Meigs, Joseph Avery

of music used in Renaissance drama during Shakespeare's
time and immediately afterward. Check the index for frequent references to Ford, Massinger, Jonson, and others.

694   MEIGS, JOSEPH AVERY. "Three Bold Gentlemen in Elizabethan
        Comedies." *DAI*, 32:1481-82A (University of Florida), 1971.
        174pp.
            The third play Meigs considers is Shirley's *The Lady of
        Pleasure* because it has "a hero who is an educated gentle-
        man of good birth, who is capable of proper behavior" even
        though he "breaks numerous rules."

695   MELLERS, WILFRED. *Harmonious Meeting: A Study of the
        Relationship between English Music, Poetry and Theatre,
        1600-1900*. London: Dennis Dobson, 1965. 317pp.
            Part One of this work is "From Mass to Masque"; Part Two
        is "From Masque to Musical Comedy." Mellers gives some at-
        tention to James Shirley, as well as "the Choral Ayre and
        the Caroline Anthem" and "Henry Lawes and the Caroline
        Ayre." The work is a thorough "exploration of the relation-
        ship between English music, poetry, and theatre by way of
        a detailed commentary on specific pieces."

696   MENDELSOHN, LEONARD RICHARD. "The Legends of Troy in English
        Renaissance Drama." *DAI*, 27:1033A (University of
        Wisconsin), 1966. 326pp.
            Mendelsohn extends his study as far as Shirley's *Conten-
        tion of Ajax and Ulysses* (1640). His dissertation "concen-
        trates on the Troy plays specifically. In its larger
        implications, it suggests that theme, so often considered
        pliable, possessing stuff which an author shapes at whim,
        may be in fact an active and controlling force."

697   MIGNON, ELISABETH. *Crabbed Age and Youth: The Old Men and
        Women in the Restoration Comedy of Manners*. Durham: Duke
        University Press, 1947. viii, 194pp.
            An excellent study of a particular set of characters and
        their relationships: Mignon's study is pertinent not only
        to the Restoration drama, but also to late Caroline drama
        as well. There are discussions of *The Lady of Pleasure*;
        The Wild Goose Chase; *The Parson's Wedding*; and others.

698   MILES, THEODORE. "Place-Realism in a Group of Caroline Plays."
        RES, 18 (1942), 428-40.
            Miles acknowledges that "the preservation of adequate
        external evidence of a play's relationship to the fads of
        its age is . . . purely accidental. For this reason, a
        group of six realistic plays of the Caroline period, which

catered, demonstrably, to certain transitory interests of
the seventeenth-century Londoner is of more than usual interest and significance." He proceeds to thoroughly analyze
the vogue of place-realism in *Holland's Leaguer; Hyde Park;
Covent Garden Weeded; The Sparagus Garden;* Nabbes' *Covent
Garden,* and *Tottenham Court. See also* Richard Perkinson's
"Topographical comedies in the Seventeenth Century," *ELH,*
3 (1936); and Albert Wertheim's "Games and Courtship in
James Shirley's *Hyde Park*," *Anglia,* 90 (1972) for a different treatment of *Hyde Park.*

699   MILLER, EDWIN HAVILAND. *The Professional Writer in
      Elizabethan England: A Study of Non-Dramatic Literature.*
      Cambridge, MA: Harvard University Press, 1959. xii, 282pp.
         Miller's study of professional writers and publishers is
      outside the date of this work, but it is valuable as back-
      ground material for a study of the professional writer dur-
      ing the Caroline period. He deals with the authors in their
      milieu, their audience and its taste, patronage, the writ-
      er's relationship with stationers and censors, and the
      "pennie knaves."

700   MILLS, LAURENS JOSEPH. *"One Soul in Bodies Twain": Friend-
      ship in Tudor Literature and Stuart Drama.* Bloomington:
      Principia Press, 1937. vii, 470pp.
         Mills found in his study that "Especially fruitful was
      the conflict that ensued when love and friendship interests
      clashed; the drama was the principal beneficiary and the
      dramatic use of the opposing themes in juxtaposition de-
      mands a large share of [this work]." Chapters V and VI,
      entitled "The Period of Shakespeare and Stuart Drama," and
      "From Socrates to Shirley" are of particular note. Check
      the index for numerous references to Caroline dramatists,
      particularly Brome, Ford, Shirley, and Carlell.

701   MISH, CHARLES C. "Comparative Popularity of Early Fiction and
      Drama." *N & Q* (June 1952), pp. 269-70.
         Between 1475 and 1642 there were approximately 717 pub-
      lished works of fiction and 881 of drama. Mish concludes
      that "Tudor-Stuart drama is artistically superior to Tudor-
      Stuart fiction," but that both were about equally popular.

702   MITCHELL, ELEANOR RETTIG. "Pronouns of Address in English,
      1580-1780: A Study of Form Changes as Reflected in British
      Drama." *DAI,* 32:4593A (Texas A & M University), 1971.
      165pp.
         "This computer-aided statistical study has examined the
      changes which took place in the pronouns of address in

Monro, John

British drama during 200 years of the Early Modern English
period." Jonson, Ford, Shirley, and Davenant are the Caroline dramatists involved.

703 MONRO, JOHN, ed. *The Shakespeare Allusion Book: A
     Collection of Allusions to Shakespeare from 1591-1700.*
     London: Chatto and Windus, 1909. 2 vols.
        Volume I contains an introduction, a chronological list
     of allusions, and the allusions themselves. Volume II,
     among other things, has an appendix of information on
     Shakespeare's influence on Jacobean and Caroline drama.

704 MOORE, JOHN ROBERT. "The Songs of the Public Theatres in the
     Time of Shakespeare." *JEGP*, 28 (1929), 166-202.
        Moore concludes that "Before 1616, the tendency toward
     off-stage singing and toward dramatic irrelevancy of the
     songs had made no great progress in the public theatres.
     The singer of the Romantic plays had ceased to be the mere
     clown of the Moralities and Interludes, without yet be-
     coming the mere singer of Caroline and Restoration drama."
     In the process, he analyzes the uses of jigs and other ir-
     relevant comic songs, ballads and popular songs, and "drama-
     tic songs written or adapted expressly for the plays." He
     also surveys the role of the major actor-musicians of the
     Renaissance.

705 MULLANY, PETER FRANCIS. "The Dramatic Use of Religious
     Materials in Jacobean and Caroline Plays." *DAI*, 28:1405A
     (Fordham University), 1967. 230pp.
        Mullany discusses the use of religious materials in
     Jacobean and Caroline plays and the various purposes to
     which they are put: occasionally as an "emotional fillip,"
     as "passionate rhetoric, contrived scenes, and the recurring
     use of surprise." Among other plays, he is concerned with
     Massinger's *The Renegado*.

706 MYERS, AARON MICHAEL. *Representation and Misrepresentation of
     the Puritan in Elizabethan Drama.* Philadelphia:
     University of Pennsylvania Press, 1931. 151pp.
        In the latter parts of the book, Myers touches on Caro-
     line attitudes to Puritans. He discusses Randolph's *Hey
     for Honesty*, and *The Muse's Looking Glass*, Cowley's *The
     Cutter of Coleman Street* and *The Guardian*.

707 NICOLL, ALLARDYCE. *The Development of the Theatre: A Study
     of Theatrical Art from the Beginnings to the Present Day.*
     NY: Harcourt, Brace and World, 1966. xix, 292pp.

Orgel, Stephen Kitay

Chapters VI and VII of Nicoll's well-illustrated history are pertinent to Caroline drama; they are concerned with the Renaissance in France, England and Spain, and the baroque drama and its legacy.

708 _____. "Origin and Types of the Heroic Tragedy." *Anglia,* 44 (1920), 325-36.
Having separated out the spurious issue of theme *vs.* blank verse in tragedy, Nicoll explores some origins of heroic plays in Elizabethan and early Caroline drama. The "mighty individualism of its heroes" is one prerequisite of heroic drama, as well as the "violent and exaggerated love-passion which characterizes the entire heroic school." These characteristics Nicoll sees as having their origins prior to Dryden and Orrery.

709 _____. *Restoration Drama, 1660-1700.* 2nd ed. Cambridge: The University Press, 1928. vi, 412pp.
In the early section of his book, Nicoll makes frequent comparisons between Caroline and Restoration audiences, their influence on the drama, scenery, actors and actresses. The work is thoroughly indexed.

710 OBAID, THORAYA AHMED. "The Moor Figure in English Renaissance Drama." *DAI,* 35:4446A (Wayne State University), 1974. 616pp.
Obaid states that "The Moorish *dramatis personnae* in English Renaissance drama are a product of certain medieval and Renaissance historical circumstances in which Christian Europe and the Muslim states traded, warred, and made peace." After an evaluation of historical materials, the author treats Milicent in Brome's *The English Moor,* Massinger's *The Bondman* and *The Renegado,* and Raymond in Thomas Randolph's *The Rebellion,* as well as others.

711 OCCHIOGROSSO, FRANK VICTOR. "Sovereign and Subject in Caroline Tragedy." *DAI,* 30:2493-94A (Johns Hopkins University), 1969. 264pp.
Occhiogrosso examines "the political vision of a number of tragedies written in the Caroline era. . . "; predominant are *The Roman Actor; Perkin Warbeck; Believe As You List; The Traitor; The Polititian;* and *The Cardinal.*

712 ORGEL, STEPHEN KITAY. *The Illusion of Power: Political Theatre in the English Renaissance.* Berkeley: University of California Press, 1975. x, 95pp.
Orgel's is a thorough examination of the machinery (both theatrical and political) that constituted a Renaissance court performance.

Orgel, Stephen Kitay

713 _____ and ROY STRONG. *Inigo Jones: The Theatre of the Stuart Court.* Berkeley and Los Angeles: University of California Press, 1973. 2 vols.
This is a definitive survey of Jones' work and that of others associated with him gleaned from the collection of the Duke of Devonshire. The texts of most masques referred to are included, and the volumes are copiously illustrated with Jones' pictoral work. Of particular note is informa- tion related to *Love's Triumph through Callipoles; Chloridia; Albion's Triumph; Coelum Britannicum; Florimène; Britannia Triumphans; Salmacida Spolia;* and *The Queen of Aragon.*

714 ORNSTEIN, ROBERT. *The Moral Vision of Jacobean Tragedy.* Madison: University of Wisconsin Press, 1960. viii, 299pp.
Ornstein's chapter on John Ford contains references to criticism of *The Cardinal; 'Tis Pity; The Lady's Trial; The Broken Heart; Love's Sacrifice; Perkin Warbeck;* and *The Lover's Melancholy.*

715 PARROTT, THOMAS MARC and ROBERT HAMILTON BALL. *A Short View of Elizabethan Drama.* 1943; rept. NY: Scribner and Sons, 1958. vi, 311pp.
Various chapters of Parrott and Ball's work are related to Caroline drama, notably VI on Ben Jonson; VII on the later comedy, both satiric and realistic, that includes discussions of the work of Middleton, Marston and Brome; IX on the Jacobean tragedies of Marston, Tourner, Webster, Middleton and Ford; and X on the work of Massinger, Shirley, Davenant, and the late court masques. There is a bibliog- raphy, by chapters, and an index.

716 PERKINSON, R. H. "Topographical Comedy in the Seventeenth Century." *ELH,* 3 (1936), 270-90.
Perkinson sees topographical comedy, in the seventeenth century, "as a genre," not because it includes plays labeled by the names of particular parks, fairs or gardens, but be- cause it is the comedy of manners and intrigues of habitués of some definite, popular locality. He gives attention to Shirley's *Hyde Park,* Nabbes' *Covent Garden* and *Tottenham Court,* and Brome's *Sparagus Garden* and *Covent Garden Weeded,* and likens them in intent and achievement with similar plays in the Restoration. There is also some commentary on Jordan's *The Walks of Islington and Hogsdon.*

717 PICKEL, MARGARET BERNARD. *Charles I as Patron of Poetry and Drama.* London: Frederich Muller, 1936. 192pp.

Reed, Robert Rentoul, Jr.

The author begins her work with an analysis of royal patronage of literature and of the character, education, and abilities of Charles I. The internal chapters are concerned with court influence and Platonic love, court and royalist poets, patronage of court drama and of the masque. The conclusion reiterates the fact that "almost all the poets and dramatists of importance were in contact in one way or another with Charles I as a patron." An appendix includes works attributed to Charles I; the book is not indexed.

718   POWELL, CHILTON LATHAM. *English Domestic Relations, 1487-
1653: A Study of Matrimony and Family Life in Theory and Practice as Revealed by the Literature, Law, and History of the Period.* NY: Columbia University Press, 1917. xii, 274pp.
Powell discusses laws, practice, and customs related to marriage through the special topics of historical controversies regarding marriage, attempted reforms of marriage and divorce laws, domestic conduct books, contemporary attitudes toward women, and domestic drama. Three bibliographies cover early books on domestic relations, books on Henry VIII's divorce, and later books of reference. The work is indexed by subject, author, and work.

719   PRIOR, MOODY ERASMUS. *The Language of Tragedy.* NY: Columbia University Press, 1954. viii, 411pp.
In his almost book-length chapter entitled "The Elizabethan Tradition," Prior gives a discussion of the tragic elements in *The Broken Heart,* and frequent passing references to other Caroline plays. He is primarily concerned with the nature of tragedy as it is exhibited in characterization, dialogue, diction, structure, theme, imagery, and allusion. The book is thoroughly indexed.

720   REED, ROBERT RENTOUL, JR. *Bedlam on the Jacobean Stage.*
Cambridge, MA: Harvard University Press, 1952. vi, 190pp.
Of particular note is Chapter VI: "John Ford and the Refinement of Bedlam," in which Reed views Ford as a Jacobean-oriented playwright of a somewhat reactionary nature. The complete volume, however, is of use as a background for the study of Bedlam on the stage and in contemporary pathological studies of madness.

721   _____. *The Occult on the Tudor and Stuart Stage.* Boston: Christopher Publishing House, 1965. 284pp.
Reed's work is a stage history of drama of supernaturalism in Tudor and Stuart England, and it deals with otherworldly characters such as witches, demons, sorcerers, and

Reynolds, Myra

> so forth. Chapter V: "Puck, Oberon and Later Demons" re-
> lates specifically to Caroline drama; however Chapters I–IV,
> which are historical surveys, are useful for background ma-
> terial. There is a comprehensive bibliography. Check the
> index for listings of individual authors and works.

722 REYNOLDS, MYRA. *The Learned Lady in England, 1650-1760.*
Boston and NY: Houghton Mifflin Company, 1920. 489pp.
In her first chapter, Reynolds gives a survey of Renais-
sance learned ladies and attitudes towards them.

723 ROGERS, KATHARINE M. *The Troublesome Helpmate: A History of
Misogyny in Literature.* Seattle and London: University of
Washington Press, 1966. 288pp.
Chapter III and IV give a good overview of particular
literary and social types, *e.g.*, the court wanton, the bossy
bourgeoise, and the insatiable strumpet. There is also an
extended discussion of Puritan attitudes toward women. The
book is indexed by author, title, and to a certain extent,
subject matter.

724 ROLLINS, HYDER E. "The Commonwealth Drama: Miscellaneous
Notes." *SP,* 20 (1923), 52-69.
The notes included here supplement those in Rollins' "A
Contribution to the History of the English Commonwealth
Drama," *SP,* 18 (1921), 267-333. Although both works are
concerned with drama slightly on the far side of this study,
both are filled with interesting notes on people, plays, and
places frequently related to Caroline drama.

725 _____. "A Contribution to the History of the English
Commonwealth Drama." *SP,* 18 (1921), 267-333.
Rollins includes many notes on plays, authors, and dramatic incidents between 1640 and 1660. His commentary is supplemented in "The Commonwealth Drama: Miscellaneous Notes"
and this article should be read in conjunction with its
companion piece (*See* 724).

726 RØSTVIG, MAREN-SOFIE. *The Happy Man: Studies in the
Metamorphoses of a Classical Ideal, 1600-1760.* Oslo and
London: Akademisk Forlag, 1954, 1958. 2 vols.
Røstvig treats the notion of the happy man, similar to
the Horatian *beatus vir* idea, which runs counter-point to
the ideas of melancholia in seventeenth- and eighteenth-
century literature. Volume I is of particular interest;
there are indices to authors and subjects.

727   RUSSELL, H. K.   "Tudor and Stuart Dramatizations of the
        Doctrines of Natural and Moral Philosophy."   *SP*, 31 (1934),
        1-27.
            Among other plays considered, Russell mentions William
        Strode's *The Floating Island*, Ford's *The Lover's Melancholy*,
        and Nabbes' *Microcosmus*. He shows how the main themes and
        issues in these plays are selected to illustrate and drama-
        tize one or more philosophical doctrines.

728   RYS, SISTER MARY ELLEN.   "The Rise of Sentimentalism in
        Jacobean and Caroline Drama."   *DAI*, 13:668-69A (University
        of Notre Dame), 1952. 401pp.
            Rys considers the major romantic tragicomedies of Beau-
        mont and Fletcher, Shakespeare, Massinger, Sherby, Ford,
        Davenant, Killigrew, Glapthorne, Carlell, Cartwright,
        Berkeley and Suckling. The purpose of the study is to in-
        vestigate the origin of romantic and philosophical senti-
        mentalism and the significant rise of the phenomenon in the
        romantic tragicomedies and the middle-class drama of the
        Jacobean and Caroline periods.

729   SABOL, ANDREW J.   "Recent Studies in Music and English
        Renaissance Drama."   *SRO*, 4 (1968-69), 1-15.
            Sabol reviews the scholarship related to song and music
        in Renaissance drama, and predicts what direction scholar-
        ship in this field will take.

730   SCHELLING, FELIX E.   *Elizabethan Drama:* 1558-1642. 2nd. ed.
        Boston and NY: Houghton Mifflin Co., 1908. 2 vols.
            In Volume I, note the latter segments of Chapter VI,
        "National Historical Drama," Chapter VII, "Domestic Drama,"
        and Chapter XII, "Romantic Tragedy." In Volume II, note
        Chapters XII, on Thomas May and Richards' *Messalina;* XIV,
        on "College Drama" and Thomas Randolph; XV, on "The English
        Masque"; XVII, on "Tragi-comedy and 'Romance'"; XVIII, on
        "Later Comedy of Manners"; XIX, on "Decadent Romance"; and
        XX, on "The Drama in Retrospect" in which Schelling surveys
        the impact of "Carolan" drama. The index follows Volume II.

731   _____. *Elizabethan Playwrights: A Short History of English
        Drama from Medieval Times to the Close of the Theatre in
        1642.* NY and London: Harper and Row, 1925. 335pp.
            Of general interest is Chapter XIII, "The Cavalier Drama-
        tists," and the effect it has had on later critics and his-
        torians of Caroline drama. Note the "List of Important
        Dates" as well as the index.

Schelling, Felix E.

732   _____. "Features of the Supernatural as Represented in Plays
        of the Reigns of Elizabeth and James." *MP*, 1 (1903),
        31-47.
           Schelling concludes his study with an examination of
        Heywood and Brome's *The Late Lancashire Witches*.

733   SCOTT, FLORENCE R.   "Teg: The Stage Irishman." *MLR*, 42
        (1947), 314-20.
           In opposition to points made by J. O. Bartley in "The
        Development of a Stock Character in *Hyde Park*. . . ." *MLR*
        (1942), 438-48, Scott establishes new criteria for determin-
        ing the nature of stock Irishmen on the English stage. The
        article focuses on four types of characters: the Irish in
        the dumb shows, the sham Irishman, the Irish soldier, and
        the Irish serving man. *See also* W. J. Lawrence's "Irish
        Types in Old-Time English Drama," *Anglia*, 35 (1912), 347-56.

734   SEATON, ETHEL. *Literary Relations of England and Scandinavia
        in the Seventeenth Century*. Oxford: Clarendon Press, 1935.
        xv, 384pp.
           Seaton gives general attention to the works of Ford,
        Massinger and Shirley, particularly the latter, while she
        traces the influence of these dramatists in Scandinavia.
        There is an extensive bibliography and an index to persons
        and places.

735   SHARMA, R. C. *Themes and Conventions in the Comedy of Manners*.
        London: Asia Publishing House, 1965. 354pp.
           Sharma's book is concerned with comedy of manners in the
        Restoration period, and more specifically, with the charac-
        ter types and conventions associated with comedies of manner.
        Nonetheless, his early discussion of fops, fools, and sty-
        lized behavior is applicable to late Renaissance drama.

736   SHARP, CECIL J., comp. *The Country Dance Book*. London:
        Novello and Company, 1909-16. 2 vols.
           In his introduction to Part I, Sharp distinguishes between
        the Morris dance and the country dance, and discusses the
        nomenclature and configurations he uses to illustrate the
        various dances. The majority of this section is devoted to
        eighteen country dances, and the notation of their steps and
        figures. Part II is a collection of thirty-five more dances;
        Part III is an amplification of Part II; Part IV contains
        fifty-two dances.

737   SILVETTE, HERBERT. "The Doctor on the Stage: Medicine and
        Medical Men in Seventeenth-Century English Drama." *Annals
        of Medical History*, n.s., 8-9 (1937-38); vol. 8:   35-47;
        vol. 9:   62-87; 174-88; 264-79; 371-94; 482-507.

Silvette's study is a thorough examination of dramatic literature and the characterization of doctors. An extensive bibliography follows the work.

738   SINGLETON, CHARLES SOUTHWARD. *Art, Science and History in the Renaissance*. Baltimore: Johns Hopkins University Press, 1967. vii, 446pp.
The work, through various essays, shows the correspondence between art, music, science, and history during the continental Renaissance, and the English Renaissance.

739   SMITH, G. C. MOORE. *College Plays*. Cambridge: University Press, 1923. 110pp.
Smith is concerned preeminently with Cambridge plays from the late 1400's until 1641/42. He gives an outline of the history of college plays, discusses the manner of their production, and concludes with a chronological table of plays by title, author, date and location (when such information is available), as well as a list of actors and some bibliographical notes.

740   SMITH, HOMER. "Pastoral Influence in the English Drama." *PMLA*, 5 (1897), 355-460.
After defining pastoral drama, Smith devotes the majority of his article to early Renaissance drama; however, he does make references to Thomas Goffe's *The Careless Shepherdess*, Ralph Knevet's *Rhodon and Iris*, Walter Montague's *The Shepherd's Paradise*, Randolph's *Amyntas*, Joseph Rutter's *The Shepherds' Holiday*, Cowley's *Love's Riddle*, and others. He discusses the differences between pastoral-constructed plays on Italian models, and those from original plots. He concludes that "Some of the plays are redeemed by occasional passages of genuine poetry, or by satiric or allegorical significance and are historically interesting because they show the extreme interest in the pastoral *motiv*, and especially the extraordinary influence of Tasso and Guarini."

741   SMITH, JOHN HARRINGTON. *The Gay Couple in Restoration Comedy*. Cambridge, MA: Harvard University Press, 1948. 252pp.
The first chapter of Smith's work, "The Love Duel in English Comedy before the Restoration" is a witty, well-documented analysis of patterns in middle and late Caroline dramas. Chapters II and III, on Platonism and "Love as a Game," should be consulted, as well as the general index. Smith gives particular attention to *The Parson's Wedding*; *Aglaura*; *The Temple of Love*; *The Platonic Lovers*; *Hyde Park*; and *A Mad Couple Well-Matched*.

Soet, Frans Dirk, De

742   SOET, FRANS DIRK, DE. *Puritan and Royalist Literature in the
        Seventeenth Century.* Delft: J. Waltman, Jr., 1932. 163pp.
            Chapters on Prynne, Carew, Suckling, Denham, and Cowley
        are included in this volume, as well as a discussion of
        songs and ballads. The Table of Contents concludes the
        work.

743   SORELIUS, GUNNAR. *"The Great Race before the Flood": Pre-
        Restoration Drama on the Stage and in the Criticism of the
        Restoration.* Uppsala: Almquist and Wilksells, 1966. 227pp.
            Despite the title, Sorelius' book is devoted more to Res-
        toration than to Caroline drama. The book is useful primar-
        ily for its discussion of Restoration adaptations of earlier
        works, and for the sense of continuity and flow which it
        stresses. It is well indexed.

744   SPEK, CORNELIUS, VAN DER. *The Church and the Churchman in
        English Dramatic Literature before 1642.* Amsterdam: H. J.
        Paris, 1930. vii, 188pp.
            The latter chapters of this work (VIII-XIII) are of value
        here for the discussion of Roman Catholic and Anglican char-
        acters on the late Renaissance stage. The work has a bibli-
        ography, a list of plays before 1642 in which church
        characters play roles, and an index by author and title.

745   SPENCER, THEODORE. *Death and Elizabethan Tragedy.* Cambridge,
        MA: Harvard University Press, 1936. xii, 288pp.
            Spencer includes frequent discussions of works by Ford
        and Massinger in his analysis of conflict, language, idea
        and dramatic technique in Renaissance tragedy. His final
        chapter, "The Drama and the Renaissance Mind" is an overview
        of dramatic theory related to tragedy directed toward a
        specific period.

746   SPINGARN, JOEL ELIAS, ed. *Critical Essays of the Seventeenth
        Century.* Vol. I. Oxford: Clarendon Press, 1908-09. cvi,
        255pp.
            Spingarn's introductory chapters, from II, "Early Caro-
        line Tentatives," through IX, "The School of Taste," are a
        distillation of late Renaissance attitudes toward the arts,
        particularly literature. The volume also includes critical
        essays, some from 1627-1642.

747   STEELE, MARY SUSAN. *Plays and Masques at Court during the
        Reigns of Elizabeth, James and Charles.* 1926; rept. NY:
        Russell and Russell, 1968. xii, 300pp.
            Steele's work is a fairly comprehensive checklist of as
        much source material related to any given performance as the

author has been able to locate. In this work, the term
"court performance has been extended to include all dramatic
representations before the sovereigns and other members of
the royal family, on progresses as well as in their resi-
dences." *See also* Chapter II: "The Reign of Charles I."

748   STENTON, DORIS MARY. *The English Woman in History*. London:
       Allen and Unwin, 1957. 363pp.
           The book surveys "the place women have held and the in-
       fluence they have exerted" from the earliest writing of
       Tacitus through John Stuart Mill's *The Subjugation of Women*
       in 1869. Chapters IV through VII are of particular note.
       The book is well indexed.

749   STONEX, ARTHUR B. "The Usurer in Elizabethan Drama." *PMLA*,
       31 (1916), 190-210.
           Stonex is concerned with the way in which the character
       of the usurer effects the plot of Renaissance literature.
       Except for R. J. Kaufmann's discussion of usury in *Richard
       Brome: Caroline Playwright* (1961), this is the most thor-
       ough discussion of the topic as it relates to Renaissance
       drama exclusive of Shylock. Stonex discusses literary and
       social attitudes toward usury, chronologically traces the
       usurer in Renaissance drama, and focuses on Brome's *The
       Damoiselle*; *The English Moor*; *The Night Walker*; Marmion's
       A Fine Companion; Cartwright's *The Ordinary*; Shirley's *Love
       Tricks*; *The Wedding*; and *The Constant Maid*; Jonson's *The
       Staple of News*; and *The Magnetic Lady*; and Davenant's *The
       Wits*. The majority of the article is concerned with Caro-
       line drama and how the theme of usury climaxed it. He notes
       that seventy-one plays, written between 1553 and 1642, have
       a usurer character.

750   SYPHER, WYLIE. *Four Stages of Renaissance Style:
       Transformations in Art and Literature 1400-1700*. NY:
       Doubleday, 1955. 312pp.
           Sypher's is a thorough introduction to systems of thought
       and practice in regards to the relationship between art and
       literature. The particular emphasis is on general Renais-
       sance style, mannerism, and baroque styles. The work in-
       cludes a bibliographical note, and is well indexed.

751   THOMAS, DONALD. *Long Time Burning: The History of Literary
       Censorship in England*. London: Routledge and Kegan Paul,
       1969. xii, 546pp.
           Thomas' work is an overview of censorship in England from
       1476 through the twentieth century. Chapters I and II, "The
       Fear of Literature," and "Censorship before Publication:

Ure, Peter

> 1476-1695" are of value, particularly because of the dis-
> cussion of licensing systems, the recognition of obscene
> literature, and the end of the licensing system. There is
> a selected bibliography, an index, and an appendix consist-
> ing of "a collection of documents . . . to illustrate
> various aspects of the history of literary censorship."

752 URE, PETER. "The 'Deformed Mistress' Theme and the Platonic
     Convention." *N & Q* (June 1948), pp. 269-70.
        Ure makes reference to Shirley's *The Duke's Mistress* and
     Walter Montague's *Shepherd's Paradise,* and concludes that
     "Shirley's use of the theme of the deformed mistress in
     [his] play indicates a consciousness of the relevance of
     the theme to Platonic préciosité, and that his scope was
     large enough to handle the type of subject that may be re-
     garded as particularly the property of a courtier like
     Suckling." *See also* Samuel Schoenbaum's "The 'Deformed
     Mistress' Theme in Chapman's *Gentleman Usher*," *N & Q*
     (January 1960), pp. 22-24.

753 WARD, A. W. and A. R. WALLER, eds. *Cambridge History of
     English Literature.* Vol. VI, Part II. NY: Putnam, 1910.
     vii, 593pp.
        Of concern in this volume of the *CHEL* is Chapter VI,
     "Philip Massinger," Chapter VIII, "Ford and Shirley," and
     Chapter IX, "Lesser Jacobean and Caroline Dramatists," par-
     ticularly for the discussion of the works of Nathaniel
     Field, Richard Brome, Thomas Randolph, Thomas May, and
     Thomas Nabbes; some attention is also given to Davenport,
     Cartwright, Mayne, Suckling, Marmion, Carlell, Glapthorne,
     and Davenant. Chapter X, "The Elizabethan Theatre," is
     concerned with Tudor and early Stuart dramatic conditions
     and policies; there is also a discussion of later private
     theatres, performances at court, Jacobean and Caroline
     audiences, and the social position of the actor.

754 WEDGWOOD, C. V. "Comedy in the Reign of Charles I." In
     Studies in Social History: A Tribute to G. M. Trevelyan.
     Ed. by J. H. Plumb. London: Oxford University Press,
     1955. Pp. 111-37.
        Wedgwood gives a general survey of Caroline comedy, al-
     though he confuses Mayne's *The City Match* with Brome's *The
     City Wit.*

755 WELSFORD, ENID. *The Court Masque: A Study in the Relationship
     between Poetry and the Revels.* Cambridge: University
     Press, 1927. 434pp.

Winslow, Ola Elizabeth

In Part I, Chapter VII, "The Caroline Masque," Welsford
discusses Platonic influences, the roles of Inigo Jones and
Prynne in dramatic history, and many Caroline masques, particularly those of Shirley, Davenant, and Carew. Part II
traces the influence of the masque, and those themes and
ideas which influenced the masque. There is a comprehensive
index.

756 WEST, ROBERT HUNTER. *The Invisible World: A Study of
Pneumatology in Elizabethan Drama.* Athens: University of
Georgia Press, 1939. 275pp.
West's work is a comprehensive and well-documented study
of witches, ghosts, magic, and demonology, focused primarily
on drama prior to 1620. However, there are many citations
to *The Late Lancashire Witches* and Massinger's *The Unnatural
Combat,* and the work serves as a foundation for further
studies of demonology in Caroline drama.

757 WHITE, H. O. *Plagiarism and Imitation during the English
Renaissance.* Cambridge, MA: Harvard University Press,
1935. x, 209pp.
Chapter IV of White's work, "The Theory of Imitation
from Jonson Onward," is of particular note, although the
study ostensibly ends at 1625. Numerous late Renaissance
sources are cited in regards to the theory of imitation.

758 WILEY, MARGARET LENORE. *The Subtle Knot: Creative Skepticism
in Seventeenth-Century England.* 1952; rept. NY:
Greenwood Press, 1968. 303pp.
Wiley is concerned with the intellectual rather than the
dramatic history of the seventeenth century but the book is
of value when associated with the patterns of blatant skepticism expressed in Caroline tragedies and tragicomedies.
The work sheds light on the social and intellectual atmos-
phere which is either ironically or satirically portrayed
in the late comedies.

759 WILSON, RODNEY EARL. "The Influence of Stoicism on Jacobean
Drama." *DAI,* 36:8038A (North Texas State University),
1973. 234pp.
Wilson, in Chapter III of his dissertation, identifies
stoicism at its "purest" in Massinger's *The Roman Actor* and
Believe As You List. Chapter IV is concerned with the
works of Jonson, Ford, and others.

760 WINSLOW, OLA ELIZABETH. *Low Comedy as a Structural Element in
English Drama from the Beginnings to 1642.* Menasha, WI:
George Banta, 1926. xi, 186pp.

Wright, Celeste Turner

>   Chapters V and VI, "Low Comedy in New Types of Drama,"
> and "Low Comedy in Relation to English Techniques and to
> Dramatic Theory," are of particular note. There is no in-
> dex, but in later chapters Winslow refers to *Tottenham
> Court; Perkin Warbeck; The Fancies; St. Patrick for Ireland;
> The Lady Mother; The Queen and the Concubine; The Staple of
> News; The Triumph of Peace; The Doubtful Heir; The Unfor-
> tunate Lovers;* and others.

761   WRIGHT, CELESTE TURNER. "Some Conventions Regarding the
         Usurer in Elizabethan Literature." *SP*, 31 (1934), 176-98.
         Wright discusses "important conventions regarding the
       stage usurer in the light of non-dramatic literature, es-
       pecially the writings of the moralists," giving particular
       attention to Thomas Wilson, Gerard de Malynes, Samuel
       Rowlands, and others.

762   _____. "The Usurer's Sin in Elizabethan Literature." *SP*, 35
         (1938), 178-94.
         Wright suggests that the plots of dramas in which a
       usurer is a character "fall into two or three patterns; ac-
       counts of his methods have a family likeness, and almost
       every detail of his person and habits can be predicted."
       Many Caroline plays are cited for examples.

763   WRIGHT, LOUIS B. "Animal Actors on the English Stage before
         1642." *PMLA*, 42 (1927), 656-69.
         Of particular note is Wright's commentary on Shirley's
       The Bird in a Cage and *St. Patrick for Ireland,* and Brome
       and Heywood's *The Late Lancashire Witches*. He concludes
       that "The evidence goes to show that animal acts on the
       English stage before 1642 were more frequent than the texts
       of the plays prove."

764   _____. "Extraneous Song in Elizabethan Drama after the Advent
         of Shakespeare." *SP*, 24 (1927), 261-74.
         Wright's article was, for a long time, upheld; now it is
       frequently questioned because he believed that song in plays
       after Shakespeare were as extraneous as songs in plays pre-
       Shakespeare. He sees them as "important entertaining fea-
       tures of the play," used only for variety, allowing the
       actors a chance to use their musical skills." The latter
       part of the article is devoted primarily to song in Caroline
       plays.

765   _____. "Juggling Tricks and Conjuring on the English Stage
         before 1642." *MP*, 24 (1927), 28-34.

Wright, Louis B.

Wright points out the uses of legerdemain in Renaissance plays; of note is his discussion of *The Magnetic Lady; Covent Garden Weeded; The Late Lancashire Witches; The Chances;* and plays produced at the Red Bull.

766 _____. "The Male Friendship Cult in Heywood's Plays." *MLN,* 42 (1927), 510-14.
Of particular note is Wright's statement that "In none of Heywood's plays . . . is the ideal of loyalty in friendship between men carried to more exaggerated extremes than in *A Challenge for Beauty.*"

767 _____. "The Reading of Plays during the Puritan Revolution." *HLB,* 6 (1934), 73-108.
Wright's article is a narrative checklist of plays available and being read during the Interregnum. He mentions works by Massinger, Brome, Jonson, Davenant, Peaps, Shirley, Carlell, Mayne, Suckling, Tatham, Cartwright, Randolph, and others.

768 _____. "The Reading of Renaissance English Women." *SP,* 28 (1931), 671-88.
Wright surveys women's reading tastes from the 1570's to 1641, and elaborates on social standards and attitudes towards women's education. Special attention is given to women of serving classes, governesses, school mistresses, and the contemporary penchant for "romances of all types."

769 _____. "Social Aspects of Some Belated Moralities." *Anglia,* 54 (1930), 107-48.
Among other things, Wright discusses the literary background for and use of the usurer in dramatic works. He notes that morality, by 1600, "had become a vehicle for social and political propaganda [and] the tradition, carried over into Jacobean and Carolinian drama, found favor in academic circles."

770 _____. "Variety-Show Clownery on the Pre-Restoration Stage." *Anglia,* 40 (1928), 51-68.
Wright's purpose is "to show how dramatists and producers catered to the taste of an uncritical audience by inserting comic material irrelevant and unrelated to dramatic needs." This he does, briefly, through Tudor and Stuart dramas, focusing on Fletcher, Shakespeare, Heywood, Shirley and Brome. He also analyzes the types of "clownery," slapstick, and farce that were popular during the period.

Yates, Frances Amelia

771 YATES, FRANCES AMELIA. *Theatre of the World*. London:
     Routledge and Kegan Paul, 1969. xiv, 218pp.
          Of particular note are Yates' final chapters, "The
     Theatre as Moral Emblem," and "Public Theatre and Masque:
     Inigo Jones on the Theatre as a Temple."

772 YEARSLEY, MacLEOD. *Doctors in Elizabethan Drama*. London:
     John Bale, Sons and Danielsson, 1933. 128pp.
          Yearsley refers to Brome's *The Antipodes*, Jonson's *The
     Magnetic Lady*, Ford's *'Tis Pity*, Massinger's *The Roman Actor*
     and *A Very Woman*, and Shirley's *The Ball* (attributed to
     Chapman).

773 ZIFF, LAZER. "The Literary Consequences of Puritanism."
     ELH, 30 (1963), 293-305.
          Ziff notes that Abraham Wright "gained everlasting if
     small distinction by amusing himself with considerations of
     what was happening to [literary] style under the Puritans."
     Also discussed is Wright's play *Love's Hospital*.

Stage History

774 ADAMS, JOSEPH QUINCY, JR. *Shakespearean Playhouses: A History of Eight Theatres from the Beginning to the Restoration.* Boston: Houghton Mifflin, 1917. xiv, 473pp.
   Adams is concerned with the site, plan, interior, and exterior of Renaissance playhouses. The book is "the result of first-hand examination of original sources, and represents a [new] interpretation of the historical evidence. . . ." Much scholarship since 1917 of stage history is related to Adams' early work. Included is a map of London showing the locations of the playhouses.

775 ARMSTRONG, WILLIAM A. "The Audience of the Elizabethan Private Theatres." *RES, n.s.,* 10 (1959), 234-49.
   Armstrong's article is an overview of private theatres from 1575-1642. He makes passing references to *The Staple of News, The Careless Shepherdess* (which he attributes totally to Goffe), *The Magnetic Lady; The Lady's Privilege; The City Madam; The City Match; The New Inn; The Court Begger;* and *The Doubtful Heir;* he is also concerned with the types of people who attended the private theatres as reflected in the characters on stage.

776 BACHRACH, A. G. H. "The Great Chain of Acting." *Neophilologus,* 33 (1949), 160-72.
   Bachrach's initial rhetorical question is "Why did those Elizabethan schoolboys and students have to learn the use of voice and body as seriously as any aspiring actor training for the professional stage?" In answering the question, he passes through multiple types of information and subject matter. Inferences can be drawn as to the effect of this training on the theatre-going audience, the language and acting of Tudor and Stuart plays, and other matters. He is concerned primarily with the theatres pre-1650.

777 BAKER, H. BARTON. *History of the London Stage and Its Famous Playwrights (1576-1903).* London: Routledge, 1904. xxii, 557pp.

Bentley, Gerald Eades

Baker's is an interesting, if emotional, account of the
London stage; only the first two chapters are relevant to
this study. Baker is particularly disparaging toward audiences during Charles II's reign, while he glorifies the
accoutrements of the Blackfriars Theatre "from 1609 until
its suppression under the Commonwealth."

778   BENTLEY, GERALD EADES. "The Diary of a Caroline Theatregoer."
      MP, 35 (1938), 61–72.
      Bentley comments on and gives many extracts from the
      diary and account book of Sir Humphrey Mildmay. He says
      "So far as I know, it is the most complete account of any
      individual's theatre attendance which exists for the Eliza-
      bethan period." The account book opens January 1631/32 and
      records about sixty entries related to drama before the
      theatres closed. It is an excellent record of the changing
      tastes of the Caroline audience.

779   _____. *The Jacobean and Caroline Stage*. Oxford: Clarendon
      Press, 1941–68. 7 vols.
      Volumes I and II: "Dramatic Companies and Players."
      Bentley gives "a history of the London dramatic companies
      and the biographies of the actors, focusing on the period
      between 1616 and 1643" although he briefly summarizes the
      activities of the older companies. For each actor he quotes
      "every scrap of biographical evidence (except for the
      careers of English actors in Germany), in chronological
      order." Volume I treats the following companies: The
      King's, the Palsgrave's or King of Bohemia's, Queen Anne's
      (Players of the Revels), Lady Elizabeth's (Queen of Bo-
      hemia's), Prince Charles', I and II, Queen Henrietta's, the
      King and Queen of Bohemia's, the Red Bull-King's, the King's
      Revels, and the King and Queen's Young Company (Beeston's
      Boys). Volume II is the alphabetical and chronological
      listing of actor's biographical materials. These volumes
      conclude with an appendix of source materials related to
      wills, the closing of the theatres because of plagues, the
      records of Sir Humphrey Mildmay, Marckham's suit, Heton's
      papers, theatrical notes from Crosfield's Diary, and a mis-
      cellany. Volumes III, IV, V: "Plays and Playwrights."
      Bentley's general purpose is "to consider all plays, masques,
      shows and dramatic entertainments from 1616-1642." For a
      comprehensive statement on the way to use these reference
      volumes, *see* the author's Preface to Volume III. He con-
      cludes Volume V with the materials related to anonymous
      plays. Volumes VI and VII: "Theatres." Bentley gives ex-
      tended discussions of the private theatres, the public
      theatres, theatres at court, and projected theatres in

Bergeron, David M.

Volume VI. Again, *see* the Preface in Volume VI for a general introduction to the material in these two volumes.
Volume VII contains the appendices to Volume VI, notably
information on Lenten performances in the Jacobean and
Caroline theatres, Sunday performances in general, and Sunday performances at court, and an annal of the Jacobean and
Caroline theatrical companies. This volume concludes with
the thorough general index for all seven volumes.

780   ____. *The Profession of Dramatist in Shakespeare's Time,*
1590-1642. Princeton: Princeton University Press, 1917.
ix, 329pp.
Bentley's book "is an explication of the normal working
environment circumscribing the activities of those literary
artists who were making their living by writing for the
London Theatres [until 1642]." He discusses amateur and
professional dramatists, the status of dramatists, plays,
actors and theatres, the dramatist's relationship with the
acting companies, their pay and contractual obligations,
regulation and censorship, and the nature of collaboration,
revision, and publication. The work is thoroughly indexed.

781   ____, ed. *The Seventeenth-Century Stage: A Collection of*
Essays. Chicago: University of Chicago Press, 1968. xvi,
287pp.
Of particular note are F. P. Wilson's article, "Ralph
Crane, Scrivener to the King's Players," in which Wilson
discusses Crane's career and includes five facsimiles of
his hand; Louis B. Wright's "Stage Duelling in the Eliza-
bethan Theatre," in which he notes stage directions and
their interpretations, from *The Goblins, The Cardinal,*
Love's Cruelty, and *The Unfortunate Lovers;* Charles J.
Sisson's thorough "Introduction to *Believe As You List*";
and William A. Armstrong's "The Audience of the Elizabethan
Private Theatres," in which he mentions *The Magnetic Lady;*
The Staple of News; The Court Begger; The Doubtful Heir;
The New Inn; and works by other Caroline authors.

782   BERGERON, DAVID M. "Actors in English Civic Pageants."
Ren P, ed. by Dennis G. Donovan and A. Leigh Deneef (1972),
pp. 17-28.
The intention of Bergeron's paper "is to bring together
all the evidence . . . about who performed in the pageants
of Tudor-Stuart England." What is revealed "is a degree of
professionalism too often overlooked."

783   ____. "The Christmas Family: Artificers in English Civic
Pageantry." *ELH,* 35 (1968), 354-64.

Bergeron, David M.

Bergeron notes that "the Christmas family's work in the mayoral pageants is unique. For one thing no other father-son team serves as artificer for any civic entertainment; furthermore, no one else has had as long an association with the pageants as the Christmas family – a twenty-one-year span from 1618-1639." Some Caroline works given special attention are *The Triumphs of Health and Posterity; Wars, Wars, Wars; London's Tempe; Triumphant-Day; Londoni Ius Honorarium; Londoni Sinus Salutis; Porta Pietatis;* and *Londoni Status Pacatus.* This article is the one referred to in the *CBEL* as "The Emblematic Nature of English Civic Pageantry."

784 _____. *English Civic Pageantry, 1558-1642.* London: Edward Arnold, 1971. 325pp.
Bergeron has a chapter in Part One on progresses and royal entries from the reign of Charles I to the close of the theatres in 1642; in Part Two he treats, among other things, the Lord Mayors' shows of John Taylor and Thomas Heywood. In Part Three he analyzes staging techniques and dramatic problems related to pageantry. The book is well indexed and well documented. A good list of primary and secondary sources is included.

785 BOAS, FREDERICK S. "Crosfield's Diary and the Caroline Stage." *Fortnightly Rev* (1 April 1925), pp. 514-24.
Boas discusses a manuscript diary of Thomas Crosfield "preserved in the library of Queen's College, Oxford, which gives valuable information concerning the activities of and payments to travelling companies playing for academic and civic entertainments."

786 BORDINANT, PHILIP. "A New Site for the Salisbury Court Theatre." *N & Q* (February 1956), pp. 51-52.
Bordinant includes a diagram of the Salisbury Court Theatre area, *ca.* 1629-66.

787 CAMPBELL, LILY B. *Scenes and Machines on the Elizabethan Stage: A Classical Revival.* 1923; rept. NY: Barnes and Noble, 1960. x, 302pp.
Campbell's book, in four parts, surveys and analyzes stage machinery and production from the sixteenth century through the Restoration. Of particular note is Part I: "The Classical Revival of Stage Decoration in Italy" and its influence on the English stage; and Part II: "Stage Decoration in England, 1600-1650"; special topics in Part III are progress in the theory of architecture and perspective, the work of Inigo Jones and his contemporaries, and

Chambers, E. K.

the use of spectacle in the theatres. Campbell treats the
perspective stage as an invention generated by Vitruvius.
Text-figure and plate illustrations are included for a Jones
staging of Davenant's *Salmacida Spolia* and for *The Pastoral
of Florimène*, possibly by Queen Henrietta Maria. *See* Harbage's *Cavalier Drama*, p. 18. The book is well indexed.

788 CHAMBERS, E. K. *The Elizabethan Stage*. Oxford: Clarendon
Press, 1923. 4 vols. + index vol.
Chambers' first volume "is devoted to a description . . .
of the Elizabethan Court, and of the ramifications in pageant and progress, tilt and mask, of the instinct for spectacular. . . . The Second Book gives an account of the
settlement of the players in London, of their conflict,
backed by the Court, with the tendencies of Puritanism, and
of the place which they ultimately found in the monarchical
polity." To the third and fourth books "belong the . . .
fortunes of the individual playing companies and the individual theatres, with such fullness as the available records
permit. The Fifth deals with the surviving plays . . . as
documents helping to throw light upon the history of the
institution which produced them." Specifically, Book I
deals with the courts of Elizabethan and James, the revels
office, pageantry, the masque and the court play. Book II
deals with the control of the stage: Humanism and Puritanism, the struggle of court and city, the actor's quality
and economics. Book III is a list and analysis of the boy
and adult companies, by name, and concludes with a discussion of Italian players in England, English players in
Scotland, English players on the Continent, and an analysis
of the actors themselves. Book IV, entitled "The Playhouses," after a brief introduction, treats the individual
public and private theatres, and ends with a discussion of
the structure and conduct of the theatres, staging at court,
and staging in the theatres of the sixteenth and seventeenth
centuries. Book V includes a discussion of the printing of
plays, the playwrights, anonymous works by title, and
thirteen appendices related to a court calendar, court payments, documents of criticism, documents of control, plague
records, the Presence-Chamber at Greenwich, Serilio's
Trattate sopra le Scene, The Gull's Hornbook, Restoration
testimony concerning the early seventeenth century, academic
plays, printed plays, lost plays, and manuscript plays. The
five books in four volumes are indexed separately at the
conclusion of Volume IV, by plays, persons, places and subjects. *See also* Beatrice White's *An Index to* The Elizabethan Stage, Oxford: Clarendon Press, 1934, 161pp.

161

Freehafer, John

789   FREEHAFER, JOHN. "Brome, Suckling and Davenant's Theatre
      Project of 1639." *Texas St Lit & Lang,* 10 (1968), 367-83.
         Freehafer comments on the controversies initiated by
      Brome's banned *Court Begger,* and its attack on the court
      establishment "because he resented the theatrical ventures
      of two royal favorites, Sir John Suckling and his crony
      William Davenant." Freehafer shows the results of this
      controversy when, in the 1660's, Davenant refused to pro-
      duce the plays of Brome.

790   ____. "Perspective Scenery and the Caroline Playhouse." *TN,*
      27 (1973), 98-113.
         Freehafer supports the theory of moveable scenery and
      perspective scenery in pre-Restoration playhouses. His
      article is an excellent review and analysis of criticism
      related to the subject. His notes read, essentially, like
      a bibliography of Caroline stagecraft. *See also* Kenneth B.
      Richards' "Changeable Scenery for Plays on the Caroline
      Stage" in *TN,* 22 (1968), 6-21; Andrew Gurr's *The Shakes-
      pearean Stage 1574-1642* (1970), pp. 132-33; and Mrs. L. R.
      Starr's "A Note on the Use of Scenery at the Cock Pit-in-
      Court," *TN,* 26 (1972), 89.

791   G., G. M. *The Stage Censor: An Historical Sketch, 1544-1907.*
      London: Sampson Low, Marston, 1908. 128pp.
         Chapter II gives a good introductory survey of the ad-
      ministration of revels under the Stuart kings. Engravings
      of Massinger, Shirley, Davenant and Killigrew are included.

792   GILDERSLEEVE, VIRGINIA CROCHERON. *Government Regulation of
      the Elizabethan Drama.* NY: Columbia University Press,
      1908. 259pp.
         Gildersleeve's work is a comprehensive study of materials
      on censorship regulations from 1543-1642, of the Master of
      Revels, of the nature and development of censorship, of
      local regulations in London, and of the Puritan influence
      and ultimate victories in terms of censorship. An appendix
      on royal patents to companies of players is included, as
      well as a bibliography and thorough index.

793   GREG, W. W. *Dramatic Documents from the Elizabethan
      Playhouses: Stage Plots, Actors' Parts, Prompt Books.*
      Oxford: Clarendon, 1931. 2 vols.
         Volume I is commentary on dramatic documents related to
      plots, actors' parts, prompt books, as well as a descriptive
      list of manuscript plays. Included is a specific discussion
      of Massinger's *Believe As You List* and Glapthorne's *The Lady
      Mother.* Volume II is a series of reproductions with tran-
      scripts. Portions from the two plays are included.

794   HAMMER, GAEL W. "The Staging of Elizabethan Plays in the
       Private Theatres 1632-1642." *DAI*, 33:3836A (University of
       Iowa), 1973. 198pp.
           Hammer deals primarily with staging at Blackfriars, the
       Phoenix, and at Salisbury Court. Numerous conclusions are
       drawn concerning staging there; she gives evidence from the
       plays produced there, and from the house records of the
       three theatres.

795   HARBAGE, ALFRED. "Elizabethan Acting." *PMLA*, 54 (1939),
       685-708.
           Harbage notes that the anonymous manuscript play "The
       Cyprian Conqueror, or The Faithless Relict" contains the
       "earliest specific instructions for acting extant in Eng-
       lish." The play dates *ca.* 1633-42.

796   HART, ALFRED. "The Time Alloted for Representation of
       Elizabethan and Jacobean Plays." *RES*, 8 (1932), 395-413.
           Hart mentions allusions in plays of Shirley and Davenant
       to the duration of plays and concludes that "climatic con-
       ditions and the structure of the unroofed theatres combined
       to limit the duration of the performance [pre-1616] in win-
       ter to about two hours and a quarter, and no good reason
       has been advanced why this should have been exceeded in the
       summer months." In conjunction with this article *see* Hart's
       "The Length of Elizabethan and Jacobean Plays," *RES*, 8
       (1932), 139-54.

797   HAZLITT, W. CAREW. *The English Drama and Stage under the Tudor
       and Stuart Princes 1543-1664.* London: Roxburghe Library,
       1869. xvi, 289pp.
           Hazlitt's book is an illustration of the period through
       a series of documents, treatises, and poems related to Eng-
       lish drama from about 1553 to 1660. Forty-five works are
       included; the book is indexed.

798   HEWITT, BARNARD, ed. *The Renaissance Stage: Documents of
       Serlio, Sabbattini and Furttenbach.* Coral Gables:
       University of Miami Press, 1958. 256pp.
           Included are selections from Nicola Sabbattini's *Manual
       for Constructing Theatrical Scenes and Machines*, Joseph
       Furttenbach, the Elder's *Civil Architecture*, as well as
       from *Recreational Architecture* and *The Noble Mirror of Art*.
       There is also a general introduction to the Renaissance
       stage and an index to the 125 illustrations from the origin-
       al texts.

Hosley, Richard

799   HOSLEY, RICHARD. "Three Renaissance English Indoor Playhouses."
       ELR, 3 (1952), 166–82.
           Hosley notes that "During the Renaissance in England the
       kind of building that was most often used as an indoor play-
       house, whether temporary or permanent, was the English great
       hall, which enjoyed the advantage for theatrical purposes
       of being furnished (usually) with a 'screen' having two en-
       tranceways to the hall proper and, in a majority of in-
       stances, a musicians' gallery over the 'screen's passage.'
       In [his] essay [he] distinguishes five classes of hall
       screen." He is not concerned with "analysis of function, or
       with origins, or with forms taken by the hall screen before
       or after the period from about 1500 to about 1660. Rather,
       the classification is simply a convenience for the purpose
       of describing the hall screen during the period indicated."

800   HOTSON, LESLIE. *The Commonwealth and Restoration Stage.*
       Cambridge, MA: Harvard University Press, 1928. ix, 424pp.
           Although outside the time span of this work, Hotson's
       study is a thorough introduction to players, playhouses,
       productions, and acting companies during the Interregnum
       and the Restoration. The frontispiece is a portrait of
       Thomas Killigrew, age twenty-six.

801   JOSEPH, BERTRAM LEON. *Elizabethan Acting.* 2nd ed. Oxford:
       Oxford University Press, 1964. 115pp.
           This manual surveys movement, rhetorical patterns and
       figures, cadence, voice modulations, rhythm, style and
       tone, as well as other special topics related to acting,
       such as asides and oratory as they were appropriate to early
       Stuart drama. The work is a useful comparative tool for
       judging the range of Stuart variations in actors and audi-
       ences. Joseph makes passing references to Randolph, May
       and Massinger, and their attitudes toward contemporary
       actors.

802   KING, T. J. *Shakespearean Staging, 1599-1642.* Cambridge, MA:
       Harvard University Press, 1971. 157pp.
           King's work is a "systematic survey of theatrical re-
       quirements for 276 plays first performed by professional
       actors in the period between the autumn of 1599 . . . and
       2 September 1642. . . ." Accompanying the survey are appen-
       dices on major scholarship from 1940-1970, on plays printed
       from 1600-1659 not included in the text, and on dramatic
       texts from 1600-1659 which are not plays. Indexes to plays,
       persons, and subject matter follow.

Leech, Clifford

803 _____. "The Staging of Plays at the Phoenix in Drury Lane
1617-42." *TN*, 19 (1965), 146-66.
King re-evaluates criticism related to the Phoenix,
analyzes what is known about those plays presumably performed there before 1642, and questions the relationship
between actual performance and the texts of printed works.
He also gives evidence culled from eighty extant plays
known to have been associated with the Phoenix's history
to support his conclusions.

804 LAWRENCE, W. J. *The Elizabethan Playhouse and Other Studies.*
2nd ser. Stratford-upon-Avon: By the Author, 1913. 261pp.
Of general interest are discussions on "light and dark-
ness in the Elizabethan Theatre," stage dimensions and theatre plans, the origin of theatre programs, "early systems
of admission," the origin of the English Picture-Stage, and
the persistence of Elizabethan "conventionalisms." The
book is indexed by author, performer, work, stage, and
theatre location.

805 _____. "The Seventeenth Century Theatre: Systems of
Admission." *Anglia*, 35 (1912), 526-38.
Lawrence shows how the system of paying admissions in
playhouses is related not only to the wages of the actors
and maintainance of the playhouse, but also to the
architecture of the playhouse and the payment of rent. He
concludes by showing that the old system straggled on into
the Restoration.

806 LEACROFT, RICHARD. *The Development of the English Playhouse.*
Ithaca, NY: Cornell University Press, 1973. 354pp.
Chapters I through II are of particular note; Leacroft
focuses on court masques, Inigo Jones, actor-audience relationships, and on a reconstruction of *The Pastoral of
Florimène*. Photographic and line illustrations are given,
as well as a good index.

807 LEECH, CLIFFORD. "The Caroline Audience." *MLR*, 36 (1942),
304-19.
Leech's article is a thorough and provocative analysis
of evidence related to the Caroline audience, without being
moralistic or sententious. His working hypothesis is that
"A dramatist cannot work without some consideration, even
if scournful, of his audience, and his 'tone' will arise
from his attitude to their expectations." Leech liberally
salts his study with substantiation from contemporary works.

McIlwraith, A. K.

808   McILWRAITH, A. K. "Patrons of *The City Madam*." *BQR*, 5 (1928), 248-49.

      McIlwraith notes Dekker's reference "to the dishonest practice of offering a fresh patron for a second fee a book already dedicated to someone else," in his *II The Honest Whore*, I.i. Then McIlwraith applies the condemnation to the 1658 and 1659 publications of Massinger's *The City Madam*. He supplements the list of patrons during 1658 and 1659 in "A Further Patron of *The City Madam*," *BQR*, 8 (1935), 17-18.

809   MEADLEY, T. D. "Attack on the Theatre *c.* 1580-1680." *London Q*, 10 (1953), 36-44.

      Meadley traces the history of the attacks and regulations leveled at theatres, actors, and plays from 1580-1680, and then catalogues the better-known attacks.

810   MULLIN, DONALD C. *The Development of the Playhouse: A Survey of Theatre Architecture from the Renaissance to the Present*. Berkeley and Los Angeles: University of California Press, 1970. 197pp.

      Chapter III, "*The Triumph of Albion*: English Pre-Restoration Playhouses," and its accompanying illustrations is a good overview of late Renaissance theatrical architecture.

811   MURRAY, JOHN TUCKER. *English Dramatic Companies, 1558-1642*. London: Constable and Company, 1910. 2 vols.

      Volume I is a discussion of the greater and lesser men's companies and the childrens' companies in London during the Renaissance. Volume II is a discussion of the 155 provincial companies. There are numerous appendices of documents related to the companies.

812   NICOLL, ALLARDYCE. "The Rights of Beeston and D'Avenant in Elizabethan Plays." *RES*, 1 (1925), 84-91.

      Although Nicoll is concerned primarily with drama after the re-opening of the theatres, he does trace Beeston's and Davenant's theatre activity *ca.* 1639-41. He also discusses Killigrew's relationship to acting companies in 1640 and 1660, as well as the proprietary ownership of Caroline or earlier plays. Evidence Nicoll gives contributes to publication data for Caroline plays.

813   _____. "Scenery between Shakespeare and Dryden." *TLS* (15 August 1936), p. 658.

      Nicoll is concerned generally with the introduction of scenery to the stage between 1625 and 1640, and specifically with the designs which give "the ground-plan and a side

view of the wings used for the setting in Mildman Fane's
Candy Restored." Nicoll quotes the stage directions, gives
the stage plan and the plan for the side wings, and sets
the stage directions in context with other contemporary
plays.

814 _____. *Stuart Masques and the Renaissance Stage.* 1937; rept.
NY: Benjamin Blom, 1963. 224pp. and 197 illustrations.
The thrust of Nicoll's book is toward staging and theatre
history and much of it is devoted to Caroline productions
and Inigo Jones' involvement in them. Of particular note
is his comparison and contrast of the staging of such Caroline masques as *Chloridia; Albion's Triumph; Coelum Britannicum; Comus; Florimène; Britannia Triumphans; Luminalia;*
and *Salmacida Spolia.*

815 ORDISH, T. FAIRMAN. *Early London Theatres* [In the fields].
London: Elliot Stock, 1894. 298pp.
Ordish's work is a comprehensive and early survey of
stage and theatrical history. He covers many subjects which
have dropped out of contemporary critical evaluation of the
Caroline period, such as drolls, pickpockets in the theatres, Morris dances, and acting techniques, to name a few.

816 PALME, PER. Triumph of Peace: *A Study of Whitehall
Banqueting House.* London: Thames and Hudson, 1957. xviii,
327pp.
In this well-illustrated study, Palme includes the draw-
ings and preliminary plans for the Whitehall banqueting
house, by Inigo Jones, as well as many other plates and
figures. Palme surveys the literature of sources related
to Whitehall, discusses, among other things, the masques
and their audiences, and gives a thorough architectural
study of the banqueting house. A lengthy bibliography and
index are provided.

817 [SIMPSON, PERCY, ed.]. *Shakespeare's England.* London:
Oxford University Press, 1917. 2 vols.
This two volume work contains numerous essays, by various
hands, on the general nature of life and learning during the
English Renaissance. Volume I contains essays on religion,
the court, the military, travel, education, scholarship,
handwriting, commerce, agriculture, law, medicine, the sciences, and folklore. Volume II contains essays on the fine
arts, heraldry, costume, home life, London life, authors
and patrons, booksellers, printers, stationers, actors,
acting, the masque, sports, pastimes, rogues, vagabonds,

Simpson, Percy

and ballads and broadsides. Three individual indexes, in Volume II, contain passages cited from Shakespeare, proper names, and subjects and technical terms.

818   SIMPSON, PERCY and C. F. BELL. *Designs by Inigo Jones for Masques and Plays at Court.* Oxford: Walpole and Malone Societies, 1924. viii, 158pp.
       In the introduction to their work, Simpson and Bell discuss the masque and its setting in terms of moveable and unmoveable scenery and properties. They also treat lighting, costuming, cost of production, and the sources for Inigo Jones' inspiration. Part II is a catalogue of drawings from 1605-1640, related to masques by Jonson, Townshend, Montague, Shirley, Carew, Davenant, Carlell, Habington, and others. They list doubtful and unidentified drawings, and give an appendix of theatrical designs, not by Jones, in the Chatsworth Collection and the Library of the Royal Institute of British Architects. 401 plates are included.

819   SISSON, C. J. "The Theatres and Companies." In *A Companion to Shakespeare Studies.* Ed. by H. Granville-Barker and G. B. Harrison. Cambridge: The University Press, 1934. Pp. 9-43.
       Sisson, among other things, is concerned with the condition of the stage in the late 16th century to around 1660. He discusses private and public theatres, typical stage structures, various elevations and floor plans of the Fortune, and he discusses the masque and the stage, the repertory of plays, the actors and performances, and the audience.

820   SORELIUS, GUNNAR. "The Rights of the Restoration Theatrical Companies in the Older Drama." *SN*, 37 (1965), 174-89.
       The early sections of Sorelius' article are concerned with those actors and playwrights who made the transistion from Caroline to Restoration drama, preeminently Killigrew and Davenant, and the issue of whether or not Beeston's Boys became a part of Davenant's company. To follow this discussion, *see* first Allardyce Nicoll's "The Rights of Beeston and D'Avenant in Elizabethan Plays," *RES*, 1 (1925), 84-91, and Hazelton Spencer's reply, "The Restoration Play Lists," in the same issue, pp. 443-46.

821   SOUTHERN, RICHARD. *Changeable Scenery*. NY: Faber and Faber, 1952. 411pp.
       Part I of Southern's study, "The Rise of Changeable Scenery at Court," is concerned essentially with scenery used in the masque (pp. 17-106). The book is well indexed and illustrated with 115 illustrations and plates.

Thaler, Alwin

822   _____. "A 17th-Century Indoor Stage." *TN*, 9 (1954), 5-11.
In conjunction with this article, *see* the double-paged
plate following p. 14, of a theatrical print from Van de
Venne's *Taferell*, 1655. Southern thoroughly analyzes
twenty-eight points related to the engraving and concludes
that "the points of the scene, taken together suggest . . .
evidence of considerable importance about the early seventeenth century indoor theatre, of which this picture seems
to have claim to be one of the earliest examples so far
found."

823   STONE, L. "Companies of Players Entertained by the Earl of
Cumberland and Lord Clifford, 1607-39." In *Malone Society
Collections*. Vol. V. Oxford: The University Press,
1959/60. Pp. 17-28.
Stone transcribes entries related to midsummer shows,
the Lord Mayors' Shows and miscellaneous entries from 1605-
1638/39.

824   THALER, ALWIN. "The Elizabethan Dramatic Companies." *PMLA*,
35 (1920), 123-59.
The latter part of this article focuses on Caroline
dramatic companies; it notes that "Richard Brome was in all
probability . . . a sharer in the Lady Elizabeth's Men as
early as 1628." Thaler notices "how the dramatic companies
toward the close of the . . . period gradually lost their
powers of self-determination, and how the ground was pre-
pared for the coming of the star system and theatrical mono-
poly of the Restoration." Thaler concludes with a discussion of the financial status of the actor-sharers.

825   _____. "The Players at Court, 1564-1642." *JEGP*, 19 (1920),
19-46.
Thaler's concern is with the exhorbitant amount of money
spent on court spectacles from the time of Henry VIII
through Charles I's reign, and with "the fact that the
players derived substantial sums of money from their associations with the court and nobility." He methodically attempts to determine "how much a company sharer may have
drawn each year from court and public performances" adding
to that sum amounts he may have received as casual gifts.
He also touches on the amounts a playwright, who was not
also an actor, might receive. It may be interesting for
the reader to compare this article with J. Lough's "The
Earnings of Playwrights in Seventeenth-Century France,"
MLR, 42 (1947), 321-36.

Thaler, Alwin

826   ____. "Strolling Players and Provincial Drama after
         Shakespeare." *PMLA*, 37 (1922), 243-80.
              Thaler discusses strollers and provincial drama "in
         light of their practical contribution to the stage history
         of their time," and the fact that they broke the London
         monopoly on drama. He makes passing references to Thomas
         Nabbes' *Covent Garden*, and its discussion of strolling
         players. He concludes with a discussion on the subject
         post-1660. Refer also to Louis B. Wright's "Variety Enter-
         tainment by Elizabethan Strolling Players," *JEGP*, 26
         (1927), 294-303.

827   ____. "Was Richard Brome an Actor?" *MLN*, 36 (1921), 88-91.
              Thaler's is an early discussion of the evidence related
         to Brome's supposed career on the stage and his association
         with Ben Jonson. Thaler's study is only pre-dated, in
         depth, by C. E. Andrews in *Richard Brome, A Study of His
         Life and Works* (1913). For a modern evaluation of the
         issue *see* Ann Haaker's "Introduction" to her critical edi-
         tion of Brome's *The Antipodes*.

828   UNWIN, GEORGE. *The Guilds and Companies of London*. 4th ed.
         London: Frank Cass and Company, 1963. xvi, 397pp.
              Unwin's is a thorough survey of the history and develop-
         ment of guilds from the time of Henry Plantagenet to Vic-
         toria. Of particular interest are Chapter XVI, "The Lord
         Mayors' Show," and Appendix B, "List of Sources for the
         History of the Existing London Companies." The work is
         indexed.

829   WICKHAM, GLYNNE. *Early English Stages 1300-1660*. London:
         Routledge and Kegan Paul; NY: Columbia University Press,
         1959, 1963, 1972. 3 vols.
              Wickham's Book II is a thorough collection of materials
         and ideas related to the regulation of the theatres, state
         control of British drama, 1530-1642, of the actors, authors,
         and theatres under state control, and of the playhouses
         themselves. The use of stage furniture is also covered.
         The volume is thoroughly indexed and illustrated. Appendix
         F is a list of Jacobean and Caroline Lord Mayors' shows.
         Book III discusses the gamehouses, inn playhouses and the-
         atres, as well as their origins as playing grounds, their
         development and disintegration. The final chapter discusses
         houses for plays, masques, and banquets. Book IV is con-
         cerned with stages and stage directions, Elizabethan,
         Jacobean and Caroline stage conventions as they relate to
         scene and stage, with stage managers, dressing rooms, en-
         trances, exits, and musicians. There are forty-six figures
         and plates. The appendices, notes, bibliographies, and
         indexes for Books II-IV are at the end of Volume II.

Subject Index

A

abbreviations, 011
academia, 769
acting, 616, 776, 817, 829
--contemporary instructions, 795
--methods of, 801, 815
acting companies, 036, 043, 061,
    095, 279, 501, 612, 779-780,
    819, 824
--childrens', 811
--Davenant's, 820
--documents of, 811
--entertainment of, 823
--finances of, 825
--Interregnum, 800
--men's, 811
--provencial, 811
--relationship to Killigrew, 812
--sources, 828
--travel of, 785
    see also fees, individual
    companies and wages
action, 319, 332, 666
actors, 012, 036-037, 501, 522,
    545, 566, 739, 764, 780,
    798-800, 806, 817, 819, 827,
    829
--and actresses, 709
--amateur, 432, 505, 659
--attacks on, 809
--biographies of, 779
--and dramatists, 801
--finances, 824-825
--lists of, 012, 052, 095, 252
--and music, 044, 612, 704
--in pageants, 782
--professional, 432, 782

--social position, 753
--in transition, 820
--variations in, 801
--wages, 805
    see also costs, lists of
    and players
adaptations, 341, 349, 355, 367,
    408, 436, 491, 743;
    see also revisions
adaptors, 143
admissions, 804
advertisements, play, 052
aesthetics, 217
afterpieces, 084
agriculture, 029, 817
airs, or ayres, see music and
    song
ale houses, 096
allegory, 474, 740
alliteration, 252
allusions, 045, 093, 220, 229,
    232, 491, 513, 529, 542,
    548, 607, 669, 719; see also
    analogues and sources
amateurs, 432, 505, 659, 780
amusements, 617
analogues, 351; see also
    allusions and sources
animals, as actors, 763
--imagery of, 426
--in productions, 681
anonyma, 042, 059, 077, 113, 119,
    137-138, 143, 147, 505, 510,
    530, 560, 591, 639, 779;
    see also pseudonyma
antimasque, 474, 637

Antiquaries, Society of, 651
anthems, 695
apologetics, 631
architecture, 093, 617, 798, 810,
    816; see also buildings
aristocrats, 131; see also court
art, 092, 738
arts, 035, 817
--attitudes toward, 746
--and music, 142
astrology, 004
atlas, 028, 034
audience, 135, 296, 337, 391,
    395-396, 409, 454, 459, 487,
    503-504, 581, 602, 612,
    681-682, 699, 704, 709, 753,
    770, 775-778, 781, 801,
    806-807, 819
--for books, 605
--decadence of, 602
--French, 633, 685
--relationship with actors, 806
--at Whitehall, 816
authors, 043, 073, 739, 817
--bibliography of, 041
--biography of, 005, 010, 012,
    019, 022, 042, 077, 082, 118,
    132, 140-141
--Elizabethan, 699
--heterodox, 181
--lists of, 005, 009, 052-054,
    061-062, 065, 068, 081, 111,
    113, 119
--role of, 098; see also
    individual authors
authorship, 146-147, 177, 182,
    270, 290, 306-307, 340, 370,
    385, 390, 397, 408, 423,
    445, 451, 465, 484, 490-491,
    501, 505, 508, 520, 522,
    531, 539, 541, 547, 553,
    562, 569, 570-571, 589, 594,
    616, 699
--attribution of, 252
--multiple, 150, 169
autographs, 062, 161, 251, 284,
    384, 453
--corrections, 162

B

ballads, 014, 023, 027, 046-047,
    079, 089, 105, 108, 704,
    742, 817
banqueting houses, 816
banquets, 177, 829
--of love, 595
--scenes, 196, 208
banter, 676
baroque, 309
beauty
--religion of, 646
Bedlam, 720
beggar-books, 623
beggars, 598
bibliography
--descriptive, 152
--general, 005, 137
biography, 005, 044, 073, 118,
    146
--criminal, 623; see also
    individual authors,
    biographies
Blackfriars, 794
blank verse, 110, 410
bookbinding, 178
books, 605, 616, 681, 718
--jest, 623
--prompt, 793
booksellers, 037, 102, 137, 139,
    290, 817
brides, boy, 648
bridges, 096
broadsides, 089, 817
buildings, 063

C

Cambridge Platonists,
    see Platonism, Cambridge
casts, lists of, 084, 545
Catholicism, 358, 394, 422, 442,
    682
Cavalierism, 496, 659
Cavaliers, and Puritan conflicts,
    691
censors, 647, 699, 791
censorship, 003, 288, 583, 610,
    647, 780, 829

--development of, 751, 792
--and obscenity, 751
characterizations, 259, 296, 320,
   379, 389, 409, 426, 429, 535,
   561, 612
characters, 624, 719, 749, 761
--Anglican, 744
--doctor, 737, 772
--Irish, 733
--lists of, 111
--Roman Catholic, 744
--types of, 635, 735
charities, 078
chastity, 600
chorus, 688
chronicle plays, see plays,
   chronicle
church
--in literature, 744
Church of England, 469
churchmen
--in literature, 744
Civil War, 048, 424, 590, 659;
   see also Interregnum
class structure, 287
classics, 064, 348, 351, 460,
   473, 519, 550-551, 561, 576,
   663, 689-690, 787
clergy, 046; see also Catholicism,
   church, and churchmen
closet drama; see drama, closet
closing of theatres; see
   theatres, closing of
clothes, 619
--imagery of, 334
--symbolism of, 383; see also
   costume and fashion
clowns, 134-135, 770
collaborations, 122, 182, 191,
   205, 281, 291, 299, 306, 340,
   346, 355, 372, 390, 404, 484,
   680, 780
Collier controversy, 631
colonies, 035, 118
comedians, Italian, 645
comedy, 027, 244, 256, 282, 317,
   332, 338, 359, 363, 379, 402,
   425, 427-428, 440-441, 444,
   456, 481, 496, 525, 584,
   592, 615, 694, 770
--academic, 587

--Cavalier, 659
--court influence on, 686
--of intrigue, 716
--Jonsonian, techniques of, 632
--low, 760
--of manners, 652, 697, 716,
   730, 735
--and music, 695, 704
--Restoration, 634
--ridicule of melancholy, 599
--structure of, 615
--survey of, 754
--topographical, 698, 716
commedia dell' arte, 388, 523
commedia improvvisa, 626
commendatory verse, 030, 052,
   126-127, 137, 668; see also
   epistles, of editors, and
   prefatory material
commerce, 130, 817; see also
   economics and trade
Commonwealth; see Interregnum
companies; see acting companies
   and individual companies
compilations, 482
composers, 044, 056, 058, 098;
   see also music and song
compositors, 167, 170, 321, 472
conflict, 195, 435, 745, 765
conjuring, 765
constitutional history; see
   history, constitutional
control
--documents of, 788
--of theatres, 829
conventions; see dramatic
   conventions
copyrights, 164
copytext, 150, 157
corrections
--in books, 173
--textual, 189; see also textual
   considerations
costume, 033, 070, 090-092, 100,
   817-818
--academic, 031
--French, 633; see also clothes
   and fashion
coteries, 050, 065, 328, 496,
   504
counterfeiters, 598

country, state of, 096; see also
    life, country
couplets, 110
court
--attack on, 789
--Elizabethan, 788
--gross elements, 646
--influence of, 686, 717, 755,
    779, 825
--invasion of, 659
--Platonism, 557; see also life,
    court
court life; see life, court
court plays; see plays, court
courtiers, 498, 504
courtship, 457, 698
crafts, 029
criticism, 015, 022, 064, 126,
    146
--contemporary, 081, 084, 746,
    773
--documents of, 788
--nineteenth-century attitudes
    toward, 005
culture
--levels of, 617
--middle class, 605; see also
    middle class and upper class

D

dance
--Morris, 736, 815
--sword, 214; see also games
dating, problems of, 003, 008-009,
    036, 041, 052-054, 060-062,
    068, 102, 104, 111, 139, 146,
    196, 270-271, 280, 292, 299,
    311, 347-348, 350-351,
    353-355, 373, 378, 381, 397,
    402, 414, 418-419, 433, 447,
    449, 451, 466, 477, 499, 510,
    519, 526, 531, 534, 539, 547,
    575, 586
death, 345, 745
decadence, 035, 225, 236, 257,
    277, 309, 320, 322, 326, 342,
    360, 363, 366, 386, 393, 396,
    409, 429-430, 446, 602, 604,

614, 616, 631, 646, 652-653,
    661, 730; see also moral
    codes
dedications, 052, 137, 269, 360,
    433, 662
demonology, 756
demons, 721
dialogues, 125, 476, 512
--Platonic, 660
--précieuse, 427-428
diaries
--of theatre attendance, 778
--theatrical, 084, 785
diction, 508
didacticism, 248, 441
directions, stage, 781
disguises, 587, 648
doctors, characterization of,
    737, 772
doctrines, philosophical, 727
documents, 003, 109, 793,
    797-798, 811
drama, 609, 732
--anti-form in, 626
--attacks on, 809
--baroque, 707
--Caroline, 777
--Cavalier, 659
--closet, 504, 550, 659
--court, 003, 317, 447, 717
--development of, 622
--domestic, 448, 718, 730
--Elizabethan, 261, 273, 594-595,
    600, 608, 610, 613-614, 621,
    639, 648-650, 652, 661, 671,
    682, 706, 708, 715, 730, 732,
    747, 749, 756, 777, 784, 792,
    796
--French, 635, 685, 707
--historical, 730
--Interregnum, 724-725, 800
--Jacobean, 286, 330, 595, 602,
    608, 613, 618, 636, 639,
    640-641, 644, 649-650, 652,
    666, 683, 703, 705, 714-715,
    720, 728, 730, 732, 747, 759,
    769, 777, 784, 792, 796
--mediaeval, 731
--and music, 601, 693
--non-dramatic elements, 688

--pastoral, 657, 678, 740
--philosophical, 727
--popularity of, 605, 701
--pre-Restoration, 680
--professional, 659
--provincial, 826
--Renaissance, 596
--Scandanavian, 734
--Spanish, 707
--Stuart, 073, 594, 683, 700,
   753, 797
--survey of, 674
--trends in, 686
--Tudor, 038, 603, 662, 683, 701,
   721, 727, 753, 770, 797
dramatic conventions, 195, 223,
   282, 285, 296, 313, 320, 326,
   332, 334, 336, 384, 401, 428,
   430, 462, 494, 587, 612-613,
   616, 663, 688, 735, 752, 761,
   804, 829
dramatic techniques, 145, 282,
   298, 304, 307, 368, 484,
   612-613, 666-667, 745
dramatis personae, 591
dramatists
--profession of, 029, 035, 569,
   595, 613, 673, 753, 779, 780
--and music, 612
dress; see clothes, costumes
   and fashion
dressing rooms, 829
drolls, 815
duelling, stage, 781

                E

economics, 025, 029, 035, 055,
   078, 089, 092, 103, 109,
   130-131, 137, 664, 675;
   see also commerce, money
   and trade
editions; see textual
   considerations
education, 035, 092, 228, 617,
   619, 768, 817
elves, 027
employment, 029
enchantments, 027
England, 663

engravings, 679
entertainments, 015, 050, 054,
   084, 094, 097, 273, 476,
   510, 612, 785; see also
   Lord Mayors' shows, pageants
   and shows
entrances, 286, 784, 829
epilogues, 562, 589, 613
epistles, of editors, 137;
   see also commendatory verse
ethics, 066, 195, 225; see also
   moral codes and decadence
evil, theme of, 221, 224, 236
exemplary plays; see plays,
   exemplary
exits, 829

                F

fairies, 027
farce, 511, 667, 770
fashion, 464; see also clothes
   and costume
favoritism, 504
fees, 003; see also employment
   and wages
fiction, 605, 641, 701
folklore, 817
folk music; see music, folk
folk plays; see plays, folk
fools, 134-135, 735
fops, 735
foreign relations, 035
France, 633, 666, 679
freaks, 655
friendship, 700
--male cult of, 766

                G

gallery, musicians, 799
gamehouses, 829
games, 051, 457, 698
geography, 028, 034, 063, 096,
   240; see also topography
ghosts, 027, 756
grammar, 403
great chain of being, 129
greed, 426

Greenwich, 788
guilds, London, 828
gypsies, 598, 692

H

handwriting, 168, 196, 781, 817
--Elizabethan, 156
harlequin, 134-135
Henry VIII, 718
heraldry, 817
heroes; see protagonists
heroines; see protagonists
highway men, 096, 520, 531
history
--constitutional, 035, 092
--intellectual, 067, 146, 531,
    627, 758
--literary, 129, 134, 137, 182
--natural, 071
--Renaissance, 738
--political, 288, 344, 350-351,
    424, 482
--social, 004, 025, 027, 029,
    035, 044, 050, 055, 078, 089,
    092, 096, 103, 109, 129-131,
    134-137, 142, 228, 287-289,
    316-317, 361, 379, 435, 455,
    529, 576, 675, 749
--theatrical, 818
history of stage; see stage
    history
holographs, 062, 151, 154, 540
home life; see life, domestic,
    and householding
honor, 261, 574, 600
hookers, 598
householding, dissolution of,
    692
houses, for plays, 829
humanitarianism, 130
humors, 361, 687

I

iconography, 422
idealism, 409
ideas
--evolution of, 067, 146, 627

--movement of, 181
imagery, 196, 262, 334, 357, 392,
    426, 437, 506, 719
imitation, 757
imposters, 209; see also
    disguises
imprints, 164
incest, theme of, 399, 422
induction plays; see plays,
    induction
industry, 130; see also commerce
inns, 096
--theatres in, 829
Inns of Court, 656
institutions, 004
--as buildings, 063
instruments, 044, 693
intellectuals, melancholy of, 599
interludes, 645
Interregnum, 106, 800
--plays read during, 767
intrigue, 359, 644
irony, 196, 258, 313, 496, 676,
    692, 758

J

jester, 134-135
jigs, 601, 704
journalism, early, 310
jugglers, 598, 765

K

kingship, 197
knaves, 692

L

language, 198, 339, 344, 402,
    587, 719, 745
--dramatic, 401
--figurative, 304
--influenced by science, 670
law, 025, 103, 344, 619, 817
learned ladies, 405, 722;
    see also women
licenses, 003, 052, 751

life, 455, 817
--in cities, 092
--in the country, 050, 078, 092, 617
--court, 359, 408-409, 428, 584, 617, 817
--domestic, 072, 228, 619, 718, 817
--in London, 050, 092, 361-362, 380, 457, 617, 817
--Stuart, 498; see also householding
lighting, 804, 818
Lismore Papers, 567
listening, 616
literature, 004, 009, 024, 035, 064, 086, 092, 098, 134-136
--American, 065
--Elizabethan, 599, 620, 699
--Jacobean, 692
--non-dramatic, 699
--popular, 068
--Puritan, 742
--Tudor, 692, 700
lodgings, 096
logic, 075
London life; see life, in London
Lord Mayors' shows, 624, 784, 823, 828-829; see also entertainments and pageants
love, duel, 741
--game of, 741
--Platonic, 203, 301, 405, 409, 428, 438, 447, 557, 646, 653, 717, 741, 752
--romantic, 223, 608
--theme of, 027, 233, 261, 322, 339, 342, 344, 359, 411, 422, 426, 428, 435, 438, 447, 597, 611, 682, 700, 708
--tyrannic, 452
--versus honor, 574; see also Platonism and romance
lovers, in disguise, 648
lyrics, 612, 629; see also music and song

M

machinery, stage, 787, 798

madness, 720
madrigal, 310; see also music and song
magic, 756
male, superiority of, 597; see also misogyny
manners, 333, 359, 361, 363, 379, 484, 617, 652
manuscripts, 046, 060, 062, 153-154, 156, 166, 184, 196, 253, 303, 347, 475, 480, 526, 539-540, 545, 547, 557, 580, 585, 659, 679, 785, 788, 793
maps, 034, 063; see also geography and topography
marriage, 344, 448, 534, 597, 619, 718
--enforced, 223, 608
masques, 015, 054, 097, 100, 113, 206, 214, 275, 376, 390, 425, 440, 450, 458, 460, 474, 482, 500, 507, 510, 521, 558, 577, 580, 609, 637-638, 656, 677, 684, 695, 713, 715, 717, 730, 747, 755, 771, 806, 814, 817-819, 821, 829
--Italian, 645
--lists, 113, 285
--order of, 680
--at Whitehall, 816
masses, 695
medicine, 050, 344, 737, 817; see also doctors
melancholy, 202, 263, 393, 411, 599, 687, 726
memoirs, 464; see also authors, biography of, and diaries
metaphors, 506
meter, 535
middle class, 130, 287, 289, 448, 455
military, 817
mind, Elizabethan, 627
minstrels, 598; see also music, song and vagabonds
miscellanies, 482
misogyny, 723; see also male, superiority of
money, 357, 504, 584; see also commerce and economics
monopolies, 824, 826

moors, in drama, 710
moral codes, 050, 195, 217, 225,
    233, 236, 248–249, 257,
    276–277, 289, 298, 300, 337,
    342, 360, 363, 386, 390, 393,
    396, 400, 409, 429, 430, 435,
    438, 446, 461, 469, 474, 577,
    594, 602, 604, 614, 616, 631,
    646, 652–653, 661, 714, 727,
    730, 761, 769, 771
morphology, 097
Moslems, influence, 624
mottoes, Latin title-page, 177
murder, 089, 594; see also death
music, 003, 014, 023–024, 027,
    037, 044, 046–047, 050–051,
    056, 079, 092, 105–108, 142,
    255, 275, 310, 485–486, 601,
    617, 642, 695, 704, 729, 764
—composers of, 044, 056, 058,
    098
—and drama, 044, 684, 693
—folk, 044
—and poetry, 098
—theory, 642; see also song
musicians, 003, 044, 056, 142,
    693, 829; see also waits
myth, 460, 587

N

narcissicism, 587
newspapers, 084
notations, act-end, 192
nut-cracking, 681

O

occult, 721; see also demonology
    and demons
oratory, 801; see also rhetoric
order, theme of, 129
outlaws, 027

P

pageants, 015, 054, 094, 125, 467,
    472, 476, 482, 782–784, 788;
    see also entertainments

pages, female, 639, 648
palimpsest, 166
pamphleteers, 424
pamphlets, 089, 508, 590, 623,
    654, 796
paper, 080, 185
papermaking, 080
parody, 241, 427–428
parts, actors', 793; see also
    actors and performance
pastorals, 499
patents, 164, 645
patriotism, 344
patronage, 137, 328, 349, 668,
    699, 717, 817
—multiple, 808
pedlars, 598
performance, 003, 009, 036, 041,
    043, 061, 084, 095, 505,
    616, 625, 633, 659, 712, 819,
    824
—amateur, 659
—court, 753
—length of, 796
—Lenten, 779
philanthropy, 078; see also
    patronage
pickpockets, in the theatres,
    815
plagiarism, 166, 757
plagues, 658, 779, 788
Platonic love; see love,
    Platonic
Platonism, 136, 464, 496, 557,
    642, 741, 752, 755
playbills, 084
players, strolling, 826;
    see also actors
playhouses, 003, 819
—construction of, 774
—Caroline, 790; see also
    theatres
playing grounds, 829
plays, 450, 779–780
—amateur, 154, 504, 609, 739,
    788
—attacks on, 809
—Caroline, survey of, 674
—Cavalier, 659
—chronicle, 198, 299, 319, 576
—court, 043, 818
—domestic, 606

--exemplary, 248
--folk, 015
--foreign, 061
--induction, 145
--interregnum, 534
--lack of vitality in, 652
--Latin, 052, 060
--length of, 796
--lists of, 005, 009, 020, 022,
   036, 041, 052-054, 060-061,
   068-069, 077, 082, 102, 104,
   120, 139, 143
--lost, 052, 113, 147, 166, 476,
   788
--non-extant, 061
--ownership of, 812
--plagiarism of, 166
--pretender, 386
--registering of, 531
--re-writing of, 041
--school, 032, 038, 587, 730,
   785; see also performance
playwrights, 372, 428, 504, 613,
   779, 820, 829
--court, 659
--Elizabethan, 731
--finances of, 825
--foreign, 061
playwriting, 317, 331, 337, 395,
   428, 455, 613, 652, 659
plot, 198, 223, 259, 280, 296,
   332-333, 342, 389, 402, 426,
   429, 447, 504, 509, 536, 550,
   608, 666, 793
--disguise, 648
--multiple, 683
pneumatology, 756
poetry, 064, 068, 092
--and drama, 796
--dramatic, history of, 625
--and music, 098, 695
--pastoral, 657
poets, court, 717
politics, 025, 029, 035, 050,
   055, 078, 092, 103, 109,
   130-131, 137, 288, 651, 664
population, 096
postage, 096
praise, theme of, 064
précieuse tradition, 686

prefatory materials, 052; see
   also commendatory verse,
   dedications, epistles, of
   editors, and inductions
preferment, 360; see also
   patronage
Presbyterianism, 508
presses, 003, 176, 180, 183
printers, 037, 085, 102, 137,
   176, 193, 348-349, 354, 817
printing, 016, 018, 068, 087-088,
   158-160, 163, 176, 180-181,
   193, 308, 321, 387, 788
--devices, 085, 087
--shared, 148
--simultaneous, 159
privileges, 164; see also
   patronage
prodigal son, theme of, 603
production, 536, 588, 787, 800,
   818; see also properties and
   setting
professions, 029, 072, 130; see
   also work
progresses, 747, 784; see also
   entertainments and pageants
prologues, 459, 531, 589, 613,
   688
promptbooks, 680
pronouns, of address, 702
proofing, 160, 167, 183
propaganda, 769
properties, 818; see also
   setting
prose, 092, 643
prosody, 110, 179, 193, 217,
   393, 404
protagonists, 027, 337, 399,
   447-448, 463, 581, 623, 708
Protestants, 682
proverbs, 007, 021, 115
pseudonyma, 059, 113, 119,
   137-138; see also anonyma
psychology, 299, 454, 470, 612,
   661
public records; see records,
   public
publishers, 037, 084, 087-088,
   102, 137, 269, 348, 354,
   699

publishing, 137, 164, 187, 362, 780, 812
--clandestine, 181
Puritanism, 317, 482, 584, 664, 723
--satire of, 665; see also Puritans
Puritans, 035, 217, 424, 508, 643, 691, 706, 723, 742, 773; see also Puritanism

Q

quacks, 520

R

raillery, 676
reading, 768
realism, 280, 333, 359, 362, 391, 396, 484, 612, 686, 698, 715
receipts, 084; see also fees
records
--household, 142
--public, 003, 008, 025, 029, 036, 052-053, 105, 142
--stationers', 008, 052-053, 105, 164, 269
recreation, 817
regulations, 780, 792, 809, 829
--of book trade, 605
religion, 035, 066, 089, 092, 130, 136, 344, 664-665, 817; see also individual religions
religious materials, 705
Renaissance
--continental, 076
--counter, 066
--English, 004
repertory, 819
reputation, 600
research, methods of, 146, 150, 152, 156, 165, 170, 176, 181-182, 186, 190, 193, 600
Restoration, 041, 261, 341, 379, 408, 452, 468, 504, 554, 573, 606, 611, 635, 644, 650, 659, 661, 666-667, 678, 686, 697, 709, 716, 735, 743, 777, 800, 805, 812-813, 820

revels, 755
--administration of, 791
--court, 624
--master of, 161, 164, 645, 792; see also Herbert, Sir Henry
revenge, theme of, 345, 614
revisions, 171, 281, 306, 346, 350, 397, 408, 466, 547, 583, 780; see also adaptations
rhetoric, 075, 401, 670, 689, 820
roads, 096
rogues, 598, 623, 817
--in disguise, 648
--in fiction, 623
romance, 359, 363, 392, 426, 492, 495, 576, 730, 738
--Cavalier, 555
--court, 299
royalists, 424
rufflers, 598
running-titles, 148, 472

S

sacrifice, human, 554
salons, literary, 405
satire, 217, 241, 243, 313, 318, 331, 359, 379, 469, 623, 644, 665, 672, 715, 740, 758
scenery, 709, 798
--moveable, 521, 790, 818, 821
--and perspective, 790
scholarship, 817; see also education
science, 035, 050, 092, 670, 738, 817
screens, hall, 799
Scudamore family, 640
sensibility, drama of, 606
sentimentality, 396, 581, 606, 728
sermons, 654
setting, 404, 409, 712, 818, 829
shows
--midsummer, 823
--water, 624; see also entertainments, Lord Mayors' shows and pageants
sin, 129
singer, 037

skepticism, 561, 758
slapstick, 770
society, 664; see also history,
    social, middle class and
    upper class
song, 014, 023, 027, 037, 044,
    046-047, 051, 056, 079,
    105-108, 142, 255, 310, 474,
    486, 612, 629-630, 642, 693,
    695, 704, 729, 742
--Elizabethan, 601
--extraneous, 764
--wedding, 681
song books, 024, 037
sons of Ben, 454, 478, 652, 690
sorcerers, 721
sources, 146, 171, 343, 348,
    353-355, 361-362, 378, 381,
    384, 387, 389, 398, 413, 417,
    419, 436, 449, 451, 460, 473,
    488, 491-492, 494, 502, 511,
    519, 536, 539, 547, 549-551,
    578, 640, 779, 818
--contemporary, 288
--identification of, 169
--printed, 679
--prose fiction, 641
spectacle, 336, 391, 787, 825
speech, 616
spelling, 170
spies, 598, 648
sports, 092, 817
stage, 829
--architecture, 787
--attendants, 095
--construction, 804
--decorations, 681, 787
--dead removers, 681
--design, 816
--French, 679
--history, 003, 012, 041, 060-062,
    065, 068, 081-082, 084, 111,
    271, 340, 348, 350, 355, 381,
    395, 419, 421, 468, 521, 526,
    588, 594, 625, 777, 788, 800,
    804, 815, 819, 829
--London, 043
--managers, 829
staging, 362, 391, 521, 588, 613,
    784, 787, 790, 794, 798, 803,
    805

--French, 633
--requirements for, 802
--structures, 819
--Stuart masques, 814
Star Chamber, 651
stationers, 699, 817
stationers' register; see records,
    stationers'
stoicism, 759
streets, 063
structure, dramatic, 223, 298,
    314-315, 336, 338, 342,
    353-354, 395, 402, 416, 429,
    441, 447, 462, 505, 511,
    535-536, 550, 577, 608, 615,
    635, 643, 667, 719, 760
style, 337, 339, 750, 773
stylistics, 011
subplot, 398, 462, 544
supernatural, 721, 732
superstitions, 027, 050, 089
suppression, problems of, 647
symbolism, 313, 315, 383, 400

                    T

tales, popular, 623
techniques, 760
terms, obsolete, 033, 093, 114,
    144
testimony, Restoration, 788
textiles, 029
textual considerations, 155,
    162, 181, 188, 421, 465,
    468, 473, 475, 479, 482,
    487, 502, 524, 531, 534,
    536, 544, 551, 562, 585,
    587, 613
theatres, 043, 092, 296, 501,
    504, 654, 774, 780, 786,
    800, 803-804, 818, 822
--admissions, 805
apurtenances, 625
--architecture, 805
--attacks on, 631, 809
--attendance, 778
--closing of, 035, 424, 779
--court, 712, 713
--development of, 707, 806, 810
--early, 681

--French, 633, 685
--house records of, 794
--indoor, 799
--Irish, 432
--lists of, 043, 061
--London, 625, 815
--maintenance of, 805
--old, 625
--private, 753, 775, 779, 794, 819
--public, 704, 771, 779, 819
--and Puritans, 654, 666
themes, 221, 224, 236, 298, 342, 392, 402, 412, 426, 429, 435, 438, 454, 457, 461, 470, 474, 494, 496, 504, 511, 544, 576-577, 584, 587, 611, 616, 620, 635, 672, 675, 682, 696, 719, 726, 745, 749, 755
theory
--dramatic, 760
--musical, 642
time, 350
tinkers, 598
title pages, 177, 321
titles, 011
tone, 446, 508
topography, 063, 698, 716
trade, 029, 035; see also commerce and economics
tragedy, 027, 120, 221, 232, 299, 300, 314-315, 322, 330, 337, 363, 374-375, 392, 410-412, 440, 446, 456, 458, 481, 525, 614, 616, 689, 708, 719, 730, 745
--domestic, 594
--illusion of, 719
--Jacobean, 714-715
--political, 711
--rhetorical, 689
--Senecan, 550
--skepticism in, 758
tragicomedy, 281, 330, 392, 416, 429, 456, 502, 511, 525, 663, 730, 758
translations, 349, 481, 489, 491, 499, 516

translators, 143
travel, 050, 096, 413, 576, 817
tunes; see music or song
type, 087, 321

U

universities, 539, 610
unthrifts, 692
upper class, 287, 326
usurer, 749, 761-762, 769
usury, 317, 357, 496, 534, 749 762

V

vagabonds, 598, 692, 817
Virginia Company, 489
virtue, 600
voyages, 620-621

W

wages, 780, 785; see also fees
waits, 142
war of the theatres, 503
wardship, 224
watermarks, 185
water-sprights, 027
widows, 597
witchcraft, 089, 217
witches, 202, 721, 756
wives, 072, 448
women, 029, 228, 281, 344, 435, 448, 461, 463, 470, 496, 597, 617, 619, 650, 718, 722, 748, 768
--and misogyny, 723
--reading tastes of, 768
--on stage, 655; see also learned ladies and wives
work, 029, 072, 768
writing, mechanics of, 156

Persons, Plays and Places

A

Adams, John Quincy, Jr.,
    bibliography of, 002
Agas, Ralph, 034
Aglaura, 497, 595, 649, 741
Agrippina, 535
Albertus Wallenstein, 367, 451,
    506, 682
Albion's England, 371
Albion's Triumph, 713
--staging of, 814
Albovine, 614, 618
Alchemist, The
--influence of, 329, 560
All for Love, 488
Amorous War, The, 163, 536
Amyntas, 329, 518, 527, 547, 564,
    678, 740
Anacreon, 690
Anatomy of Melancholy, The,
    281, 411, 437
Antigone, 519
Antipodes, The, 199, 232, 234,
    250, 256, 264, 282, 318, 335,
    413, 455, 634, 649, 772, 827
Antiquary, The, 565, 651, 669,
    682
Apollo room, the, 478
Apology for Actors, The, 507
Arcadia, 290
Argalus and Parthenia, 188, 506
Aristippus, 149, 564
Aristophanes, 491, 575
Arviragus and Philicia, 554-556
--manuscript, 557, 580
Astrophel and Stella, 238

As You Like It, 250
Aubrey, John
--works of, 010
--on Jonson, 200

B

Bacon, Sir Francis, 075, 197,
    230, 436, 493
Bacon, Robert, 553
Ball, The, 333, 340, 361, 380,
    772
Bandello, Matteo, 212
"Banished Shepherdesse, The,"
    580
Bartholomew Fair, 444
Bashful Lover, The, 341
"Bastard, The," 580
Bedingfield, Thomas
--influence of, 398
Beeston, William, 318, 498,
    820-821
Beeston's Boys, 820
Believe As You List, 184, 189,
    192, 252, 270, 286, 341, 347,
    453, 711, 759, 781, 793
Believe It Is So and It Is So,
    270
Benefice, The, 192
Benlowes, Edward, 621
--biography of, 668
Berkeley, Sir William, 468
Bible
--allusions to, 045

Bird in a Cage, The, 763
Birkhead, Henry, 580
Blackfriars, 545, 777
Bloody Banquet, The, 177, 595
Boleyn, Anne, 046
Bondman, The, 162, 232, 252,
    348, 461, 710
--parallel with The Royall
    Slave, 549
Boyle, Richard, Earl of Orrey,
    245, 708
Brennoralt, or The Discontented
    Colonel, 486
Bride, The, 485, 529, 579
Britannia Triumphans, 255, 713
--staging of, 814
Broken Heart, The, 073, 123,
    195-196, 203, 212, 223, 225,
    233, 236-239, 263, 268, 276,
    279, 301, 304, 312, 315,
    319, 337, 365, 368, 372-375,
    393, 400, 409-410, 416-417,
    429-431, 447-448, 595, 608,
    671, 689, 714, 719
Brome, Richard, 179, 199, 205,
    220, 250, 256, 282, 315, 320,
    367, 377-378, 412, 439, 455,
    496, 580, 594, 599, 606, 609,
    613, 620-622, 632, 634, 649,
    658, 665, 673, 675, 681,
    692, 700, 710, 715-716, 732,
    749, 753-754, 763, 767, 770,
    772, 789, 824, 827
--collaboration of, 346
--influence on, 199, 264, 274
--life of, 199, 335
--quartos of, 267
--reputation, 234-235, 256, 264,
    317
--sources, 413
Brothers, The, 339
Browne, Sir Thomas, 071
Burton, Robert
--influence of, 263, 281, 408,
    411, 437
Butter, Nathaniel, 310
Byland, Ambrose, 501
Byron's Revenge, 510

C

Calverley, Walter, 224
Candy Restored, 524, 813
Cane, Vincent, 442
Captain Underwit, or The Country
    Captain, 569
Cardano, Girolamo
--influence of, 238
Cardinal, The, 073, 221-222, 272,
    314, 339, 344, 361, 363, 392,
    419, 630, 649, 711, 714, 781
Careless Shepherdess, The, 562,
    740, 775
Carew, Thomas, 474, 479, 503,
    621, 673, 742, 745
--masques of, 818
Carlell, Jean, 502
Carlell, Lodowick, 412, 495, 502,
    554-557, 580, 618, 621, 700,
    753, 767, 818
Carlisle, Countess of, 557
Cartwright, William, 116, 158,
    160, 352, 412, 480, 487, 497,
    537, 549, 554, 621, 632, 673,
    690, 749, 753, 767
Case Is Altered, The, 426
Castiglione, Baldassare, 237, 312
Cavendish, William, Duke of
    Newcastle, 569, 632
Challenge for Beauty, A, 544, 766
Chamberlaine, Robert, 496
Chamberlaine, William, 554
Chances, The, 765
Chapman, George, 314, 340, 345,
    380, 446, 471, 571, 651, 653,
    752, 772
Charles I, King
--reign of, 048, 067, 130, 318,
    359-360, 376, 464, 503, 651,
    717
Chloridia, 285, 458, 677, 713,
    814
Christ's Passion, 489, 516, 559
Christmas family, the, 783
City Madam, The, 173-174, 248,
    252, 262, 280, 287, 289, 334,
    341, 349, 461, 529, 603, 652,
    671, 775, 808
City Match, The, 163, 536, 584,
    754, 775

City Night Cap, The, 492, 509
City Wit, The, 264, 282, 455,
    682, 754
Civil Architecture, 798
Claracilla, 475
Clavell, John, 328, 520, 531
Cleopatra, 232, 470, 473, 488,
    561
Clifford, Lord, 823
Cockayne, Sir Aston, 320, 328,
    510, 524
Cockayne, Sir William, 280
Cock Pit-in-Court, 790
Coelum Britannicum, 474, 713, 814
Cole, Francis, 589
Combat of Love and Friendship,
    The, 537
Complete Armour against Civill
    Society, 654
Comus, 657, 814
"Conceited Peddler, The," 580
Constant Maid, The, 361, 749
Contention of Ajax and Ulysses,
    369, 696
Converted Robber, The, 678
Cooke, William, 187
Corneille, Thomas, 393, 685
Cornelianum Dolium, 563
Coronation, The, 321
Corporal, The, 591
Court Begger, The, 250, 264, 775,
    781, 789
Court Secret, The, 192, 247, 303
Covent Garden, 485, 579, 698,
    716, 826
Covent Garden Weeded, 250, 264,
    335, 698, 716, 765
Cowley, Abraham, 499, 528, 541,
    589, 606, 678, 706, 740, 742
Crane, Ralph, 781
Crede Quod Habes et Habes,
    see The City Night-Cap
Crooke, Andrew, 187
Crosfield, Thomas, 779, 785
Cruel Brother, The, 255, 325,
    618
Cumberland, Earl of, 823
Cupid and Death, 677
Cupid and Psyche, 483
Cupid's Revenge, 451
Curiosities of Literature, 388

Cutter of Coleman Street, The,
    541, 606, 706
Cynthia's Revels, 383
"Cyprian Conqueror, The, or The
    Faithless Relict," 795

D

D., J., 618
Damoiselle, The, 250, 264, 318,
    329, 749
Dankerts, Cornelius, 034
Davenant, Sir William, 050, 161,
    179, 228, 246, 254-255, 293,
    297, 318, 325, 360, 366, 412,
    427-428, 443, 492, 497, 503,
    601, 609, 611, 614, 618, 620,
    632, 637, 646, 656, 663, 681,
    702, 715, 749, 753, 755, 767,
    787, 789, 791, 796, 812, 818,
    820
Davenport, Robert, 177, 320, 439,
    494, 509, 532, 542, 673, 753
Day, John, 439
Dekker, Thomas, 039, 179, 199,
    291, 299-300, 390, 577, 675,
    808
Dempster, Thomas, 019
Denham, John, 232, 742
Descartes, René, 075
Deserving Favorite, The, 502,
    556, 618
Devil Is An Ass, The, 227, 242,
    257, 324, 332, 356, 478
Devil Tavern, The, 423, 478, 565
Dick of Devonshire, 177
Digby, Sir Kenelm, 292, 464, 498,
    527
Disraeli, Isaac, 388
Distresses, The, 325, 428, 682
"Don Manuell," 303
Donne, John, 512, 592
Doubtful Heir, The, 247, 363,
    760, 775, 781
Downes, John, 069
Drinking Academy, The, 153, 478,
    490, 530, 546-547, 552-553,
    564
Drunkard's Character, The, 654
Dryden, John, 260, 331, 452, 488,
    554, 613, 708, 813

Duke of Lerma, The, 372, 334, 408
Duke of Milan, The, 618
Duke's Mistress, The, 247, 752

E

Eclogues, 564
Edward VI, King, 046
Egers, 506
Egerton MS. 1994, 610
Ellice, Robert, 297
Ellice, Thomas, 297
Eliot, T. S., 204, 209
Emperor of the East, The, 162, 171, 194, 252, 283, 384, 387-389, 461, 682
Enchanted Lovers, The, 499
England, 055
English Moor, The, 250, 264, 455, 580, 710, 749
Epicoene, 264
"Epistle to the Society of Florists," 654
Eumorphus sive Cupido Adultus, 587
Every Man in His Humor, 201
Every Man Out of His Humor, 383
Example, The, 339, 396, 606

F

Fair Favorite, The, 325, 428
Fair Maid of the Inn, The, 295, 329
Fair Maid of the West, The, 073, 443
Fairy Knight, The, 153, 478, 547, 564
Faithful Shepherdess, The, 657
Fancies, Chaste and Noble, The, 195, 233, 239, 263, 294, 342, 372, 402, 416, 438, 760
Fane, Mildman, Earl of West-moreland, 505, 524, 813
Farwell to Militarie Profession, A, 213
Fasti Oxonienses, 538

Fatal Dowry, The, 232, 252
"Female Rebellion, The," 580
Field, Nathaniel, 169, 320, 355, 690, 753
Fielding, Sir William, 634
Fine Companion, A, 565, 749
Fletcher, John, 122, 169, 281, 295, 306, 344, 351-352, 359, 363, 446, 497, 525, 566, 606-607, 609, 623-624, 636, 663, 673, 770
Floating Island, The, 568, 727
Florimène, Pastoral of, 713, 787, 806, 814
"Fool Would Be a Favorite, The," 580
Ford, John, 179, 195-197, 212, 223, 225, 253, 279, 294, 301-302, 304, 309, 312, 315, 319, 323, 330, 337, 342, 345, 372-375, 386, 399, 400, 408-409, 411, 422, 429-430, 435, 437-438, 446-448, 454, 577, 595, 599, 607, 609, 618, 622, 624, 636, 649, 653, 671, 673-674, 689, 692-693, 700, 702, 714-715, 720, 727, 734, 745, 753, 759, 772
--and abnormal psychology, 202
--authorship, 408, 416
--bibliography, 099, 123
--characterization, 209
--collaboration, 291, 299, 390
--comedies, 402
--devices, 198
--friends, 297
--influence of, 368
--influence on, 218, 232, 237-238, 263, 268, 300, 305, 370-371, 436
--life, 404
--modernity of, 393
--non-dramatic works, 301
--reputation, 203, 239, 270-271
--sources, 364
--themes, 198, 233, 276
--tragedies, 276, 322, 326, 412
--women in, 228
Fortunate Isles, The, 677
Fortune, the
--elevations and floor plans of, 819

France, 055
Freeman, Sir Ralph, 550
Furttenbach, Joseph, 798

G

Gainsford, Thomas
--influence of, 270, 364, 370,
    436
Gallery to the Temple, A, 514
Gamester, The, 333, 361, 396,
    682
Gaudy, Philip, 365
General, The, 245
Gentleman of Venice, The, 159,
    247
Gentleman Usher, The, 752
Gerbier, Charles, 496
Germany, 055
Gifford, William
--on Jonson, 200
Gilbert, William, 338
Glapthorne, Henry, 188, 320, 329,
    349, 367, 414, 445, 451, 465,
    471, 477, 500, 506, 570-572,
    582-583, 599, 618, 621, 632,
    673, 753, 793
Goblins, The, 486, 581, 781
Goffe, Thomas, 412, 740, 775
Goodman, Nicholas, 469
Gosse, Edmund, 366
Great Duke of Florence, The,
    248, 334, 550
Great Favorite, The, see The
    Duke of Lerma
Greene, Robert, 492, 509
Grey, Lady Jane, 046
Grotius, Hugo, 489, 516
Guardian, The, 224, 248, 341,
    381, 541, 544, 589, 606,
    652, 682, 706
Guarini, Battista, 740
Gull's Hornbook, The, 788

H

Habington, William, 497, 818
Hamlet, 524, 649
Hannibal & Scipio, 485, 578-579

Hardy, Alexander, 685
Harleian Miscellany, 436
Harper, Thomas, 149
Hausted, Peter, 486, 538, 632
Hawkins, Sir Thomas, 283
Henrietta, Maria, Queen, 405,
    557, 646, 787
I Henry IV, 542
Henry VII, 386, 436
Henry VIII, King, 046
Herbert, Sir Henry, 003, 008,
    610, 647; see also records,
    stationers'
Heton, Richard, 779
Hey for Honesty, 491, 518, 562,
    575, 706
Heywood, Thomas, 094, 177, 205,
    369, 443, 448, 476, 482, 484,
    503, 507-508, 517, 522, 544,
    574, 576, 594, 606-607, 609,
    620-622, 624, 673, 675, 678,
    732, 763, 766, 770, 784
--bibliography, 030, 040, 125
--collaboration, 211, 346
--late plays, 593
--pageants, 472
--reputation of, 593
History of the Earl of Tyrone,
    The, 370
Histrio-Mastix, 631, 654
Hobbes, Thomas, 075
Holinshed, Raphael, 230
Holland, 055
Holland's Leaguer, 469, 533, 565,
    651, 682, 698
Hollander, The, 329, 506, 682
Holy Court, The, 283
Honest Whore, The, 808
Honor Triumphant, 430
Hood, Robin, 027
Horace, 690, 726
Howard, Sir Robert, 372, 408
Humorous Courtier, The, 359, 363
Hungary, 431
Hyde Park, 333, 339, 361, 397,
    457, 698, 716, 733, 741

I

Imperiale, 550
Imposture, The, 247

Inconstant Lady, The, 466, 591
Indian Emperor, The, 554
Ireland, 336, 432, 433, 459
Iron Age I, The, 369
Istorie Fiorentine, Le, 398
Italian Night Masque, The,
    see Italian Night Piece, The
Italian Night Piece, The, 497
Italy, 055, 663, 787

J

James I, King, 048
Jealous Lovers, The, 329, 490,
    518, 547, 562, 564
Jones, Inigo, 391, 713, 755, 771,
    787, 806, 814, 816, 818
Jonson, Benjamin, 035, 096, 161,
    179, 199, 240, 278, 285,
    295-296, 310-311, 313, 324,
    332, 338, 352, 357, 359, 382,
    391, 395, 401, 423-424, 450,
    460, 462, 474, 478, 517, 527,
    546, 560, 565, 584, 595, 607,
    609, 613, 623, 632, 634,
    672-673, 675, 678, 686, 693,
    702, 715, 749, 757, 759, 767,
    772, 827
--and action, 204
--allusions to, 229, 513
--and Anglicanism, 665
--and Brome, 827
--bibliography of, 057, 117, 206
--biography of, 200
--Cavalier heroes, 201
--characters in, 204, 207, 227
--chronology, 206, 311
--comedy, 204, 206, 208, 217,
    226-227, 241-243, 257, 320,
    441, 632
--criticism, 200, 226
--devices, 227
--influence of, 213, 227,
    231-232, 268, 317, 320, 361,
    363, 458
--language, 207
--late plays, 226, 241-242, 257,
    331, 356, 440, 444
--life of, 425
--masques, 206, 214, 275, 376,
    818

--and music, 275
--plot, 227
--prose, 207
--reputation, 206, 220, 226, 229,
    632
--satire, 217
--structure, 227
--symbolism, 206
--themes, 208, 217, 258, 275
--tragedies, 232
Jordan, Thomas, 094, 432, 496,
    501, 517, 573, 716
Jovial Crew, The, 073, 235, 250,
    264, 282, 455, 692
Julia Agrippina, 232, 535
Julius Caesar, 232
Junius, R., 654
"Just General, The," 580
Just Italian, The, 325, 427
Juvenal, 690

K

Kent, 036
Killigrew, Henry, 497
Killigrew, Thomas, 161, 475, 513,
    586, 620, 673, 791, 800, 812,
    820
--influence on, 512
--life, 504
--travels, 567
King and Queen of Bohemia's
    Company, 779
King John and Matilda, 532
King's Men's Company, 279, 501,
    779
King's Revels, the, 501, 779
Kirke, John, 522
Kirkman, Francis, 069
Knave in Grave, The, 618
Knevet, Sir Ralph, 499, 514, 654,
    678, 740
--life, 515
Knight of Burning Pestle, The,
    214

L

Lady Alimony, or The Alimony
    Lady, 409

Lady Elizabeth's Men, 779, 824
Lady Mother, The, 188, 192, 760, 793
--authorship of, 570
Lady of Pleasure, The, 073, 333, 339, 361, 379, 396, 694, 697
Lady's Privilege, The, 506, 775
Lady's Trial, The, 195, 233, 239, 263, 301, 304, 342, 372, 714
Lamb, Charles, 439
Lando, Girolamo, 477
Langbaine, Gerard, 019, 069, 077
Lawes, Henry, 695
Lawes, William, 630
Late Lancashire Witches, The, 199, 205, 346, 484, 594, 732, 756, 763, 765
Launching of the Mary, 569, 610
Lawrence, W. J., 112
Lenton, Francis, 654
Lesage, Alaine Renè, 685
Life and Death of Mahomet, The, 451
Lillo, George, 351
London, 034, 240, 652, 792, 824; see also life, London
Londoni Ius Honorarium, 472, 783
Londoni sinus Salutis, 783
Londini Status Pacatus, 624, 683
London's Tempe, 783
Loose Fancies, 464
Lost Lady, The, 468, 630
"Lost Lover, The," 580
Love and Honor, 073, 254, 325, 428
Love in a Maze, 361, 396, 478
Love-Sick Court, The, 264, 282, 335
Love Tricks, 214, 295, 339, 361, 362, 363, 678, 749
Love Will Find Out the Way, 321, 397
Love's Cruelty, 221, 314, 392, 458, 682, 781
Love's Hospital, 588, 773
Love's Mistress, or The Queen's Masque, 507, 677
Love's Riddle, 499, 541, 678, 740
Love's Sacrifice, 123, 195, 203, 225, 233, 239, 263, 276, 301,

304, 342, 372, 374-375, 400, 409, 411, 429-430, 447, 618, 671, 714
Love's Triumph Through Callipolis, 458, 677, 713
Love's Victory, 554
Love's Welcome At Welbeck, 214
Lover's Melancholy, The, 123, 195, 233, 239, 263, 279, 297, 304, 309, 326, 342, 372-373, 411, 430, 437, 556, 714, 727
Lower, Sir William, 499
Lucan, 519
Luminalia, 255, 814

M

Machiavel As He Lately Appeared, 508
Machiavelli, Niccolà, 197, 227, 398
Mad Couple Well Match'd, A, 264, 741
Magnete, De, 338
Magnetic Lady, The, 201, 204, 241-243, 338, 344, 356, 426, 440, 444, 462, 749, 765, 772, 775, 781
Maid of Honor, The, 073, 175, 329, 351, 461
Maid's Revenge, The, 221, 314, 360, 392
Malade Imaginaire, 194
Malynes, Gerard, de, 761
Manual for Constructing Theatrical Scenes and Machines, A, 798
Manuche, Cosmo, 580, 585
Marlowe, Christopher, 305
Marmion, Shackerley, 483, 520, 531, 533, 565, 651, 669, 673, 749, 753
Marston, John, 715
Martial, 690
Masque, A, 510
Masque of Christmas, The, 214
Massinger, Anne, 327
Massinger, Arthur, 327
Massinger, Philip, 161-162, 169, 171-173, 175, 188, 191, 194, 212, 220, 224, 278-281,

286-289, 307, 334, 344,
347-351, 353-354, 372, 381,
384, 387-389, 431, 439, 453,
461, 497, 523, 549, 584, 595,
599, 603-604, 607, 609, 613,
618, 620, 622, 624, 631, 649,
671, 673, 675, 692-693, 705,
710, 715, 734, 745, 753, 756,
759, 767, 772, 791, 793, 801,
808
--actors in plays of, 252
--adaptations, 341
--and Anglicanism, 665
--alliteration, 252
--autograph, 172, 174, 251
--bibliography, 099, 124
--biography of, 259, 327-328,
352, 385
--collaboration, 355
--comedies, 284
--devices, 259, 298
--early editions, 219
--influence of, 452
--influence on, 232, 252
--imagery, 262
--location of plays, 219
--punctuation, 681
--reputation, 252, 259
--sources, 283
--women in, 228
May, Thomas, 050, 220, 320, 328,
470, 488, 498, 511, 561, 620,
673, 730, 753, 801
--biography of, 473, 481, 534,
535
--influence on, 232
--as pamphleteer, 590
Mayden-Head Well Lost, A, 574
Mayne, Jasper, 163, 220, 320,
349, 607, 613, 620-621, 673,
753-754, 767
--biography, 536, 584
Mead, Robert, 537
Measure for Measure, 511
Mercurius Britanicus, 358, 442
Mercury Vindicated, 677
Messallina, 232, 551, 730
Metamorphoses, 369
Microcosmus, 485, 521, 577, 579,
727
Middleton, Thomas, 467, 636, 675,
715

Mildmay, Sir Humphrey, 778-779
Mill, John Stuart, 748
Milton, John, 368, 657
Molière, 194, 635
Money Is An Asse, 573
Monster Late Found Out and Dis-
covered, A, 631
Montague, Walter, 499, 740, 752,
818
Montfort, Montague, 539, 610
Moseley, Humphrey, 158, 159, 308
Muses' Looking-Glass, The, 256,
518, 547, 564, 631, 706

N

Nabbes, Thomas, 220, 278, 320,
439, 485, 496, 521, 529, 569,
577-579, 620-621, 632, 698,
716, 727, 753, 826
--biography, 579
--reputation, 517
Naufragium Joculare, 541
Neale, Thomas
--biography, 540
Neptune's Triumph, 295
Nero, 535
New Academy, The, 264
New Inn, The, 204, 208, 231,
241-242, 258, 296, 324, 356,
382, 383, 409, 426, 444, 462,
595, 775, 781
New Trick to Cheat the Devil, A,
494, 542
New Way to Pay Old Debts, A,
248, 287, 289, 334, 461, 604
Newcastle, Duke of, see
Cavendish, William
News from Plymouth, 246, 325,
329, 427, 682
Nicoline, Francis, 645
Night Walker, The, 306, 566, 749
Noble Mirror of Art, The, 798
Northern Lass, The, 250, 264,
267, 274, 335, 409
Novella, The, 264, 413, 455

O

Octavia, 218
Old Couple, The, 534
Old Joiner of Algate, The, 651
Oldys, William, 069
Opportunity, The, 361, 363
Ordinary, The, 158, 264, 749
Orrey, Earl of, see Boyle,
    Richard
Osmond the Great Turk, 451, 580
Othello, 414, 471, 618
Ovid, 369
Oxford, 032, 087-088, 141, 587,
    588

P

Palsgrave's Company, the, 779
Paradise Regained, 368
Parliament of Love, The, 259
Parson's Wedding, The, 504,
    512-513, 567, 697, 741
Passionate Lovers, The, 495, 556
Peaps, W., 767
Pennycruicke, Andrew, 349
Pepys, Samuel, 108
Percy, Thomas, 047
Perkin Warbeck, 073, 123,
    195-198, 202, 209, 225, 230,
    232, 239, 253, 263, 270,
    276, 291, 299, 304, 323,
    364, 371-372, 374-375, 386,
    429, 430, 436, 449, 454, 711,
    714, 760
Perkin Warbeck
--lost play of, 370
Persius, 690
Pestell, Thomas, 543
Philomela, 492, 509
Phoenix, The, 794, 803
Phoenix in Her Flames, The, 499
Picture, The, 162, 175, 212, 279,
    431, 461, 556
Platonic Lovers, The, 325, 409,
    427-428, 618, 741
Pleasant Dialogues and Dramas,
    678
Plutarch, 473
Plutus, 491

P (continued)

Polititian, The, 159, 221, 265,
    308, 339, 392, 711
Pope, Alexander, 483
Porta Pietatis, 624, 783
Prince Charles' Company, 779
Prynne, William, 631, 654, 742,
    755
Purcell, Henry, 693

Q

Quarles, Francis, 621
Queen, The, 195, 225, 233, 263,
    301, 309, 326, 342, 372-373,
    404, 416, 430, 618
Queen and the Concubine, The,
    282, 760
Queen Anne's Company, 779
Queen Henrietta's Company, 501,
    779
Queen of Aragon, The, 713
Queen of Corsica, The, 192
Queen's Exchange, The, 264, 282,
    367
Queen's Masque, The, see Love's
    Mistress

R

Racine, Jean Baptiste, 393
Randolph, Thomas, 149, 151,
    153-154, 220, 388, 478,
    490-491, 493, 527, 538,
    546-547, 552-553, 562, 575,
    580, 596, 607, 620-622,
    631-632, 657, 673, 678, 690,
    706, 710, 730, 740, 753, 767,
    801
--bibliography, 058, 127
--biography, 518, 548, 564
--as critic, 256
Rape of the Lock, The, 483
Rawlidge, Richard, 631
Rawlins, Thomas, 496, 669
Rebellion, The, 669, 710
Recreational Architecture, 798
Red Bull Theatre, 522, 765, 779
Rehearsal, The, 541
Renegado, The, 162, 232, 252, 278,
    461, 624, 705, 710

Requo, De, 549
Revelation of Mr. Brightman's
  Revelation, A, 508
Revenge for Honour, 414, 445,
  451, 471, 477, 571, 618
Revenger's Tragedy, The, 233
Rhodon and Iris, 499, 654, 678,
  740
Richard II, 198
Richards, Nathaniel, 730
--biography, 551, 563
--influence on, 232
Rider, W., 618
Rival Friends, The, 486
Robin Hood, see Hood, Robin
Roman Actor, The, 162, 188, 232,
  252, 259, 341, 353, 461, 595,
  631, 711, 759, 772
Romeo and Juliet, 300, 669
Rowlands, Samuel, 761
Rowley, William, 522
Royal Exchange, The, 367
Royal Master, The, 247, 407
Royal Slave, The, 160, 487, 537,
  549, 554
Royal Society, the, 071
Rutter, Joseph, 678, 740

S

Sabbattini, Nicola, 798
Sad Shepherd, The, 324, 678
St. Patrick for Ireland, 336,
  343, 459, 760, 763
Salisbury Court, 526, 658, 786,
  794
Salmacida Spolia, 255, 637, 677,
  713, 787, 814
Sampson, William, 513
Sandys, George, 489, 559,
  620-621
Scandinavia
--influence of English drama on,
  734
Scotland, 023
Scudamore Papers, 640
Seneca, 519, 550
Seven Champions of Christendom,
  The, 522
Shakespeare, 093, 097, 155, 160,

190, 220, 250, 252, 300, 363,
424, 473, 511, 513, 519, 525,
539, 542, 581, 607, 610, 613,
618, 623, 625, 649, 669, 682,
692-693, 700, 703-704, 764,
770, 813, 817, 826
Shepherd's Paradise, The, 409,
  499, 740, 752
Shepherds' Holiday, The, 678, 740
Shirley, Henry, 269
Shirley, James, 159, 165, 179,
  187, 220-222, 228, 278, 290,
  303, 306, 308, 321, 328, 333,
  339, 344, 359-362, 372, 394,
  396-397, 399, 405, 412, 419,
  421, 439, 442, 457, 463, 503,
  569, 599, 601, 606-607, 609,
  613, 620-622, 624, 637, 649,
  656, 665, 673, 675, 678, 681,
  686, 694-696, 698, 700, 702,
  715-716, 734, 749, 752-753,
  755, 763, 767, 770, 772, 791,
  796
--bibliography of, 099, 126
--biography of, 210-211, 215-216,
  249, 260, 266, 269, 273, 358,
  363, 407, 420
--characterization, 277
--chronology, 260, 269, 273, 418
--collaboration, 340
--comedy, 244, 249, 272, 380
--devices, 273
--grammars, 403
--influence on, 245, 249, 261,
  273, 618
--in Ireland, 336, 432-434, 459
--masques, 249, 458, 818
--narration, 247
--reputation of, 216, 244, 260,
  406, 456
--tragedies, 249, 265, 314, 392
--tragicomedies, 247, 249
--sources, 213, 292, 343, 369,
  398
Short Treatise Against Stage-
  Players, A, 631
Sidney, Sir Philip, 238
Siege, The (Cartwright), 158
Siege, The (Davenant), 325
Siege of Rhodes, The, 254, 443
Silent Woman, The, 213

Smock Alley, 566
Socrates, 700
Soddered Citizen, The, 192, 520,
    531, 556
Somerset, Earl of, 046
Sophocles, 519
Sophy, The, 232
Sparagus Garden, The, 250, 264,
    335, 337-378, 698, 716
Staple of News, The, 204, 208,
    226, 241-242, 257, 295,
    310-311, 324, 333, 356-357,
    383, 426, 444, 450, 462,
    478, 749, 760, 775, 781
Statius, 519
Strode, William, 568, 727
Stuarts, the, 035, 050, 092
Subjugation of Women, The, 748
Suckling, Sir John, 050, 317-318,
    486, 497, 581, 595, 624, 649,
    690, 742, 752-753, 767, 789
Sun's Darling, The, 390, 577,
    677
Swaggering Damsell, The, 496
Swinburne, Algernon, 200, 439
Swisser, The, 554, 556, 580, 592

T

Tacitus, 748
Taferell, 822
Tasso, Torquato, 740
Tatham, John, 094, 496, 517, 767
Taylor, John, 094, 784
Tempest, The, 581
Temple of Love, The, 255, 409,
    428, 741
Thomaso, or The Wanderer, 513
'Tis Pity She's a Whore, 073,
    123, 195-196, 203, 218, 225,
    233, 263, 271, 276, 297, 300,
    304, 309, 342, 372, 374-375,
    393, 399-400, 410, 416, 422,
    429-430, 447, 595, 618, 682,
    714, 772
Tottenham Court, 485, 579, 698,
    716, 760
Tourner, Cyril, 715
Townshend, Horatio, 818
Traitor, The, 221, 361, 363, 392,
    398, 421, 711

Trappolin, Creduto Principe,
    see Trappolin, Supposed a
    Prince
Trappolin, Supposed a Prince,
    511, 523
Trattate sepra le Scene, 788
Triumph of Peace, The, 165, 558,
    629-630, 637, 656, 760, 816
Triumphant-Day, 783
Triumphs of Health and Posterity,
    The, 783
Triumphs of the Prince D'Amour,
    The, 255, 656
Troy, legends of, 696
True and Wonderful History of
    Perkin Warbeck, The
    (Gainsford), 436
Twins, The, 618

U

Underwoods XXX, 231
Unfortunate Lovers, The, 325,
    428, 760, 781
Unfortunate Mother, The, 485, 579
Unnatural Combat, The, 259, 354,
    461, 756
Unnatural Combatant, The, 233

V

Very Woman, A, 281, 341, 772
Virgil, 690
Virgin Martyr, The, 252, 452
Vitruvius, 787
Volpone, 268
Vow Breaker, The, 513

W

Wadloe, Simon, 423
Walks of Islington and Hogsdon,
    The, 716
Warde, The, 540
Warner, William, 270, 371, 436
Wars, Wars, Wars, 783
Wasp, The, 501, 526
Webster, John, 263, 636, 653, 715

Wedding, The, 247, 292, 361, 363, 749

Westmoreland, Earl of, see Fane, Mildman

"Where did you borrow that last sigh," 630

Whitehall, 816

Wild Goose Chase, The, 697

Wilde, George, 587–588, 678

Wilson, Arthur, 466, 545, 556, 580, 591–592, 607

Wilson, Thomas, 761

"Wine, Beer, Ale," 580

Winstanley, William, 081

Witch of Edmonton, The, 123, 300

Wit in a Constable, 349, 465, 506, 572, 583

Wit Without Money, 351

Wits, The, 246, 427, 749

Wit's Triumvirate, or The Philosopher, 560

Witty Fair One, The, 339, 361, 363, 396, 682

Wolsey, Cardinal, 046

Wood, Anthony à, 019, 538

Worde, Wynkyn de, 046

Wright, Abraham, 773

Y

Young Admiral, The, 261, 329

Young Gallants Whirligig, The, 654

Authors of Secondary Writings

A

Ackerman, Catherine A., 464
Adams, Joseph Quincy, Jr.,
    002-003, 229, 465, 539, 572,
    774
Adams, Henry Hitch, 594
Addis, John, 194
Agas, Ralph, 034
Aird, Catherine D., 009
Ali, Florence, 195
Allen, Don Cameron, 004
Allibone, Samuel Austin, 005
Anderson, Donald K., Jr.,
    196-198, 595-596
Andrews, Clarence Edward, 199,
    346, 827
Anklesaria, Shirin Sarosh, 200
Apperson, George Latimer, 007
Arber, Edward, 008
Armstrong, William A., 775, 781
Arnold, Judd, 201
Arnott, James F., 009
Ashley, Maurice, 597
Aubrey, John, 010
Avery, Emmet L., 084
Aydelotte, Frank, 598

B

Babb, Lawrence, 202, 599
Bachrach, A. G. H., 776
Bacon, Wallace A., 203-204
Bailey, Richard Weld, 011
Baker, David Erskine, 012
Baker, H. Barton, 777

Baker, Hershel Clay, 013
Bald, R. C., 466-468
Ball, Robert Hamilton, 715
Barber, Charles L., 600
Barber, Laird Howard, Jr., 205
Barish, Jonas A., 206-209, 226
Barnard, Dean Stanton, Jr., 469
Barry, J. W., 470
Bas, Georges, 210-211, 503
Baskervill, Charles Read,
    212-214, 431, 601
Bastiaenen, Johannes Adam, 602,
    661
Bartley, J. O., 733
Baugh, Albert C., 210, 215-216
Baum, Helena Watts, 217
Bawcutt, N. W., 218
Beard, Charles, 033
Bearline, Lester A., 146
Beck, Ervin, Jr., 603
Beckingham, C. F., 471
Bell, C. F., 818
Bennett, A. L., 219, 604
Bennett, H. S., 605
Bennett, Josephine W., 291
Bentley, Gerald Eades, 147, 220,
    550, 778-781
Bergeron, David M., 015, 472,
    782-784
Bernbaum, Ernest, 606
Berry, Joe Wilkes, Jr., 473
Berry, William Turner, 016
Besterman, Theodore, 017
Bigmore, C. W. H., 018
Bigmore, E. C., 018

Bishop, William Warner, 020
Black, A. Bruce, 607
Black, Forrest Edward, Jr.,
    221
Bland, D. S., 222
Blaney, Glenn H., 223-224, 608
Blaney, Peter W. M., 148
Blanshard, Rufus A., 474
Blevins, James Richard, 225
Blezzard, Judy, 255
Bliss, Philip, 141
Blissett, William, 226
Block, Andrew, 119
Blom, Eric, 056
Boas, Frederick S., 038, 475-476,
    539, 609-610, 785
Bode, Robert F., 611
Bohn, Henry G., 021
Boles, Margaret Cabell, 537
Bordinant, Philip, 786
Boughner, Daniel C., 227
Bowden, William, 486, 612
B[owen], G[eorge] S[pencer], 613
Bowers, Fredson Thayer, 049, 143,
    149-154, 414, 451, 477-478,
    547, 614
Bradbrook, Muriel Clara, 615-616
Bradford, Gamaliel, 228
Bradley, Jesse Franklin, 229
Brereton, J. LeGay, 230, 436
Bridenbaugh, Carl, 617
Briggs, William Dinsmore,
    231-232
Brissenden, Alan, 233, 435
Broeker, Harriet Durkee, 618
Brome, Richard, 234-235
Brown, Arthur, 155
Brown, John Russell, 155
Bruce, J., 025
Brydges, Samuel Egerton, 022
Bryne, Eva A. W., 351
Buchan, Peter, 023
Buckan, Hannah, 543
Burbridge, Roger T., 236
Burelbach, Frederick M., Jr.,
    237, 312, 365
Burriss, Mary Helen, 536
Burton, Dolores M., 011
Bush, Douglas, 024

C

Camden, Carroll, 619
Campbell, Lily B., 787
Carew, Thomas, 479
Cargill, Oscar, 291
Carsaniga, G. M., 238
Carter, John Stewart, 421
Cartwright, William, 480
Carver, Rev. Alfred J., 116
Carver, Ann Augusta Cathey, 239
Cawley, Robert Ralston, 620-621
Cazamian, Louis, 622
Chalfont, Fran Cernocky, 240
Chambers, E. K., 788
Champion, Larry Stephen, 241-243
Chandler, Frank Wadleigh, 623
Chapman, Edgar Leon, 244
Charles, Amy M., 515
Chester, Allan Griffith, 481
Chew, Samuel C., 624
Child, Francis James, 027
Chubb, Thomas, 028
Clark, Alice, 029
Clark, Arthur Melville, 030,
    482, 508
Clark, E. C., 031
Clark, William S., 245
Collier, John Payne, 625
Collins, Howard S., 246
Cook, Dorothy E., 090
Cope, Jackson Irving, 483, 626
Cosulich, Gilbert, 414
Courtney, W. L., 032
Cousins, Kathryn McCambridge,
    247
Crabtree, John Henry, Jr., 248
Craig, Hardin, 627
Crinò, Anna Maria, 249
Cromwell, Otelia, 484
Crowther, J. W., 250
Cruikshank, Arthur J., 162,
    251-252
Crum, Margaret, 253
Cunningham, C. Willett, 033
Cunningham, Dolora, 206
Cunningham, Phillis, 033
Curry, John V., 628
Cutts, John P., 485-486, 510,
    629-630

D

Dankerts, Cornelius, 034
Danton, J. Periam, 487
Darlington, Ida, 034
Davenant, Sir William, 254-255
Davies, Godfrey, 035
Davies, H. Neville, 488
Davis, Joe Lee, 256, 631-632
Davis, Richard Beale, 489
Davril, Robin, 196
Dawson, Giles E., 036, 156
Day, Cyrus Lawrence, 037,
    490-491, 546
Dean, J. S., 492
Dearing, Vinton A., 049, 157
Deierkauf-Holsboer, S. Wilma,
    633
Deneef, A. Leigh, 782
Dessen, Alan Charles, 257
Dewey, Nicholas, 038
de Worde, Wynkyn, 046
Dick, Oliver Lawson, 010
Disraeli, Isaac, 388
Dobell, Bertram, 568
Donaldson, Ian, 634
Donovan, Dennis G., 039-040, 782
Downes, John, 041
Duncan, Douglas, 258
Dunn, Thomas Alexander, 259
Dyce, Alexander, 260, 420

E

Eagle, Dorothy, 065
Eagle, R. L., 493
Eckhardt, Eduard, 494
Eliot, T. S., 204, 448, 671
Ellehauge, Martin, 635
Ellis, Havelock, 454
Ellis-Femor, Una Mary, 636
Erickson, Kenneth Jerrold, 261
Evans, G. Blakemore, 480
Evans, Gwynne B., 158
Evans, Herbert Arthur, 637
Evenhuis, Francis D., 262
Ewbank, Inga-Stina, 638
Ewing, S. Blaine, 263
Ewton, Gene Stephenson, 495

F

Faust, Eduard Karl Richard, 264
Fehrenbach, Robert Julian, 159,
    265
Feil, Doris, 639
Feil, J. P., 249, 266, 640
Ferriar, John, 352
Feuillerat, Albert, 592
Field, Bradford S., Jr., 641
Field, H., 267
Field, Nathaniel, 355
Finney, Gretchen Ludke, 642
Fisch, Harold, 643
Fitzgibbon, G., 268
Fitzgibbons, M. Simplicia, 534
Flanagan, James Donald, 644
Fleay, Frederick Gard, 042-043,
    269
Fletcher, Ivan Kyrle, 645
Fletcher, Jefferson Butler, 646
Ford, John, 270-271
Ford, Wyn K., 044
Fordyce, Rachel Poole, 496
Forker, Charles R., 272, 419
Forsythe, Robert Stanley, 249,
    273
Foster, Joseph, 141
Fowell, Frank, 647
Foxon, D. F., 160
Freeburg, Victor Oscar, 648
Freehafer, John, 497, 789-790
Freeman, Arthur, 081
Fried, Harvey, 274
Frost, D. L., 649
Fulghum, Walter B., Jr., 045
Fuller, David, 275
Funston, Jay Louis, 588
Furnivall, Frederich James,
    046-047

G

G., G. M., 791
Gabrieli, Vittorio, 498
Gagen, Jean Elizabeth, 650
Gair, W. R., 651
Galloway, David, 651
Gardiner, Samuel R., 048
Gaskell, Philip, 049

Gates, William Bryan, 499
Gaw, Allison, 688
Gebauer, August William, Jr., 276
Gerber, Richard, 277
Gibbs, A. M., 255
Gibson, C. A., 278-280
Gifford, William, 352, 420
Gildersleeve, Virginia Crocheron, 792
Gill, Roma B., 281
Glapthorne, Henry, 500
Godfrey, Elizabeth, 050
Golding, Amy M., 652
Goldstein, Leonard, 653
Gomme, Alice Bertha, 051
Goodman, Cyndia Clegg, 282
Gosse, Edmund, 418, 439
Gourlay, J. J., 501
Granville-Barker, H., 819
Graves, Thornton S., 654-655
Gray, Charles H., 502
Gray, J. E., 171-172, 283-284
Graziani, R. I. C., 285
Green, A. Wigfall, 656
Greg, W. W., 052-054, 157, 161-165, 184, 249, 241, 284, 286, 531, 539, 657, 793
Grierson, Herbert John Clifford, 055
Grivelet, Michael, 211, 503
Grosart, A. B., 567
Gross, Alan Gerald, 287-289
Grove, George, 056
Guffey, George Robert, 057-058
Gurr, Andrew, 790

H

Haaker, Ann, 234-235, 658, 827
Hales, J. W., 047
Halkett, Samuel, 059
Hall, Vernon, Jr., 291
Halliwell, J. O., 032, 060
Hammer, Gael W., 794
Harbage, Alfred H., 061-062, 166, 290-293, 299, 408, 504-505, 659, 787, 795
Harben, Henry A., 063
Hardison, O. B., 064

Hargreaves, Geoffrey D., 167
Harris, Victor, 660
Harrison, G. B., 819
Hart, Alfred, 796
Hart, D. J., 294
Hart, H. C., 295
Harvey, Paul, 065, 115
Hastings, James, 066
Hawkins, Harriet, 296, 602, 661
Hayden, Hiram Collins, 067
Hazlitt, W. Carew, 068-069, 548, 797
Hector, Leonard Charles, 168
Heffner, Ray L., 206
Heltzel, Virgil B., 662
Hensman, Bertha, 169
Herrick, Marvin T., 663
Heseltine, Janet E., 115
Hewitt, Barnard, 798
Heywood, Thomas, 507
Hibbard, George B., 226, 450, 526
Hiler, Hilaire, 070
Hiler, Meyer, 070
Hill, Christopher, 664
Hill, T. H., 170
Hinman, Charlton, 160
Hobbs, Mary, 297
Hoeniger, F. David, 071
Hoeniger, Judith F. M., 071
Hogan, Alice Patricia, 298
Hogan, Charles B., 084
Holaday, Allan, 508
Holden, William P., 665
Hole, Christina, 072
Holzknecht, Karl J., 073
Homan, Sidney P., Jr., 299-300
Hooper, Richard, 559
Hoskins, Herbert Wilson, Jr., 301
Hosley, Richard, 799
Hotson, Leslie, 800
Howard-Hill, Trevor H., 074
Howarth, R. G., 302-303
Howe, James Robinson, IV, 304
Howell, William Samuel, 075
Howgego, James L., 034
Hoy, Cyrus, 305-307, 666
Huberman, Edward, 308
Huebert, Ronald M., 309
Hughes, Leo, 667

I

Institut Pédagogique National, 076
Isham, Sir Gyles, 557

J

Jackson, William A., 049
Jacob, Giles, 077
Jenkins, Harold, 668
Jones, J. L., 669
Jones, Richard F., 670
Jones, Stephen, 012
Jonson, A. F., 059
Jonson, Ben, 310-311
Jordan, John Clark, 492, 509
Jordan, R., 237, 312
Jordan, W. K., 078
Joseph, Bertram Leon, 801
Jump, J. D., 510
Juneja, Renu, 313

K

Kalmer, Elaine Bush, 314
Kaufman, Helen A., 511
Kaufmann, Ralph James, 250, 315-318, 671, 749
Keast, William R., 512-513
Kelley, Michael J., 319
Kennedy, James, 059
Kennedy-Skipton, Letitia, 156
Kernan, Alvin, 672
Kerr, Mina, 320
Kifer, Devra Rowland, 311
King, T. J., 321, 802-803
Kinloch, George Ritchie, 079
Kirk, Rudolf, 349
Kistner, Arthur L., 322-323
Kistner, M. K., 322-323
Klein, David, 673
Knevet, Ralph, 514-515
Knight, G. Wilson, 674
Knight, William Stanley MacBean, 516
Knights, L. C., 206, 289, 675
Knoll, Robert Edwin, 324
Knox, Norman, 676

Koch, J., 517, 677
Koeppel, Emil, 213, 232
Kottas, Karl, 518

L

Labarre, E. J., 080
Laidler, Josephine, 678
Laig, Friederick, 325
Laing, John, 059
Lamb, Charles, 337
Langbaine, Gerald, 081-082
Lauren, Barbara, 326
Lautner, Edward John, 519
Lawless, Donald S., 327-328, 520
Lawless, Robert S., 385
Lawrence, T. E., 679
Lawrence, William J., 521-522, 680-681, 733, 804-805
Lea, Kathleen M., 523
Leacroft, Richard, 806
Lee, Sidney, 118
Leech, Clifford, 226, 329-330, 524-525, 682, 807
Lemly, John W., 331
Lever, J. W., 526
Levin, Harry, 206
Levin, Laurence L., 332
Levin, Richard, 333, 683
Lockert, Charles Lacy, Jr., 355
Loiseau, Jean, 528
Long, John, 684
Lough, John, 685, 825
Lovejoy, Arthur O., 129
Lurie, Dona Jean Barry, 529
Lynch, Kathleen M., 686
Lyons, Bridget Gellert, 687
Lyons, John O., 334

M

McCaulley, Martha Gause, 688
McClure, Donald Stuart, 335
McConnell, Elizabeth M., 336, 459
McDonald, Charles Osbourne, 337, 689
McEuen, Katherine Anderson, 690

McFarland, Ronald E., 338
McGrath, Juliet, 339
McIlwraith, A. K., 171–175,
    283–284, 808
McKenzie, D. F., 160, 176, 226
McKerrow, Ronald B., 049, 085
Mackie, John Duncan, 691
McKinnon, Dana Gene, 340
McManaway, James G., 143, 177,
    341, 452
McMaster, Juliet, 342
MacMullan, Hugh, 343
McNamee, Lawrence Francis, 086
McNeir, W. F., 250
McPeek, James A. S., 692
Madan, Falconer, 087–088
Magoun, F. P., Jr., 530
Maitland, Frederic William, 103
Makkink, Henri Jacob, 344
Manifold, John Streeter, 693
Manly, F., 345
Marmion, Shackerley, 531
Marshburn, Joseph H., 089
Martin, Robert Grant, 346
Massinger, Philip, 347–355
Maxwell, J. C., 532
Maxwell, Sue, 533
May, Thomas, 534–535
Mayhew, A. L., 114
Mayne, Jasper, 536
Mead, Robert, 537
Meadley, T. D., 809
Meigs, Joseph Avery, 694
Mellers, Wilfred, 695
Mendelsohn, Leonard Richard,
    696
Middleton, Bernard C., 178
Mignon, Elisabeth, 697
Miles, Theodore, 457, 698
Miller, Edwin Haviland, 699
Mills, Don, 450
Mills, Laurens Joseph, 538, 700
Mills, Lloyd Leslie, 356–357
Mish, Charles C., 605, 701
Mitchell, Eleanor Rettig, 702
Mitchell, John Arthur, 540
Monro, Isabel, 090–091
Monro, John, 703
Monro, Kate M., 091
Montfort, Montague, 539
Moore, John Robert, 704

Morillo, Marvin, 358–360, 442
Morrison, Paul G., 102, 139
Morpurgo, J. E., 092
Morton, Richard, 361
Mullany, Peter Francis, 705
Mullin, Donald C., 810
Mumper, Nixon, 362
Murray, John Tucker, 811
Murrie, Eleanore Boswell, 037
Myers, Aaron Michael, 706

N

Nares, Robert, 093
Nason, Arthur Huntington, 216,
    363
Neale, Thomas, 540
Neill, Michael, 237, 364–365,
    436
Nethercot, Arthur H., 366, 541
[Nichols, John Gough], 032, 094
Nicholson, B., 367
Nicoll, Allardyce, 245, 707–709,
    812–814, 820
Novarr, David, 368
Nungezer, Edwin, 095

O

Obaid, Thoraya Ahmed, 710
Occhiogrosso, Frank Victor, 711
Ochester, Edwin F., 369
O'Connor, John J., 370–371, 436
Olive, W. J., 542
Oliver, H. J., 372
Oras, Ants, 179
Orbison, [Theodore] Tucker,
    373–375
Ordish, T. Fairman, 815
Orgel, Stephen Kitay, 376, 712,
    713
Ornstein, Robert, 714

P

Pafford, John Henry Pyle, 520,
    531
Palme, Per, 816

Palmer, Frank, 647
Panek, Leroy Lad, 377–378
Papousek, Marilyn Deweese, 379
Parker, William Riley, 140
Parkes, Joan, 096
Parlin, Hanson T., 380
Parrott, Thomas Marc, 414, 715
Parssinen, Carol Ann Miller, 381
Partridge, A. C., 097
Partridge, Edward B., 382–383
Patrick, Julian, 226
Pattison, Bruce, 098
Peel, Donald Frank, 384
Pellegrini, Giuliano, 514
Pennel, Charles A., 099
Perkinson, Richard H., 698, 716
Pestell, Thomas, 543
Phelan, James, 385
Phelps, Wayne Howe, 386
Phialas, Peter George, 387–389, 523
Pickel, Margaret Bernard, 717
Pierce, Frederick E., 390
Planché, James Robinson, 100
Plumb, J. H., 754
Pollard, Alfred William, 102
Pollock, Frederich, 103
Poole, H. Edmund, 016
Povey, Kenneth, 180
Powell, Chilton Latham, 718
Powell, Woodrow W., 544
Presley, Horton Edward, 391
Princic, Walter Francis, 392
Prior, Moody Erasmus, 719
Putt, S. Gorley, 393

R

R., W., 545
Radtke, Stephen John, 394
Ramage, David, 020, 104
Randolph, Thomas, 546–548
Read, Forrest Godfrey, 395
Redgrave, Gilbert R., 102
Reed, Isaac, 012
Reed, Robert Rentoul, Jr., 396, 720–721
Reimer, A. P., 397–398
Requa, Kenneth A., 399

Reynolds, Myra, 722
Rhodes, Dennis E., 059
Rice, Warner G., 549
Richards, Kenneth B., 550, 790
Richards, Nathanael, 551
Roberts, Jeanne Addison, 400
Robinson, J. W., 009
Rogers, Katherine M., 723
Rollins, Hyder Edward, 105–108, 546, 552–553, 724–725
Roper, Derek, 271
Røstvig, Maren-Sofie, 726
Routh, Charles Richard Nairne, 109
Ruoff, James E., 554–557
Russell, H. K., 727
Rys, Sister Mary Ellen, 728

S

Sabbattini, Nicola, 798
Sabol, Andrew J., 558, 729
Sackton, Alexander H., 401
St. Louis, Nadine Small, 294, 402
Saintsbury, George E. B., 110
Salmon, Vivian, 403
Sandedge, William Lee, 353
Sandys, George, 516, 559
Sargeaunt, Margaret Joan, 404
Sayce, R. A., 181
Schelling, Felix E., 405, 730–732
Scherrer, Gebhard Joseph, 406
Schipper, J., 407
Schmid, F. Ernst, 535
Schoenbaum, Samuel, 061, 182, 560, 752
Scott, Florence R., 733
Scouten, Arthur H., 084
Seaton, Ethel, 734
Sensabaugh, George F., 408–412
Sharma, R. C., 735
Sharp, Cecil J., 736
Sharp, Harold S., 111
Sharp, Marjorie Z., 111
Sharp, Robert Boies, 413
Shaver, Chester Linn, 414, 477
Shaw, Catherine M., 415
Shepard, Leslie, 105

Sherman, Stuart P., 416–417
Shirley, James, 418–421
Shuttleworth, Bertram, 112
Sibley, Gertrude Marian, 113
Silvette, Herbert, 737
Simonds, Peggy Munoz, 422
Simoni, Anna E. C., 059
Simpson, Percy, 183, 423,
    817–818
Singleton, Charles Southward,
    738
Sirluck, Ernest, 424
Sisson, Charles J., 184, 347,
    781, 819
Skeat, Walter W., 114
Skemp, A. R., 551
Smith, Denzell Stewart, 473,
    561
Smith, G. C. Moore, 562–564,
    739
Smith, G. Gregory, 425
Smith, Homer, 740
Smith, John Harrington, 741
Smith, Robert Metcalf, 607
Smith, W. A., 059
Smith, William George, 115
Soet, Frans Dirk, de, 742
Sonnenshein, Richard Adolph,
    565
Sorelius, Gunnar, 743, 820
South, Malcolm Hudson, 426
Southern, Richard, 821–822
Sparkes, John C. L., 116
Spek, Cornelius, Van Der, 744
Spencer, Benjamin Townley, 348
Spencer, Hazelton, 820
Spencer, Theodore, 745
Spingarn, Joel Elias, 746
Squier, Charles LaBarge,
    427–428
Staff of Catholic University,
    026
Starr, L. R., Mrs., 790
Stavig, Mark Luther, 429–430
Steele, Mary Susan, 747
Steensma, Robert C., 117
Steiner, Arpad, 212, 431
Stephen, Leslie, 118
Stenton, Doris Mary, 748
Sternfeld, Frederick, 486
Stevenson, Allan H., 185–187,
    432–434, 566

Stockholk, Johanne M., 350
Stone, Carl Warren, 435
Stone, George W., 084
Stone, L., 823
Stonehill, Charles A., 119
Stonehill, H. Winthrop, 119
Stonex, Arthur B., 749
Stoye, J. W., 567
Stratman, Carl J., 120
Strode, William, 568
Strong, Roy, 713
Struble, Mildred Clara, 230,
    364, 436
Summers, Montague, 041
Sutton, Juliet, 437–438
Swinburne, Algernon Charles,
    398, 439–440, 569
Sykes, H. Dugdale, 188, 570–571
Symons, Arthur, 189
Sypher, Wylie, 750

T

Tannenbaum, Dorothy R., 126
Tannenbaum, Samuel A., 122–127,
    189, 546
Tansell, G. Thomas, 190
Targan, Barry Donald, 441
Taylor, Aline Mackenzie, 358,
    442
Taylor, Archer, 128
Telfer, Robert Stockdale, 354
Thaler, Alwin, 443, 824–827
Thayer, Calvin Graham, 444
Thomas, Donald L., 445, 465,
    572, 751
Thompson, Elbert N. S., 191
Thorn-Drury, G., 573
Tikriti, Khalid Mahir, 574
Tillyard, E. M. W., 129
Toback, Phyllis Brooks, 575
Tomlinson, T. B., 446
Toynbee, Margaret, 557
Trevelyan, George Macaulay, 130
Tupper, James W., 254
Turner, Robert K., 192

U

Ure, Peter, 270, 447-449, 752
Unwin, George, 828
Ustick, W. Lee, 131

V

Van Dam, Bastiaan A. P., 193
Van Lennep, William, 084
Velte, Mowbray, 576
Venn, J. A., 132
Venn, John, 132
Vienken, Heinz J., 587
Vince, R. W., 577-579
Von Fossen, R. W., 226

W

Wagner, Bernard M., 580, 585
Waith, Eugene M., 450
Waller, A. R., 753
Wallerstein, Ruth C., 581
Walter, John Henry, 451, 539,
    582-583
Ward, A. W., 753
Ward, C. E., 452
Ward, John Woodruff, 584
W[arner], G. F., 453
Watkins-Jones, A., 580, 585
Watson, George, 133
Weathers, Winston, 454
Webb, Margaret Andrews Kahim,
    455
Wedgwood, C. V., 754
Welsford, Enid, 134, 755
Wertheim, Albert, 336, 456-459,
    586, 698
West, Robert Hunter, 756
Wheeler, Charles F., 460

White, Beatrice, 788
White, Harold Ogden, 228, 757
Wickham, Glynne, 829
Wilde, George, 587-588
Wiley, Audrey Nell, 589
Wiley, Margaret Lenore, 758
Wilkinson, C. H., 590
Willeford, William, 135
Willey, Basil, 136
Williams, Arnold, 409
Williams, Franklin B., Jr., 137
Williams, William P., 099
Wilson, Arthur, 591-592
Wilson, Edmund, 206
Wilson, F. P., 781
Wilson, Rodney Earl, 759
Wing, Donald, 138-139
Winston, Florence T., 461
Winslow, Ola Elizabeth, 760
Winstanley, William, 140
Winter, De, 310
Wise, Thomas, 439
Witt, Robert W., 462
Wood, Anthony À., 032, 141
Woodfill, Walter L., 142
Woodward, Gertrude Loop, 143
Wright, Celeste Turner, 761-762
Wright, Louis B., 050, 593, 605,
    763-770, 781, 826
Wright, Thomas, 144

Y

Yates, Frances Amelia, 771
Yearsley, Macleod, 772
Young, Stephen C., 145

Z

Ziff, Lazer, 773
Zimmer, Ruth Kachel, 463